AN
INTERPRETATION
OF
THE LIFE
OF
VISCOUNT SHIBUSAWA

BY

KYUGORO OBATA

DAIYAMONDO JIGIYO KABUSHIKI KAISHA
BIJUTSU INSATSUSHO

FOREWORD

by

Baron S. Goh

President of Zaidan Hojin Shibusawa Sei-en O Kinen Kai
(The Viscount Shibusawa Memorial Foundation, Inc.)

In connection with the publication of this book written
by Dr. K. Obata under the auspices of Zaidan Hojin
Shibusawa Sei-en O Kinen Kai (The Viscount Shibusawa Memorial Foundation, Inc.), it may not be out
of place for me as its President to write a few words on
its behalf.

We, the members of the Foundation, especially the
official members, are keenly sensitive to the gravity of
our responsibility to carry out our intention expressed
in the Prospectus of the Foundation printed elsewhere
in this book. We are happy in seeing the bronze statue
of the Viscount erected in the center of the city of Tokyo,
thereby doing honor to the memory of the Viscount
and his great work. However this is but introductory to
innumerable projects we intend to carry on in accordance
with his Will.

What we would like to see soon is the Viscount's
biography written and published by an experienced
writer, so that it may serve not only to perpetuate the
precious memory of this wonderful man and his vast
achievements, but also to stimulate the future generations
of businessmen to hold the level of the business standard
high and clean. No other man had ever so much
contributed toward the emancipation of the business life

in Japan from its feudal degeneracy and thraldom on the one hand and elevated it to its present position of importance and dignity on the other as the Viscount did. His mastery behavior as a moral bulwark against the invasion and temptation of all sorts of materialism and mammonism is a priceless legacy he left to Japan's civic and industrial life.

Dr. K. Obata, who served the Viscount for many years as English private secretary, was anxious to summarize the activities of the Viscount in English, and we are glad to cooperate with him in the realization of his desire.

The Viscount's broad mindedness and his intense interest in the promotion of international good will and world peace deserve high recognition. From this point of view, the writer of this volume should be complimented in his effort to couch the narration of certain features of the many sided life of the Viscount in the English language which is so universally spoken.

We sincerely hope that this book will be a prophecy to the appearance in the near future of a more complete and thorough biography of that grand personality—Viscount E. Shibusawa.

Baron I. Y.

the Author

The glorious sun-set and its after glow have faded away. The day is done. The night is on. Not a cloud mars the clear sky studded by the millions of of luminaries. The moon and stars are vieing with each other to throw their light to the uttermost parts of the earth, trying to make darkness less dismal and the night more nearly like the day. In this brilliant galaxy of the heavenly hosts, there exists a tiny one, which is ambitious not to be ambitious, save to hold up a torch to wanderers here below.

A genius is a unique personality transcending all other men around. No single person nor a group of persons, no mater how great and renowned they may be, can take his place. When he is gone he is lost forever, and no substitute can be found. But this is also true that a genius neither lives nor dies to himself alone. Intentionally or unintentionally, he creates around him circles of his admirers. Confidential secretaries and business associates form the inner circle, and the multitudes of admirers the outer one. To them all the indelible impressions of the personality of that central figure are given. Later some of them, out of their grateful recognition of the privilege they enjoyed during the days of their association with that dominant personality, are impelled to pay their tributes to him. Others believing that such a wonderful character should always be upheld before the eyes of the coming generations for their encouragement and guidance, would try to prepare his memoirs. Thus books, booklets, pamphlets, novels, and dramas are written to describe the various phases of his comprehensive and complex life.

Viscount Eiichi Shibusawa, " A grand old man of Japan " was that kind of a genius. As was characterized in the Imperial Condolence, he was a " Shakai jin

no gikei " (A princely civilian). Since his death on the
Armistice Day of November 11, 1931, accounts of his
life have been published by his admirers, and many
books had been written during his life time, of which
the " Sei-en Sensei Rokujyu nen Shi " (Sixty Years'
Career of Viscount Shibusawa) written by Baron Sakatani
is the outstanding and authoritative work. Among the
new productions the most stimulating and instructive
are : a booklet entitled " Shibusawa Shishaku " (Viscount Shibusawa) written by Mr. T. Watanabe, first
Secretary of the Viscount and Chief Director of "Shibusawa Dozoku Kabushiki Kaisha " (Shibusawa Holding
Company, Ltd.) founded by the Viscount ; a voluminous and resourceful book (octavo) of nearly one thousand pages entitled " Shibusawa Eiichi O " (Eiichi
Shibusawa the Grand Old Man), and another one (royal
octavo) entitled " Shibusawa O no Omokage " (Vestiges
of Viscount Shibusawa) of 400 pages, both written by
Mr. K. Shiraishi, second Secretary of the Viscount and
Associate Director of the same company. These are
written in the Japanese language.

The author of this little book has been ever since
the death of the Viscount anxious to write his memoirs
in English, as he had been for twelve years English Secretary to the Viscount. But circumstances have so far
prevented him from taking up the work. Recently
assistance for the enterprise was promised to him by
the authorities of Zaidan Hojin Shibusawa Sei-en O
Kinen Kai (The Viscount Shibusawa Memorial Foundation, Inc.). After all it was better for the author to
have waited, as he can now have free access to the
immortal biographies prepared by the above writers,

who have most generously consented to place their works at his disposal.

In sending forth this humble work into the world, the author will be satisfied if it may find a place among the many volumes written about the Viscount, as that tiny star above referred to does among the celestial luminaries.

Kyugoro Obata.

INTRODUCTION

My friend Dr. Kyugoro Obata for many years acted as English private secretary to the late Viscount Shibusawa. He lived almost every day in close contact with the Viscount: he listened to the Viscount's resourceful talks many a time; interpreted the conversations that took place between the Viscount and foreign visitors; and translated his remarks, addresses, and letters into English. He accompanied the Viscount when the latter made a trip abroad. Naturally he came to know the Viscount as few men could know him. Dr. Obata looked upon the Viscount as one does upon his own father or teacher.

Dr. Obata was greatly affected and deeply mourned when he faced the grim reality of the death of the Viscount on the eleventh of November, 1931—Armistice Day of the great World War. Very soon after books and pamphlets written about the life and work of the Viscount began to come out almost in an endless succession, but no work of the kind in English appeared. Dr. Obata did not like this, because he thought that the account of a life like that of the Viscount should not be confined within the bounds of his own country. The Viscount was so internationally minded that his contributions to the promotion of world peace made the entire world a debtor to him. Dr. Obata feared that the blame of negligence and disloyalty must fall upon the English secretary, if something was not soon done to initiate the work of the internationalization of the knowledge of the marvellous career of the Viscount.

Driven by such a high sense of obligation, Dr. Obata strove to enlist an interested group in support of his project and began to re-examine various available data about the Viscount and coordinate them in a readable form. The work has been done after several years' labor, and I have not the slightest doubt that the facts mentioned in this volume together with the observations and opinions given by him are fair and sound.

Through this volume the Viscount will long live on the stage of international drama. His merits and contributions will be handed down from generation to generation in a world-wide fashion, thus stimulating and elevating humanity to a higher level.

As one of the nearest relatives and friends of the Viscount, I owe an unpayable debt of gratitude to Dr. Obata, whose loyalty and devotion to the Viscount has at last been crystalized in this handy book.

Baron Y. Sakatani

At this moment I vividly recall the scene at the celebration of the sixtieth birthday of the late Viscount Shibusawa at his Asukayama home, some thirty five years ago. Scholars, statesmen, businessmen, social workers, and diplomats gathered together to felicitate the one whose vision and wisdom had made him a great man of Japan. It is not for me to appraise the worth of the Viscount as a great statesman and as a prince of industry. There are others who can discuss those phases of the life of the Viscount far more competently than I can. As my life has been largely confined within the field of diplomacy, it may not be out of place for me to scan the international activity of the Viscount from this angle.

Baron d'Anethan of Belgium was present on the occasion just referred to. Being the doyen of the accredited diplomats of the different countries then stationed in Japan, the Baron made congratulatory remarks on behalf of his colleagues. A few other notables addressed and congratulated the Viscount. Then the time for the Viscount to respond came, and it was in this reply that he for the first time made public his intention to withdraw from the business world and to devote the rest of his life to such public activities as education, social improvement, and international work.

It was quite natural for me to pay special attention to the words of the Viscount regarding international activity. He gave a very emphatic statement of his determination to promote better understanding and good will among nations. Perhaps no one was more pleased than I in hearing the declaration of the Viscount, because I was then feeling the need of diplomacy conducted by laymen of my country. The peoples' diplomacy was what I wanted to see inaugurated, and the fact that the cause was championed by a man of great prestige like the Viscount gave me unspeakable joy.

With this impression upon me, I watched the international activities of the Viscount. His initial move toward the peoples' diplomacy was to head a party known as the Honorary Commercial Commissioners of Japan to the United States of America in the year 1909 in return for the similar visit to Japan of the American businessmen in the previous year. The party consisted of members more than fifty in number, including a few ladies. The party reached Seattle early in September. Needless to say the party received a loyal welcome from the officials and civilians of the city. The reception Committee did every thing in their power to make the visit of the party pleasant and profitable. A good start was made. A fine precedent was established. A special train was placed at the disposal of the party during its entire journey of three months, visiting more than fifty cities in the States.

The leader of the party, the Viscount, then seventy years of age, sized up the situation in every city, where programs of welcome in forms of personal contact, luncheons, banquets, and inspections of public institutions awaited him and his associates. Every city struck its own medals and prepared badges to honor and commemorate the occasion. The party was greeted by leading citizens in every city and by President Taft. A colossal opportunity for carrying on the peoples' diplomacy presented itself to the visiting party. Thus

the name of Baron Shibusawa was indelibly impressed
upon the minds of leaders in various spheres of
American life. It would be impossible to rightly estimate the permanent and salutary influence of this
enterprise on the promotion of mutual understanding
and friendship between our two countries.

The Japanese American Relations Committee, of
which I have honor to be a member of the Executive
Council, was organized by the Viscount when he returned from his American trip in 1916. Moreover, it was
largely due to his influence that a group of businessmen, headed by the late Baron Dan of the Mitsui
company, visited England in the years 1921–1922.

But the international and diplomatic activities of the
Viscount were not confined to the two countries above
mentioned. The doors of his heart were wide open to
all nations on earth. The stories of his unselfish
interest in China for China's sake and for what he
actually did for her would swell into a volume if
told.

The Viscount always insisted that in personal dealings one should faithfully observe the moral principles
of Chyu-jo, inward honesty and sympathy. He insisted that there was no reason why these principles
should not be applied to international dealings also.
In other words he scathingly criticised the secret and
Machiavelian diplomacy then in vogue. I never forget
the honor the Viscount accorded me soon after I
returned from my mission in America in 1917, calling
on me at my house, and complimenting me on the
frank and open attitude in which I had collaborated
with Mr. Lansing, Secretary of State.

The strong sense of justice and fairness in the Viscount and his steel-like faith in their ultimate triumph over all human relationships would have made him a model diplomat, if he had turned his energy and wisdom into that channel.

The writer of this book and his supporters should be highly congratulated on having made it possible to introduce the name of the Viscount and a summary of his career to the whole world through the language most widely spoken.

Viscount K. Ishii

It was my good fortune to be a member of the delegation from the Pacific Coast Chamber of Commerce that visited Japan at the invitation of the Japanese Chambers of Commerce in the Fall of 1908. The reception afforded the Delegation not only by the Japanese Chambers of Commerce but by the Japanese nation at that time was marvelous in the extreme. It was not merely a courteous gesture of good will from the business representatives of one nation to another but a generous outpouring of a nation's sincere desire to demonstrate the friendship that Japan had for the people of the United States.

The entertainment offered us was royal in every way and I recall with particular pleasure the banquet tendered us at the residence of Baron Shibusawa in the Nihonbashi District, Tokyo. This was the first time I had had the pleasure of meeting the Baron. His kindly personality, his generosity, his friendship freely offered, made an indelible impression on the American party as well as on myself. Our meeting was the beginning of a cordial association for the betterment of the relations between our two countries which has continued unabated during a period of over thirty years.

After the visit of Baron Shibusawa to the Panama Exposition in San Francisco in 1915, we were elected the respective heads of organizations designed to further and promote friendship between our two nations; in Tokyo the Baron became the Chairman of the Japanese American Relations Committee and in San Francisco I was appointed the Chairman of the Japanese Relations Committee of the San Francisco Chamber of Commerce and later also President of the Japan Society. As heads of our respective organizations we were in constant correspondence and promoted visits of friendship committees between our two countries.

Baron Shibusawa, later elevated to the rank of Viscount by the Emperor, was one of nature's noblemen. In one of our confidential interviews he related to me how he became such a firm friend and admirer of the United States. At the time that Admiral Perry made his historical entrance into Tokyo Harbor with his fleet, Viscount Shibusawa was a young samurai of strong nationalistic tendencies. He was a member of a band of young Japanese of noble birth who protested with all the vehemence in their power against this foreign invasion and he continued this attitude of mind up to the time of his acquaintanceship with Consul Townsend Harris, afterwards American Minister to Japan. Mr. Harris proved not only an able envoy of the United States, but also a sincere friend and adviser to Japan and succeeded in winning Baron Shibusawa's complete friendship and confidence to such an extent that later on the Baron devoted his life to the promoting of friendly relations between the two nations. Possessed of great wealth and influence his power for peace and better understanding can hardly be estimated. His was an international mind, that could comprehend the point of view of other nations, a grasp of economic and social questions that was truly astounding. Never tiring, never discouraged, endowed with infinite patience, he never deviated throughout his long and useful life from the course he had set out for himself of bringing Japan and the United States closer together.

I can frankly say that no man I have ever met has influenced my life more than did my good friend Viscount Shibusawa.   William Shakespeare sums it up in a few words: "His life was gentle and the elements so mix'd in him that Nature might stand up and say to all the world 'This was a man'."

My acquaintance with Viscount Shibusawa extends
to many decades. We used to meet at different places
and on various occasions, where we came to know each
other well. Among many incidents which transpired
between us during our intercourse, I can recall three
which show how our minds ran parallel in public
questions.

The first incident was this: Before and after the
Sino-Japanese war, I was Vice-Minister of the Department of Agriculture and Commerce, Viscount Enomoto
being the Minister. Japan emerged the victor in this
war and obtained an enormous sum of money as a part
of the war spoils. Generally speaking, war brings a
curse both upon the victor and the vanquished. The
curse which falls upon the victor is an economic disturbance—inflation first and then deflation. I was fully
aware of such an outcome in this particular case if
we did not guard against it, as I had studied the
financial panic which upset the economic life of America
after its civil war and of Germany after the Franco-
Prussian war. I was a student at Harvard University
not long after the close of the civil war, when America
was suffering from "hard times". Germany secured
the indemnity of 500,000,000 francs from France,
which maddened her financial world with a victory
boom for a period, but soon sent her down into an
unprecedented financial panic. I knew all this to be
true in a general way, but without statistical data on
hand to sustain my argument. So I took steps to
send an expert to America and Germany to investigate
their financial and economic conditions. Later on a
report about Germany was submitted. It strongly sup-

ported my opinion. I had it translated and, adding
my views to the translation, I published it in the form
of a pamphlet. I showed a copy to Viscount Shibusawa, who was then the president of Dai Ichi Ginko
and the president of the Tokyo Chamber of Commerce.
He heartily endorsed the views expressed in it which
immensely strengthened my position on the question.
Moreover he took the report to the gathering of
the Ryumon Sha held in his Asukayama home and
read it to those assembled. Copies were widely
distributed in the branch offices of Dai Ichi Ginko.
Then Baron Takashi Masuda the former chief direct-
or of the Mitsui Company came out in agreement with
my views. He asked me to reprint the pamphlet for
the use of the company and its branch offices. It
was also widely circulated through local governments
and chambers of commerce.

So far so good. But I was confronted with a strong
foe. Viscount C. Watanabe, the Minister of the Finance
Department, and Mr. K. Kawada, the Governor of the
Bank of Japan, held decidedly an opposite view. They
condemned me as an enemy of progress and prosperity
by warning the people against a panic. Threats were
made to compel me to resign my office but I turned
a deaf ear. Within one year of the so-called boom, its
reverse began to show in a gloomy aspect of trade.
In Osaka, many banks had to face runs, and failures
followed one after another. The epidemic spread to
Kyoto and Nagoya, playing the same kind of havoc
there as in Osaka. Governor Kawada was obliged to
go to Osaka to attempt readjustments. He made but
little headway there. In the meantime the panic wave

reached Tokyo and ruined various financial institutions. But Dai Ichi Ginko and the Mitsui Company received no shock from it. This coincidence of our foresight and its wholesome effect upon the financial world of the day made our mutual appreciation deeper and our friendship firmer.

The second instance was of an international nature. Having received my early education in Harvard University as I said above, it was quite natural for me to be deeply concerned in questions which affect Japanese American relations. Viscount Shibusawa's interest in America was created in him by his study of the life and work of Townsend Harris during the latter's diplomatic service in Japan. The Viscount and I were in perfect accord in the belief that friendly relations between America and Japan have a far reaching significance in the promotion and maintenance of world peace. But from the time the Russo-Japanese war was concluded, a bitter anti-Jepanese movement in California began to manifest itself. The questions of Japanese school children and the leasehold of agricultural land by Japanese farmers were brought before the Legislature of the State of California. In 1913 the California Alien Land Law was enacted by the Legislature in spite of the vigorous protest presented by Japanese farmers and their American sympathizers. In the fall of 1920, a more drastic law was to be enacted by the referendum of the citizens of California. This measure, if adopted, would have driven Japanese farmers into despair and ruin. For them it was a question of life or death. Hence they rose up to a man to defeat the referendum movement. Letters were addressed and personal emissaries sent to political and business leaders of Japan. The Japanese American Relations Committee and the America-Japan Society were deeply stirred by the news. Being president of the Society and a member of the Committee, I could not be indifferent to such a serious event. This emergency caused the Viscount and some of us to meet together and discuss the matter. It resulted in our inviting some influential Americans to come to Tokyo and freely discuss the pending question as well as other Japanese American questions. We organized the Welcome Society to American Guests early in the spring of 1920, and extended our invitations to two parties. One was headed by Mr. Wallace M. Alexander of San Francisco, and the other by Mr. Frank A. Vanderlip of NewYork. Devoting one week or more to each conference, we held the Japanese American Unofficial Conference in the auditorium of the Bankers' Association. The object of the Conference was to study and get light on the questions at hand, but not to form any resolutions to bind us.

One of the most important results of these meetings was the unanimous consent of the conference members to create a Japanese American Joint High Commission to deal with these questions. This idea of a Joint High Commission was suggested by the historical precedent that America and England solved the most difficult question of the Newfoundland fishery dispute by this method. Mr. Vanderlip and Mr. Alexander were asked to influence their Government, while the Viscount and I ours. A tactful campaign was carried on on both sides of the Pacific, but it failed. Time went swiftly by and the fall of 1920 came. The referendum was forced through to our disappointment. Four years later the Immigration Law was introduced in Congress. This being a national question unlike the problems of California, it created a great sensation in Japan. Despite strong opposition, the law was passed. This law stirred the minds of leaders of Japan to a high pitch of resentment and indignation, because it clearly demonstrated a discriminatory attitude of America toward Japan. We the members of the America-Japan Society and of the Japanese American Relations Committee, were deeply disappointed. I could not stand the disgrace and resigned the Presidency of the America-Japan Society, issuing a public statement as to my attitude toward the American action. But the Viscount, deeply hurt though he was, begged me not to withdraw my name from the membership of the two organizations. In deference to his courteous entreaty I consented only to retain my membership, but since then I have ceased to attend the meetings. For sixty long years I have endeavored to promote better understanding and good will between our two countries, but the reward I received was "a stone for bread and a scorpion for a fish." My patience was exhausted, and even now I cannot look upon America as I used to in the days of President Theodore Roosevelt, who was a great champion of fair play and the square deal.

The third occasion may be stated thus: Toward the close of September of 1931, the year the Viscount passed away, I went to Asukayama to inquire after his health. When I presented my card to the house-steward who knew me, he begged me to wait in the parlour until he took the card to the Viscount, saying it would make the Viscount angry, if he did not report to him that I was there. To my great surprise the Viscount left his room and being accompanied by his nurse walked into the room where I was waiting. There he spoke to me:

"It is very unlikely that I shall rally to take part in any active work. The Immigration Law of 1924 will remain as an irritant if not revised. You are much younger than I am and will be able to work out the final solution of this ominous problem. So far as I can see now, there is nothing which would jeopardize the historic good relations between our two countries if only this law were removed or revised. I sincerely hope that the American friends and you will closely cooperate to accomplish this object."

I never thought that this visit was to be the last, and that what he told me would be his final words—his last will and testimony to me!

Viscount Shibusawa was truly a great man. He was a patriot, statesman, educator, philanthropist, and businessman of whom Japan can be justly proud. He was a national treasure which will increasingly shed lustre on Japan as the years roll on.

Count Kentaro Kaneko.

My acquaintance with Viscount Eiichi Shibusawa spanned a period of many years. During this time we were intimately associated in various organizations and activities. In my capacity as president of the following organizations I had his hearty cooperation as vice-president—The Society which Promoted the Founding of the Meiji Shrine, The Capital and Labor Harmonization Association, The League of Nations Association of Japan, The Society for Aiding Reconstruction Following the Great Earthquake, The Society for Rebuilding the Confucian Hall in Tokyo, The Society for Promoting the Study of the Chinese Classics, and The Medical Association of Japan.

This list of organizations in which the Viscount was a moving spirit and to which he gave unsparingly of his thought, time and energy speaks eloquently of the catholicity of his mind and the breadth of his interests.

Every phase of the nation's life came within the scope of his creative thinking and constructive endeavors. He recognized no barriers of culture or class and gave himself without stint to lifting the total life of the Empire to higher levels. He felt that in every realm of life the best was none too good for the land that he loved and passionately gave himself to its realization.

The Viscount did not however confine his outlook and interest to his own nation. He was a true patriot. But so large was his mind and heart that his interests and concern leaped across the national frontiers and made the world's problems and its needs his own. His love for his country and his internationalism were so blended that it took both to give expression to the full measure of the man.

Although he took the whole world into his mind and heart it was the bettering of American-Japanese relations and Japanese-Chinese amity to which he gave himself with crusading zeal. America has never had a truer friend than Viscount Shibusawa. Throughout his long life he left no stone unturned in his efforts to build a bond of understanding and good will between America and Japan. This was one of the major goals of his life.

He was also one of China's most understanding friends. An earnest and consistent follower of Confucius and an ardent student of the Chinese Classics enabled him to look deep into the Chinese soul and comprehend the true inwardness of the Chinese people. He yearned that these two sister nations of Eastern Asia which have had so much in common across the centuries should speedily settle their differences and become a united and mighty force in the building of a better world.

The Viscount had the mind and the mood of a pioneer. In his own special field as a banker and an industrialist he blazed new trials in many directions. In his interest in woman's education and in the large role he played in the founding of the Japan Woman's University he helped to inaugurate a new day for the nation's womanhood.

In the international realm, through his innumerable and intimate contacts with outstanding leaders in practically every nation and his unceasing endeavors to build a world brotherhood, he took his place by the side of those in every land who have pioneered in the interests of world peace and international good will.

The Viscount was not only a pioneer. He was a

builder. He not only ventured into new fields and helped lay foundations for new movements and new enterprises but he devoted himself to the more difficult work of making these permanent and fruitful. In many fields he left movements and institutions which are monuments to his patience and skill as a true builder.

The Viscount was a man with an open mind. He was not obsessed with a thing simply because it was new. On the other hand he was not afraid of any thing because of its newness. He turned upon it an open and inquiring mind and if it revealed intrinsic values he gladly welcomed it. He believed that progress constantly points forward to new experiences and new attainments in every field and did not hesitate to keep step with every advance.

He did not however turn his back upon the old. He was loyal to the illustrious and heroic souls who from time immemorial have guided Japan toward its destined goal. He was deeply appreciative of his nation's ancient culture. He believed that there is much that is unique and of infinite worth in Japan's past and he strove to conserve these values and make them contribute to the nation's and the world's future growth.

In the spiritual realm he believed that the ancient meditative East has much to give to the young energetic West. Thus to the end of his days he was a keen student of the Chinese Classics and a devout follower of such sages as Mencius and Confucius.

Although Viscount Shibusawa was one of the most conspicuous figures modern Japan has produced he was one of the most modest and approachable of men. He had a sympathetic heart for every good and needy cause. In proportion to his wealth he was one of the nation's most generous givers but many of his philanthropies were known only to those whom he helped and to a few of his closest associates.

He was truly great in the breadth of his mind, the scope of his interests, the warmth of his sympathies, his powers of leadership, his spirit of service and the genuineness of his character. A nation's most precious treasures are its full blown manhood and womanhood. Viscount Shibusawa will stand through the years as one of the finest representatives of Japanese manhood.

Tokugawa Iyesato

ACKNOWLEDGEMENT

Generally speaking this book itself is an acknowledgement of the author's indebtedness to many persons and
groups both at home and abroad. His debt is domestic
as well as foreign; national and international.

The author-debtor, balancing the amount of the debts
he has incurred during the last two years and a half,
is amazed at the vastness of the amount and the enormous
number of the creditors. He wonders at the liberality
of the creditors. But in a calmer moment he under-
stands the reason why such unmortgaged transactions
were possible and concludes that it was the strength
of the personality of Viscount Shibusawa which made
the debtor bold and the creditors liberal, for his fair
name could command an immense measure of credit in
men. So the first acknowledgement of the author's indebtedness should be made to the central figure of the
book—Viscount Shibusawa himself.

Next there are a few persons and organizations without whose generous aid this work could not have been
completed.

The late Mr. Z. Horikoshi, who was a great admirer
of Viscount Shibusawa and a member of the Board of
Directors of Zaidan Hojin Shibusawa Sei-en O Kinen
Kai (The Viscount Shibusawa Momorial Foundation,
Inc.), strongly endorsed the author's plan to write a
memoir of the Viscount in English. This voice of Mr.
Horikoshi found its echo in Mr. T. Watanabe, a Director
of Shibusawa Dozoku Kabushiki Kaisha (The Shibusawa
Holding Company) and another member of the Board

of Directors of the Foundation. It was through their
recommendation that the Board favorably acted upon
the author's proposal.

Baron Sakatani's moral support has been a constant
inspiration to the author. Its value can never be over-
estimated.

The advice, suggestions, and correction of the manuscripts freely given to the author by Mr. K. Shiraishi,
another Director of Shibusawa Dozoku Kabushiki Kaisha
and the author of the "Shibusawa Eiichi O," have
been indispenable assets. The author's conviction that
he could send out this volume at a specified time came
from the magnanimous offer of Mr. Shiraishi to make
free use of his book.

The author is greatly indebted to Mr. Cabot Coville,
the Second Secretary of the American Embassy in
Tokyo for his aid in securing the photographs of the
American Presidents and of Judge Gary, used in this
book.

Last of all the author owes a debt of gratitude to
Dr. Arthur D. Berry, class mate at Drew Theological
Seminary, 1895–1898, and Dean-Emeritus of the Theological Department of Aoyama Gaku-in. He has will-
ingly and cheerfully corrected the entire manuscript
and has read the proof in the midst of his arduous
duties. The author little dreamed in those old academic
days in the "Drew Forest" that after forty years he
should be associated with and assisted by Dr. Berry
in a work like this.

Then there are organizations to which the author is
heavily indebted. They are Shibusawa Jimusho, The
Japanese American Relations Committee, and Zaidan

Hojin Shibusawa Sei-en O Kinen Kai. Time and expense, the necessary requisites for carrying on the work, have been generously provided by them.

The Compilation Office of the Biographical Data of Viscount Shibusawa of Ryumon Sha was very generous in furnishing many pictures to be inserted in the book as illustrations.

Now it remains to be seen whether "An Interpretation of the Life of Viscount Shibusawa" will satisfy the claims of the innumerable creditors, and fairly relieve the author from the heavy burden of his long standing debt!

K. OBATA

CONTENTS

CONTENTS

ILLUSTRATIONS

AN INTERPRETATION

OF

THE LIFE

OF

VISCOUNT E. SHIBUSAWA

BY

KYUGORO OBATA

CHAPTER I

THE ENVIRONMENT

THE soul of man is by no means a passive automaton. It is highly active, initiative, selective, appropriative, assimilative, and retentive. These are the qualities which make the soul quickly responsive to its environment either for acceptance or rejection of its influence. For a newly born babe as it grows, the mother, the home, the schools both primary and secondary, history, literature, art, music, society, the nation, heaven and earth, constitute one vast complex environment—an inexhaustible source for the soul's own expansion and enrichment.

But it would be a sad mistake for us to believe that the environment, in order to be helpful, should always and unquestionably be a favorable one or that we should expect it to be such. There are hard facts and tragic events in human history, and wise men summarise them in such epigrammatic expressions as " A big tree is exposed to the envy of the wind " ; " Adversity makes a jewel out of you " ; " People of sterile soil prosper, but those of fertile soil lag behind." In taking such views as these regarding human environment, we would study the one that surrounded Viscount Shibusawa in his younger days.

Viscount Shibusawa was born in the year 1840 in a village called Chiarai-jima, which now forms a part of Yatsumoto-mura. The place is about 50 miles north of Tokyo. It occupies a small section of the famous Musashi-no, a broad plain in mid-Japan, where it was said that the sun rises from and sinks down behind its tall grasses. Far away toward the north-west, such mountains as Akagi, Myogi, and Haruna stand like mighty castles. In the winter season, the piercing wind known as *Akagi oroshi* swept across the village. The local tradition has it that even the winebibber of the worst sort, whose feet could hardly perform their normal duty on account of intoxication, would not have to walk a block or two before he would be brought down to his sober senses. All along the entire north side of the village, the river Tone, one of the three largest rivers of Japan, runs. In the early days of the history of the village, the river did for it two contradictory things —it threatened the villagers with destructive floods and the next moment blessed them with enriched soil. " I wound and I heal."

The third Shogun, Iyemitsu Tokugawa, was one of the ablest statesmen, if not the ablest in the Tokugawa regime, which lasted more than 250 years. He conducted the State affairs from 1623 until 1651, under the reigns of the three emperors, Go Mizunoo, Meisho, and Go Komyo. In the year 1634, Shogun Iyemitsu issued a drastic proclamation to drive out of the country all foreigners. The prohibitory law reads as follows :

" Sending ships to foreign countries is strictly forbidden ; he shall be put to death, who secretly enters into a ship and is later detected. The captain of the said ship shall be detained for judgement from the Shogun ; he shall be executed, who goes to a foreign country, stays there and later returns home. The reward of 200 or 300 pieces of silver according to the merit shall be given to the one who searches for, detects, and reports Christians. The descendants of the Southern barbarians shall be driven back to their own countries. If one shelters them, he shall suffer capital punishment, and his relatives shall be punished according to the degrees of the crime."

This law was often referred to by the later Shoguns and Daimyo as the unalterable ancestral law.

Owing to this anti-foreign measure, Japan lived a hermit life during more than 200 years, almost completely isolating herself from foreign relations, until 1853, when Commodore Perry finally succeeded in persuading Japan to give up the time honored policy of isolation.

Now what were the political conditions in foreign countries during the 40 years preceding the year 1868, when the Meiji Restoration took place ? Although Japan was cut off from communication with the western nations, yet she could not have been wholly insulated to what was going on in those nations. For, as the earth is divided into islands, peninsulas, and continents on the surface but is one solid mass at the bottom, so humanity divided into tribes, races, and nationalities is in reality an indivisible spiritual entity. The mighty ocean of world politics which rocked the ships of State in the western nations must have affected spiritual and political affairs in the Far East. Moreover Japan was never absolutely cut off from the rest of the world as Nagasaki was left open as an international port.

It was when Viscount Shibusawa was 27 years old that he started for France, where he stayed two years 1867–68. During these twenty eight years of the life of the Viscount, the following events transpired in foreign countries : December 10th, 1848, Louis Napoleon, a nephew of the great Napoleon was chosen President of the second Republic of France. After three years a contest between the President and the National Assembly arose. This contest resulted in the extension of the Presidency of Napoleon for the term of ten years, and finally he was made Emperor, taking the title of Napoleon III., in year 1852. In 1854, the Crimean War broke out, in which Turkey assisted by England and France fought Russia, and won the victory. In 1857, the Sepoy Mutiny took place. In 1861, the great Civil War of America broke out, and two significant events resulted from it at the conclusion of the struggle : (1) national unification, and (2) abolition of slavery throughout the country.

In order to clearly understand the significance of the facts above cited, we must go back to the causes which led up to them. We shall have to trace them as far back as to the Renaissance which originated in Italy in the Medieval Age. This revival of Greek and Latin literature and learning was introduced into Germany by many young students who went to Italy to acquire the knowledge of the classical learning. In Germany the

Humanism nurtured by classical culture took a sterner turn as it was influenced by an intense interest in Hebrew and Christian antiquity. In other words, what was the Renaissance in Italy, became the Reformation in Germany. The balmy air of the South produced the Humanist, and the cold clime of the north the Reformer.

The Father of the Reformation was Martin Luther. The heroic stand he took against the Catholic Church at the Diet of Worms stirred up the Catholic world to a very wide extent in the year 1521. With this beginning, Protestantism whose creed is the freedom of conscience and sanctity of personal belief took deep root in Germany, and spread to France and to England. In France, the sect called the Huguenot arose. Some of the Nobles imbibed this faith, while the Crown remained Catholic. In England, there arose Puritanism and Separatism which opposed many religious forms and practices of the Church of England as well as the Catholic Church. Famous men like John Milton, Oliver Cromwell, and John Bunyan became followers of the new cults. The Established Church of England persecuted Puritans, especially Separatists, many of whom escaped to Holland whence they sailed as the passengers of the Mayflower for the New World. There as the Pilgrim Fathers, they laid the foundations of civil liberty.

The thirteen colonies of America grew out of the Early Settlers, and in 1775 they waged war against their mother country in defense of their rights and liberties. The war was ended by the Peace of Paris in 1783, England acknowledging the independence of America. George Washington was the Founder and Father of the New Republic. Now in connection with this

Revolutionary war, there is a very important fact which bridges it with the French Revolution. It is the fact of Lafayette, a French aristocrat of whom Myers the author of the "General History" thus writes: "Among the nobility was the patriotic Lafayette, who had won the admiration of his countrymen by splendid services rendered the struggling republic in the New World. His influence at this time was probably greater than that of any other man." It was the same Lafayette who sent the key of the Bastille, the destruction of which was the signal for the beginning of the great French Revolution, to Washington, "as a trophy of the spoil of despotism." He sent a letter accompanying the key and it reads : " That the principles of America opened the Bastille is not to be doubted, and therefore the key goes to the right place." The French Republic was established September 21, 1792, and the following day, the 22nd, was made the beginning of a new era, the first day of the first year of the French Republic. The Republic thus established had to suffer many obstacles, but a lasting contribution to the promotion of human rights among common people was made. Myers again writes : " The republics established, it is true, were short lived : for the times were not yet ripe for the complete triumph of democratic ideas. But a great gain for freedom was made. The re-established monarchies, as we shall see later, never dared to make themselves as despotic as those which the Revolution had overturned."

The great Napoleon, the Emperor of France, was distinctively a personal embodiment of the spirit and idea of the French people. He was the man of the hour at the time of the Revolution. His popularity was so unlimited that the people of France could not be satisfied without offering him the best and highest France could afford, and it was the throne. Napoleon did not become, but *was made*, the Emperor of France in 1802, almost by the unanimous votes of the people. As we already saw, Louis Napoleon Bonaparte, the President of the second Republic was so popular that, like his illustrious uncle, he too *was made* Emperor, in 1852. His reign lasted till 1870.

In Russia, Tsar Alexander 11., (1855–1881) made himself famous by emancipating the serfs in 1861, and the whole number of the serfs liberated was about 46,000,000. This act of the Tsar appears on the surface like a gracious gesture to the people of Russia, but fundamentally it was the yielding of the ruler to the popular demand that they should have a part in the affairs of the empire—the political trend after the fashion of the French Revolution.

The Crimean War was ostensibly an engagement between Russia and Turkey, but in reality it was a grand demonstration in organized form of those liberal movements which had been fostered all over Europe, England, and America during the long period from the 16th to the first quarter of the 19th century. The creation of the Balkan States is its incontrovertible proof.

The Sepoy Mutiny too points toward the rise of liberalism against despotism. Mutiny is a deplorable method to be resorted to, none the less it is an indication of the struggle of a ruled class for the assertion of the inalienable rights of man—the right to live and the pursuit of happiness.

Rebellions, Revolutions, and Reformations in the political, social, and religious world are the outbursts of the death struggle of the oppressed against the oppressors, when the latter, their conscience smirched by wanton indulgence in pomp, luxury, and licentiousness, not only ignore and forget the welfare and security of the former but cause their burden of life to increase by levying arbitrary and heavy taxes upon them. In other words, when the oppression, injustice, and unreasonableness of the privileged class jeopardize the security of the people, the peace and order of society is upset, calling for some kind of readjustment and restoration.

We shall next observe the political conditions at home during the period under discussion. In Japan under the Shogunate from the time of Shogun Iyeyoshi down to Shogun Yoshinobu, the last one of the regime, namely from 1837 to 1867, her national life mirrored, in a small scale, the scene which was enacted on the political stage of Europe from the close of the 18th century to the middle of the 19th century. The privileged class had fattened themselves on the fruits of labour of the lower class. The tyranny, corruption, and arbitrariness of the former set up one camp, and the dissatisfaction, indignation, and resentment of the latter, another camp. However, this contrast in Japan did not loom up as strikingly as it did in Europe, because in Japan, the masses, that is to say, farmers, tradesmen, and artisans, were long trained to live satisfied in their own spheres of life, no matter how hard their lot might be. They were socially and politically doctrinated by the Confucian teaching : " The people may be made to follow a path of action, but they may not be made to understand it."

For them such a fatalistic formula as "Your Excellency's very unreasonableness is the very reasonableness for me, your humble servant," was a precept written on the tables of their hearts. They were as docile as sheep. But in Japan there existed a class of men known as the *samurai*. They were, as a class, indifferent to the question of the material side of life, but keenly alive to any moral issue. They were the salt of Japan. They formed a middle class to mediate between the privileged class and the masses, leaning toward the latter in sympathy as chivalry was one of their cardinal virtues. Being intelligent they could give an articulate expression to the atmosphere created by the masses, thus serving them as self-constituted attorneys.

During the last fifty years of the Tokugawa regime, the financial conditions of Japan were frightfully bad. There were four causes for it. First, the extravagant life of the Shoguns; second, the enormous expenditures incurred because of the institution of the "Sankin Kotai" (half of the provincial Daimyo all over the country with their families and retainers lived in Yedo, the seat of the Shogunate, for one year and the other half under the same conditions the next year, thus alternating their residences every other year); third, the large expense of building mansions for some of the provincial Daimyo living in Yedo; fourth, the expense of the removal of Daimyo from one province to another as punitive measures. Scholars and patriots like Kumazawa Banzan, Ogyu Sorai, and Yokoi Shonan, sounded alarms for the improvement of the financial situation but in vain. This universal adversity, enhanced by the complications with foreign countries and aggravated by the assasination of the chief minister Ii Kamon no kami in the year 1860, stirred those who had been feeling for a long time the oppression to assert their own rights and liberty. As for the means to the end, the first thing they wanted to do was to tear down the Tokugawa regime. So they branded the regime with a weak policy toward foreign powers and the long infringement upon the sanctity of the Imperial Throne, whose sacred right it should have upheld and safe-guarded but had in reality desecrated by over-shadowing it. Hence three terms which most aptly characterized the conditions of the national life of Japan in those turbulent days were coined: Son-no (Suprem-acy of the Emperor); Jo-i (Anti-foreign); and To-baku (Down-with-Tokugawa-regime). Here and there through-out the country, public spirited men joined together in plot and insurrection for the purpose of overthrowing the existing regime. Young men of high thinking and plain living like Viscount Shibusawa could not hold their peace under the circumstances and were only too anxious to lay down their lives by resorting to direct action for the removal of the ills of their coun-try. "To hate despotism and crush tyranny," was their slogan.

Right here it may be argued that one can hardly see the logical connection between the restoration of the Throne to its rightful place and the idea of the personal rights and liberty of the people. It is true that the status of His Majesty the Emperor of Japan among His subjects is august and incomparable, but it is equally true that there is another side to His status, which is His fatherhood to us all. No father would withhold good things from his children, such as rights and liberty.

The Japanese as a people are religious. Every village has its patron deity enshrined in a temple. In connection with the temple or shrine a certain feature of the social life of the community is picturable. In the case of Chiarai-jima, the village where the Viscount was born and grew up, the religious and social life is clearly seen. Once a year in the fall, the villagers hold an enthusiastic festivity in the compouud of Suwa Jinja—the shrine dedicated to their patron deity. They carry on a dance known as " Sasara." The entire village turn out to enjoy the celebration. The participants in the dance are young men, full of life and vigor. Viscount Shibusawa in his younger days took part in the celebration many autumns. Preceding the public exhibition, the participants spend many evenings in drill and practice. Before and after the rehearsal they gossip and talk about current topics, thus fraternizing with one another. This annual event became the center of interest for the men of the village, stimulating and elevating their moral, social, and political life. Throughout the year they look forward to it and back to it.

Regarding this amusement " Sasara " the late Baroness Hozumi, the eldest daughter of the Viscount and a lady of high literary attainments, wrote:

" On the occasion of the annual festivity of the Suwa Shrine all the participants put on a special dress. First, two persons, one holding a long wooden pole and the other a shorter one, then three persons imitating a lion, a lioness, and a lion called " Hogen," and then two others wearing head gears decorated with flowers, march toward the shrine keeping step to the music of flutes played by a group of flutists. Then on arrival at the spot, the pole holders begin the ceremony according to the established custom, which is followed by the young dancers of the year who are called "Yakusha." When this is finished, the entire group move out to the yards of the houses where the entertainment for the year takes its turn. There they performed many plays beginning with the younger players and ending with the older and more skilled ones. In this manner the festivity continues beyond midnight, every body greatly enjoying the annual occasion. It is said that the motion of the head and feet of the dancers required a lively but rhythmic carriage. Especially the lion had to be lively and aggressive, while the lion " Hogen" moved in a serene and dignified manner. The "Yakusha" is a group of actors who for the first time appear before the patron deity for the dance. The custom of the village is to give to every young man of twelve or thirteen years of age a chance to be one of the " Yakusha." The home where the Viscount was born and spent his early years enjoyed the right to furnish the lion instead of the lioness for generations. Hence he at the age of twelve years participated in the dance as a " Yakusha" and continued during the following eight or nine years to take part in the play, so that he became quite an expert."

Viscount Shibusawa firmly believed that the custom of this lion dance was an important factor in keeping the life of the villagers pure and high. As to how wholesomely it affected the social life of the community, the Viscount has this to say : "It is a beautiful custom for the old and young to spend several evenings for the rehearsal of this play, trying to develop the best that is in them for the dance and music. In these gatherings they may promote mutual understanding and the exchange of knowledge, which fact may go far to influence the autonomy of the village government."

Domestic influence played an important role in the life of the Viscount as it does in all youths. His father who, by his industry and diligence, brought about prosperity and elevated the status of his home in the community to the second rank, was a just and stern man, while his mother was a very incarnation of mercy. The Viscount being the only male child who survived, the mother lavished upon him the most intense and ardent love. How great her influence was upon him can be seen from the following incident: the birth day of the Viscount was registered in the local government as the 14th of February, but he always insisted that it was the 13th instead of the 14th, because his mother used to tell him so. As we shall see later, we have a reason to believe that the Viscount's deep interest in the welfare of lepers, that most unfortunate class of mankind, was early roused in him by her and thus it was a manifestation of his filial loyalty to his mother.

Among the relatives and associates of the Viscount, there were several promising young men who stimulated him to seek after the higher and nobler life of patriotism and chivalry. He had a famous teacher in fencing and admirable associates in developing it. Also he had first rate tutors in Chinese classics. In those days, it was quite customary for a well-to-do farmer's home conspicuous in the community to be frequented by political wanderers, who would remain in the home for several days as self-styled guests. They would drop in unexpectedly, but were not necessarily unwelcomed. They would discuss politics and give vent to their complaints about what was going on in the moral, social, economic, and political field. It was inevitable for the impressionable dispositions of the young people of the community to receive indelible influences from such contacts either for good or bad.

CHAPTER II

CHILDHOOD AND YOUTH

IN the childhood days of Viscount Shibusawa, there was no such institution as the primary school in the modern sense of the term in Japan. The schooling of boys was limited to reading, writing, and using the *soroban* (calculating instrument), conducted by private tutors. *Gekken* (fencing) and *Jyudo* were taught quite extensively, and primarily as arts of selfdefence, which meant not so much physical training as spiritual training.

The Viscount was early inspired by his father, who was himself quite a student of Chinese classics, to take lessons in the reading of the classics. He mastered the primer known as "Sanji Kyō" at the age of six years. By the time he reached the age of 14 or 15, he had finished the reading of several classical and historical books, all written in the Chinese language, under the tutorship of Rankō Odaka. This teacher opened the eyes of Viscount Shibusawa to the charm and fascination of the study and influenced him eagerly to aspire to the cultivation and development of a chivalrous and patriotic spirit—the spirit which was not only possessed by the tutor himself, but was also manifested by the heroes and geniuses described in the books read. Of all the classics which the Viscount went through, the Lun Yu (the analects of Confucius) exerted the most powerful influence upon his entire career, because he fully and completely allowed himself to be moulded by its teachings. It may be no exaggeration to say that very few Christians have read and worn out their New Testaments as the Viscount did his pocket Lun Yu. He read Lun Yu, committed it to memory, recited it, meditated upon it, and dreamed it. He loved it for the beauty of its literary style and its highly practical and moral teachings.

There is an episode which tells how zealous the Viscount was in reading. In the New Year morning at the age of twelve, his mother dressed him in formal clothes, as is the custom with us Japanese even to this day, and he was to make calls on the relatives and neighbours for " A Happy New Year." He took with him a book to read as he walked. Soon he became intensely interested in his reading and fell into a ditch, badly soiling the newest and best clothing his mother had prepared for him for the occasion. It was too much even for the gentle mother to keep her equanimity. So she scolded him, but with tactful discrimination not to discourage the boy in the good habit of reading. In this connection, another interesting story may here be given. The author accompanied the Viscount during his tour to America at the time of the Washington Conference. He was 83 years old then, 71 years after his ditch experience. He was returning from Rochester, to New York City. He said to the author: " I have exhausted all the books and pamphlets I brought with me from home for reading. I have a Japanese Bible presented to me by Mr. John Wanamaker in my recent visit to him. You had better read it to me beginning with the first chapter of the Old Testament." This order was given in the train,

Replica of the Home of the Viscount's Birth.

while it was running at full speed and making a tremendous noise. The order was obeyed and the author read chapter after chapter to the Viscount contending against the overwhelming noise. It took two or three days for him to get rid of hoarseness. On the steamer and in the train, the Viscount never allowed spare moments idly to pass by, constantly applying himself to reading. There is an old saying in Japan: "The soul of the three year old child persists for one hundred years." The reading habit burned into the soul of the Viscount in his early years certainly remained until his death at the age of 92. He was not only an omnivorous reader, but also had a marvellous capacity of memory. The paragraphs and sentences of immortal literary merit gathered from the books he went through were stored in his brain for ready use. This made him in later years a delightful conversationalist and an effective public speaker. His exquisite taste for literature naturally led him to the study of Chinese poetry and to its composition from early days.

A few words should be used in explaining what kind of physical and moral effect the training of fencing brought to bear upon the Viscount. Fencing is a national game of Japan, handed down to us from our remote ancestors. The regular and proper exercise of this game develops the muscles of the fencer's body, together with fortitude of mind and sharpness of eyes. Its traditional prestige eliminates from it anything mean or tricky. Its training and practice should be conducted from start to finish on the basis of fairness and square deal. The Viscount was trained by an expert of local fame, and had a number of companions who stimulated him to develop the art. It was the knowledge of this militaristic art that led him to form friendships with strong men of the Mito school—the school which was considered a nursery of the loyalists of uncompromising type.

But the Viscount was a son of and heir to a farmer family whose vocation he would have to perpetuate. To this situation his father drew the attention of the Viscount when he reached the age of about 14—the year Commodore Perry entered into Uraga Bay with his squadron. The father told the son that he must not be endlessly indulging in the cultural side of life, as he was to be the heir to the Shibusawa estate. So the young heir made up his mind to harness himself to the farm life. This of course did not mean that he should set aside all the learning and the fencing to which he had attained. He kept up his contacts with such leaders as Kado Momonoi, a loyalist and a master of Chinese classics and poetry; Sheishitsu Shibusawa, his uncle, from whom he received a stimulus to develop his calligraphic taste, in which he later became an expert, although in a quite different style from that of his uncle; Kisaku Shibusawa, his cousin and close copatriot; Tonei Odaka, a rare expert in fencing; Rankō Odaka, the elder brother of Tonei to whom we have already alluded, a man of strong personality and of an intense patriotism; and scores of friends who were ready at any time to lay down their lives for the Emperor and the country.

The word " farmer " at once brings the idea of the

cultivation of the soil. In Japan, raising rice, wheat, and vegetables is the business of the average farmer. Feeding silk worms is also regarded as a part of farming life. In the case of Banko Shibusawa, the father of the Viscount, the most prominent part of the farm life was given to the manufacture of indigo—the dye stuff very extensively used throughout the whole of Japan in those days when chemicals were unknown. In fact, nearly all well-to-do farmers set apart a portion of their fields for the cultivation of indigo. Banko Shibusawa not only extensively raised indigo in his own farm, but also bought it from neighbouring farmers. Banko Shibusawa through his years of experience in this profession made himself a keen expert. And it was largely due to his success with this phase of the farm life that he accumulated wealth to the extent that his family became one of the wealthiest in the community, if not the wealthiest. The Viscount being the son of such a father took a lively interest in the indigo business and manifested great sagacity as early as his 14th year. The secret of the success rested on grading the qualities of the leaves of the plant, their price being fixed accordingly, and the instinctive sorting of the grades could be attained only through years of experience. The process of manufacturing the dye stuff out of the leaves is simple and primitive. The large quantity of leaves bought or gathered from the farm is assorted. The leaves are separated from the stem. They are spread on mats and dried by the heat of the sun to a certain degree. Then they are piled up. Water is poured on them at fixed intervals. Heat is produced which causes fermen-

tation, reducing the leaves to a pasty condition.
They are beaten in the mortar into dough, which in
turn is made into small balls. The balls are dried
and made ready for the market. The reader will
readily see that in this business the work of agriculture, industry, and commerce are involved in a mini-
ature form. The Viscount was clever enough to master
all the secrets which his father had won by his hard and
long deliberation and did the job quite satisfactorily.
The Viscount also obtained the practical knowledge of
feeding silk worms, and it was because of this knowledge that he was in later years summoned by H. M.
the Empress Dowager Shōken to counsel with Her
Majesty on the subject.

As a young farmer, manufacturer, and merchant,
the Viscount proved himself quite promising for a
large and more extended career along these lines.
But he was not satisfied in the present situation. His
inclination toward political life had been steadily
growing in him through his contact with those public
spirited men already mentioned and under the influence of the widening chasm between the Imperial
Court of Kyoto and the Shogunate his expanding
life seemed to alienate him from the narrow and
monotonous life in the village. His ambitious mind
was so set on large affairs of the nation that it
soon considered the local and regional matters quite
secondary.

The following two stories might be cited as con-
tributary, at least subconsciously, to the Viscount's
future abandonment of his inheritance. One is a
trifling incident in a way, but involves much that is

illuminating. It clearly demonstrates the positive and incredulous mentality of the Viscount, which characterized his long life. Then the whole matter must have disgusted him and made him feel the intellectual distance between him and the people of the community. He must have consciously or unconsciously been persuaded that his future life could not be fostered in the atmosphere created by people so superstitious however otherwise congenial and loving they were. The other event distinctly strengthened his desire to give up his rural life to prepare himself for the task of making impossible such revolting acts of tyranny and despotism throughout Japan. The stories are briefly these: the Viscount had an older sister who became ill. His father took her with him to a resort to cure her. During their absence, the mother and the close relatives came together for a conference over the welfare of the ailing member of the family. According to a widespread custom among country people, they agreed to invite an ascetic-medium to tell them what were the causes of the illness. The Viscount was only 16 years of age then, but he was convinced of the foolish and superstitious nature of such an attempt and was strongly opposed to inviting into his home the fortune-teller. He was overruled on account of his minority. The medium was invited and went through a certain ceremony. He was soon inspired by spirits and told the company present that the curse of certain deities had fallen on the sick daughter. Among the deities there was the departed spirit of a dead member of the family long neglected. (According to Buddhist teachings, the spirit of a dead person becomes a *hotoke,* or a deity). Though his wishes had been ignored yet the Viscount was present. He asked the medium saying: "How many years ago was it that the neglected one died and what was the name of the era?" The medium promptly replied: "About fifty years ago and it was about the third year of Tempo." The reply was suicidal because it was self contradictory. The Viscount was born in the 11th year of Tempo and now 16 years old. Therefore the third year of Tempo was 24 years back less than half of 50 years. The Viscount at once turned to his mother believing that she would remember such a serious incident in her family if it happened only 24 years ago and asked her whether or not there was any one dead in the family whose spirit had been neglected. To this she replied that she knew nothing about it. The rest needs no elaboration, save that it was a day of victory for the Viscount.

The other story runs thus: the Viscount's father received a communication from the Deputy's office to be present there at the earliest possible date. The father caught cold and was unable to go and the Viscount, then 17 years old, was to represent his father. He and the village master went together and appeared before the Deputy, who acted haughtily and overbearingly. He said: "I summoned both of you here to-day for no other purpose than to order you and other wealthy men in the village to subscribe according to their abilities the needed amount for the marriage expense of a daughter of the governor. As this subscription is to be applied to such a felicitous event you must consider it a high honor to be numbered

among the subscribers. As to the amount to be met
by Ichiroemon (the common name of the father of the
Viscount), I fix it at 500 ryo. Gratefully accept the
assessment and pay the amount as soon as possible,
even within to-day."

What high-handed robbery? How could one "consider it a high honor" in the face of such an im-
position? Thus the fire of indignation was kindled in
the bosom of the Viscount, and yet repressing his
emotion, he politely replied: "I clearly understand
Your Excellency's proposition and shall quickly report
the matter to my father." The Deputy's face flashed
fire, and he uttered the following vindictive words:
"Stop your nonsense. Haven't you come here as the
representative of Ichiroemon, your father? You cannot decide on so trifling a matter on the spot and yet
claim to be the accredited representative? Such in-
decision means disloyalty and should not be tolerated.
You are now a young man of 17 years of age and
have reached the stage of life where you are undoubtedly exercising your free will on many personal
matters. There is no reason why you cannot give a
positive reply about 500 or 700 ryo. Your reply to
me amounts to contempt of a high officer, which
should not go unpunished."

Did such intimidations frighten the Viscount and
overawe him? No. Instead, the attitude of the Deputy
roused in the soul of the Viscount a dormant fire
heretofore undreamed of by him. The Deputy appeared
to the Viscount the very personification of the corrupt
rule of the Tokugawa regime. Young though he was,
yet then and there he swore to himself to dedicate

himself unreservedly to the altar of the destruction of the Tokugawa regime. The Viscount expressing in later years the feeling roused by the Deputy said : " I was almost ready to strike him in the face."

Seven years passed by from the time the Viscount thus drank the bitter cup thrust upon him by the Deputy. During the time, the central figure Ranko Odaka, around whom the three young men, the Viscount, Kisaku Shibusawa, and Tonei Odaka moved as the stars of the Great Bear move around the North Star, was a constant inspiration, giving them opinions and criticisms about domestic and foreign affairs. The time spirit was moving onward toward the formation of the public opinion expressed in the cry : " Down with the Tokugawa regime and away with foreigners." Odaka and his henchmen caught the spirit and hastened to carry on their plot of overthrowing the existing regime by direct action. But before that, the Viscount, who was the heir to his father's estate, must get the consent of his father to give up the inheritance in order to enter into a political career. This preliminary condition was quite important but hard to achieve. The night of September 13th, 1863 was a memorable one for the Viscount, because it was then that he prevailed over his father to relieve him from the future responsibility of the the headship of the family. No sooner was he released than he joined in the formation of the plot. Needless to state that Ranko Odaka was the generalissmo in the case. The revolutionary army was to be called a band of the soldiers of the gods. The statement of declaration was prepared by him. It was couched in most furious and vehement words, containing four points—namely (1) All foreigners then living in Yokohama, Hakodate, and Nagasaki shall be exterminated; (2) Any young man who refuses to join the band shall be killed on the spot; (3) The members of the band in their own villages shall be made the direct subjects of His Majesty, the Emperor, receiving rewards for their valiant deeds; (4) Even those who had been in close association with foreigners to that time shall be readily accepted as members of the band, if they give up their past life and surrender themselves to the authorities of the band. The posters of the declaration were to be very widely distributed. Besides, swords, lanterns, and uniforms were provided. Everything for the uprising was ready. But there was one important matter which would strengthen the cause or kill it outright, and that was the report of Tonei Odaka, who had been sent as an emissary to Kyoto, the seat of the Imperial Court. But who was Tonei Odaka who held the power of life and death over the movement and his relations to the Viscount? Tonei Odaka was the next younger brother of Ranko Odaka and was two years older than the Viscount. He early left his country home and studied in Yedo fencing and Chinese classics under famous tutors in those branches. This made him quite a figure, not only in his own village, but also in a wide circle. While in Yedo he came in contact with leaders of the Mito School—the school noted in fostering the spirit of loyalty to the Imperial Household, although its founder was one of the three supporters of the Tokugawa regime. Tonei Odaka was more or less a free-lance as he could devote himself to studies without being handicapped by domestic affairs.

The Viscount being the heir to a family could not devote his time so freely and exclusively to studies as Tonei could. But the two young men being great chums, and the Viscount's taste being quite similar to that of Tonei, we can easily see how the Viscount persuaded his father to let him spend a year or so in Yedo. This request was granted to him, and like a bird set free from the cage, off he went to Yedo, where he availed himself of every opportunity his keen and absorbing mind could grasp. He made many important contacts which helped prepare him to be what he was in later years. He entered into the private school of the Chinese classics conducted by the same teacher Tonei Odaka was under. He also became a pupil in a well known private school of fencing. Then the Viscount became acquainted with a gentleman by the name of K. Kawamura, who in turn introduced the Viscount to Yenshiro Hiraoka, an influential vassal to Prince Yoshinobu Tokugawa—the Prince who later became the 15th and last Shogun of the Tokugawa dynasty. Thus Tonei Odaka became one of the links of the chain which fastened the Viscount to the last Shogun. Also it was Tonei Odaka who saved the Viscount from a most disastrous failure, because it was his report and irresistible argument that persuaded the Viscount and the others present to give up the plot almost ready for attempted execution. The plot carried out, might have cost the life of the Viscount, thus changing the whole course of the industrial civilization of Japan. Tonei Odaka killed the plot completely. What was the ground on which his argument rested? It was the great power which the Shogun was still exercising all over Japan.

In Kyoto Tonei saw it, and saw also the failure of the rebellious attempts such as the Totsugawa and Ikuno Silver Mine rebellions. He saw another possible plan which might greatly strengthen the position of the Shogun and that was the rumor of the union between the Imperial Court and the Shogun's regime. To the mind of Tonei, the onset of the "band of the soldiers of the gods" against the Shogunate was as futile an attempt as to try to destroy the Fortress of Gibralter with a pistol. His conviction was adamant and no amount of arguments could change it. But on the other hand, the mind of the Viscount was firmly set on the plot. Thus sharp and fierce debate between them took place throughout the night. The elder Odaka, who had painfully kept silence, carefully weighed the arguments exchanged between the two sides, and could read his younger brother's mind quicker than any of the others who were present. Finally he arose and said: "What Tonei says is right. The situation in Kyoto has changed. If the Satsuma and Aizu Clans back up the movement of the union of the Imperial Court and the Shogunate, there lies no alternative for us but to abandon our revolutionary movement." This decision of Ranko Odaka was final and the Viscount who always placed boundless confidence in Ranko acquiesced in the decision. This incident took place in October 1863.

This sudden change affected the future movements of all the leaders of the plot, especially that of the Viscount. One rebellion after another was started and defeated by the Shogunate agencies. But the Shogunate became so nervous and sensitive that it spread a net of vigilance against rebels all over the country. Although the adventurous movement of "the band of the soldiers of the gods" had been nipped in the bud, yet the leaders of the band could hardly escape the net. Now the time had come for the Viscount to flee in order that he might save himself from suspicion and arrest. No time for delay! But where could he go as his name was already included in the black list of rebels. Almost at his wit's end, he recalled the name of Yenshiro Hiraoka. At this time Hiraoka was in Kyoto with his Lord, Prince Yoshinobu Tokugawa, who had been appointed by the Tokugawa regime as the Commander-in-Chief of the Imperial Guards. The Viscount took the liberty to designate himself and his cousin, Kisaku Shibusawa, as two retainers of Yenshiro Hiraoka. Under that designation they could travel to any part of the country in safety. They journeyed on toward Kyoto and soon arrived there where they were welcomed by Hiraoka.

CHAPTER III

RETAINER OF PRINCE Y. TOKUGAWA

VISCOUNT Shibusawa's visit to Kyoto was another epoch making event, perhaps just as significant as that of abandoning the revolutionary movement in his native village. For, though it was undoubtedly humiliating for the Viscount and his cousin Kisaku Shibusawa to pledge their allegiance to Prince Yoshinobu Tokugawa, who stood for the regime which a few months ago they planned to destroy, yet it was exceedingly important for their safety and future success so to do. Therefore they, through the kind offices of Y. Hiraoka, became full fledged *samurai* of the Hitotsubashi Branch of the Tokugawa Family. The Viscount was soon appointed to an office of minor importance, through which however he came into contact with men of different types and idiosyncrasies coming from the four quarters of the country.

The activities of the Viscount in Kyoto 1864–1867 already reveal his wide-awake and far-sighted statesmanship.

The first thing the Viscount observed was the helplessness of Prince Tokugawa as the Commander-in-Chief of the Imperial Guard, because the Prince had hardly any army. So he made a recommendation to raise an army. He and his cousin Kisaku were sent to the North to enlist privates. They came back to their home. There they tried to rescue Tonei Odaka who was being kept in prison on account of his social and political misdemeanors. They made a desperate effort to save him, but all in vain. However, they succeeded in bringing with them some 40 strong men to Kyoto. A very disheartening event took place in Kyoto while the Viscount was away. It was the assassination of Y. Hiraoka, who had placed strong confidence in the Viscount and in whom the Viscount saw a person of extraordinary wisdom. Strong though those 40 Northerners were, yet the number was far smaller than what the Viscount expected. In order to make up the shortage of men, he was despatched to Southwestern sections of the country—the territory of the Hitotsubashi Family. In those days, the first born youths were to stay at their homes as they were to be heirs to their fathers' estates. The second born and those below were free to enlist. As the representative of Prince Y. Tokugawa, the Viscount quit himself with certain pomp and dignity. Wherever he went, he invited the leaders of the community to meet him and appealed to them to meet their obligations to send their youths to Kyoto as privates in the army of their Lord Prince Tokugawa. He travelled quite extensively for the purpose, but with slim success. Somehow or other the Viscount's eloquence and his authority did not seem to move them. He was sorely tried almost to the point of despair, but his wonted persistency and tenacity to the purpose once formed were too strong even in this case to be defeated. He struggled hard and finally conceived the idea of gaining personal favor with the foremost leaders of the community. To this new strategy he resorted when he entered into the territory of Bicchu under the jurisdiction of the Hitotsubashi Branch. In a vil-

lage called Terado there lived a famous scholar whose
name was Roro Sakatani. Being the representative of
the Lord Yoshinobu Tokugawa, the Viscount counted
himself equal to any man however great and renowned
in the territory. This aristocratic self-confidence embold-
ened him to approach Roro Sakatani. He must search to
find a way to win the heart of his new acquaintance. So
the Viscount wrote a cordial letter to the sage of Terado,
enclosing in it a Chinese poem and sending a keg of *sake*
as a present. The poem reads something like this:

"The joyful rain of Spring makes everything fresh,
    The poet's bosom swells with emotions high,
As a token of good will a keg of *sake* is sent,
    Felicitating the health of a friend soon to be seen."

Such a sentiment couched in poetic garb was sure to
rouse fraternal emotions in Roro Sakatani. Thus they
met and for them " to know was to love." The supper
was prepared. They exchanged cups.

They began to discuss current topics. The Viscount
still held the views of the closed door and " away-with-
foreigners ", but the Terado sage took the opposite side—
the open door and the anti-away-with-foreigners, making a fine distinction between " foreigners " and " barbarians." Although he lived in a rural district away
from the centers of civilization and carried on educational work in a private school, yet the sage had imbibed advanced and enlightened views on the mooted
questions of the day. He indeed transcended the nationalistic form of thought and caught the much broader
and universal view then swaying the civilized world. In
this connection, it is quite significant to see Baron Y.

Sakatani, a son of Roro Sakatani and a foremost statesman of present day Japan, firmly standing for internationalism and world peace based upon justice and
fairness. Still more significant and beautifully romantic
is the fact that the acquaintance of the two great men,
Roro Sakatani and Viscount Shibusawa, finally event-
uated in the marriage of their children, the present
Baron Y. Sakatani and Miss Kotoko Shibusawa the
second daughter of the Viscount, a lady of superior
intellect who inherited that wonderful power of memory
possessed by her father.

Another strategy the Viscount resorted to was to
compete with Sekine, the fencing expert of local
fame. This was in a way critical for the Viscount,
because if he were defeated in this match, his fencing
ability would be greatly discounted, affecting in an ad-
verse manner the prestige he had established with Roro
Sakatani. This idea nerved him. The appointed day
came and the two foes appeared on the floor, surrounded
by a host of spectators. It did not take much time for
the Viscount to find his opponent lacking in offensive.
And sure enough he won the victory.

The Viscount's great success in these two strategic
operations opened the eyes of the villagers. They
thought a young stranger who found such an easy
access to their respected sage Roro Sakatani and who
could defeat the peerless fencer Sekine must be almost
superhuman. Sensing the situation the Viscount vigorously pushed his campaign of enlistment. One day he
met a group of young people of the village and spoke
to the effect that they should be proud to be called the
Clansmen of Prince Yoshinobu Tokugawa, who is now

Prince Yoshinobu Tokugawa.

the Commander-in-Chief of the Imperial Guards in Kyoto ; that it should be a privilege and honor for any young man to be enlisted in the army ; and that there could be no better chance for him to prove himself loyal and patriotic. No doubt the Terado sage and the fencing expert gave moral support to the efforts of the Viscount. Young men of high spirit and brave heart were moved, and one after another sent in their names as volunteers. This result became the keynote to the further campaign in the neighboring districts, and at the end of his campaign he had raised nearly 500 privates whom he brought with him to Kyoto. Prince Y. Tokugawa was highly pleased over the success of the Viscount and rewarded him in an extraordinary manner. The next task which confronted the Viscount was how to drill these rustic youths to make them a regiment of military men. The Viscount adapted the French method of military training, which fact would incidentally show that his rigid anti-foreign notions had undergone a change. Otherwise he would not have allowed his soldiers to handle guns imported from a foreign country. At any rate, this army proved in the course of time quite useful to Prince Y. Tokugawa.

Another contribution which the Viscount made for promoting the welfare of the Prince was in the way of finances. The expenditures of the Tokugawa regime toward its downfall, swelled enormously and taxes levied upon the people became heavier and heavier. The Viscount saw this bad effect upon his Lord, Prince Y. Tokugawa, who had to support a large number of retainers and soldiers. During the journey for the conscription compaign, the Viscount made careful observations of the kinds of products and the trading methods in different territories under the jurisdiction of the Prince. The Viscount saw a large profit to be obtained by the unification and rationalization of the disposal of products. The result was most helpful by bringing in much money to the coffers of the Prince.

The last contribution he tried to make, but which could not be realized on account of the delicate situation Prince Y. Tokugawa then encountered, was the Viscount's recommendation to the Prince not to accept the office of the Shogunate, even if the offer was made to him. This recommendation was rather audacious and presumptuous for a petty officer like the Viscount at that time to offer to his Lord, and under ordinary circumstances it is hardly credible that such an incident should take place. We briefly quote the words of the Viscount mentioned in his " Life of Prince Yoshinobu Tokugawa."

" At this time (when the 14th Shogun Iyemochi Tokugawa died), I worried a great deal, because I caught the rumor that Prince Yoshinobu Tokugawa would succeed to the Shogunate thus becoming the 15th Shogun. I had been studying the political trend ever since I came to Kyoto, especially paying my close attention to the movement of the leaders of the Satsuma Clan. They were determined to put an end to the Tokugawa regime. I had occasions to discuss politics with Kichinosuke Saigo (the Great Saigo) in Kyoto, and saw in him a dominant figure who might play the leading role in the coming Reformation. I could clearly see how unwise it would be for Prince Y. Tokugawa to assume the office against such tremendous odds. Although I had a boundless admiration for the high statesmanship and over-flowing popularity of the Prince, yet it would be very difficult for him to resuscitate the faltering regime managed by so many soft and luxurious officers. The result would be that the entire blame of misgovernment would fall upon the Prince. Therefore, the Prince should remain as heretofore a close adviser to the government, whose head,—that is—the Shogun, should be chosen from the other branches of the Tokugawa Family. In the meantime it would be better both for the government and the Prince, as the representative of the Hitotsubashi Branch of the Tokugawa Family, to strengthen himself with man power and material resources and reside in Osaka, so that he could, together with Kyoto, resist an enemy from the south if necessity demanded it. When I confided this secret to I. Hara, the high officer of the Prince, he told me that it was a most opportune memorial and should personally be presented to the Prince. But alas! The Prince's succession to the Shogunate was unchangeably settled before I could find any chance to address him. I was never before in my life so badly disappointed, and could hardly suppress feelings of deep irritation and discontent."

Thrown into despair, the Viscount must have felt anew in his heart the feelings which he had when he and Tonei Odaka debated the plot of overthrowing the Tokugawa regime. He might have thought that he should now insist on carrying out the plan and even die rather than to have this bitter experience. This dismal feeling must have been intensified, when he found out that he together with the rest of the Prince's officers must become officers of the Tokugawa regime which he had intended to destroy a few years before and which was now surely destined to fall. However, compelled by the force of circumstances, he was assigned to a military post of the Shogunate and accepted it reluctantly. During the tenure of this office an event which tested the calm courage of the Viscount took place. It was the

arrest of one Osawa who was charged with espionage.
The Viscount's colleagues were hesitant to accept this
duty on account of the rumor that Osawa was well
prepared to resist the Shogunate agency. The Viscount who had been spending gloomy days felt that the
job might give him relief from his depression. So he
volunteered to capture the traitor, and admirably succeeded in the discharge of this precarious duty. His
fame as a military expert suddenly rose in the army
circle. But this exploit was not enough to dispel his
daily gloom. In his reminiscences, the Viscount gives
his mental picture of that time in the following words:
" The Tokugawa regime is now being exposed to danger
of down-fall. The time may not be distant when
it topples over. If I carelessly remain in my present
position, I may become a prey to the doomed system.
I should not mind to go down into ruin with the system
were I placed in a post of high responsibility. But
I am nothing more than a petty officer. It is better to
return to the former life of a political wanderer than to
die as a nameless person in the fallen government." The
Viscount fell into this melancholia in the latter part of
the fall of 1866. Could he find a remedy to dispel his
gloom?

CHAPTER IV

VISIT TO FRANCE

WHILE Viscount Shibusawa was brooding over this fog-bound life, there came a call to him which changed his mental equilibrium. It was the order from the new Shogun that the Viscount should go to France as one of the retainers of Prince Mimbu of Mito, the younger brother of the Shogun. I. Hara, the chief officer of the Shogun, invited the Viscount to his own residence on the 29th of November, 1866, and thus spoke to him:

"I am sure that you have heard that there will be opened an exposition in France next year. On that occasion, the Emperors and Kings of various countries will visit Paris to inspect it and it was proposed, through the French Minister, that the presence of a relative of the Shogun is greatly desired. After careful deliberation, the Shogun has decided to dispatch Prince Mimbu of Mito for the occasion. The Shogun also is desirous to have his brother spend five or six years in France for study after the mission to the exposition is over. For this reason, the attendants of the Prince should be limited to a very few, but the Mito officers will not have their Prince go to France unattended. So seven in number have been chosen. But those who were chosen as the attendants are, every one of them, out and out anti-foreigners, regarding foreigners as barbarians and wild beasts. There is not the slightest inclination in them to learn anything in France. What will happen in the future is a matter of considerable worry, although Governor Yamataka will be a counsellor to the Prince. At any rate Prince Mimbu may not be able satisfactorily to carry on his studies, if he be surrounded by those stiff men. The Shogun feels that you are a proper person to accompany his brother for his sake as well as for your own. I was deeply struck with the pertinency of the Shogun's choice, and have gladly concurred in it. I hope that you will promptly accept this appointment."

The Viscount most gladly accepted the offer, saying that five years or ten years would not make any difference to him. I. Hara, knowing the Viscount's anti-foreign inclination, warned him about it. The Viscount's reply to him in the form of a frank confession is significant and characteristic of the Viscount. He says: "I am decidedly an anti-foreigner, and that without knowing foreign affairs. I am now of the opinion that one should know matters at first hand before he opposes or criticizes them. Moreover, I believe that there are many things which we should learn from foreign countries. From this point of view, I am pleased to accept the appointment." This unequivocal reply of the Viscount to I. Hara dissipated every trace of suspicion from the latter's mind as to the Viscount's attitude toward foreigners and things foreign. This belief of the Viscount that there would be many things to learn from foreign countries is a prophecy of the Viscount's whole later life. In regard to the mighty influence which this two years' trip of the Viscount to foreign countries exerted upon him, Baron Sakatani has this to say:

"None of us can adequately appraise how profoundly the two years' foreign tour of the Viscount affected his thoughts and how marvellously it filled his open mind with the materials wherewith he in later years enriched his country. The most important thought he brought back with him from his foreign visit is that the source of the wealth and power of a country lies in commerce and industry."

In order that the reader may thoroughly appreciate what the Viscount accomplished for his country and what he contributed to her welfare and civilization, he should forget his present surroundings, in which he is enjoying various facilities in transportation, communication, navigation, education, and amusement, and put himself back to the time when the Viscount began his foreign journey and become his fellow traveller. This would mean that the reader would be living in a country where the Feudal System of government is still performing its functions. There is not a mile of railroad; no telegraph and telephone; neither a street car nor an automobile; no such lights as electric, gas, or kerosene; nothing except candles and seed oil lanterns; no steamship to plough the high seas; no postal system; no machine industry to speak of; and no public system of education. The high minded *samurai* with the top-knot on his head, carries with him two swords, long and short, on the left side of his body, thrusting them between his sash and kimono. If you, by any chance, should rouse his ire, you might be exposed to fatal disaster, your head slashed from your body, and yet he go unpunished, because he is a *samurai!* The value of a man's life is infinitely cheap.

Prince Mimbu and his retinue consisting of thirtyone officers and servants left Yokohama on board the French steamer Alphée on the 15th of February, 1867. Among them there were two foreigners, Alexander Siebold of the English Legation and Dury, Consul-General of France. Siebold spoke the Japanese language. The officers consisted of a physician, military experts, experts in foreign affairs, a translator, an interpreter, and an executive secretary. The Viscount was a secretary-treasurer and as such was very close to the Prince. Although the Viscount made up his mind no longer to be a blind anti-foreigner, as can be seen from his confession before I. Hara, yet he still held to his old antipathy toward foreigners, even after he had embarked on the foreign steamer. The Mito group were especially strong in their belief in the national superiority of their own country and in their contempt of things foreign. One evening, the Viscount fell into conversation with Taichi Tanabe, one of the experts in foreign affairs and made derogatory remarks about foreigners, charging them as being imperialists and aggressors. At such a time it was customary for the Viscount to cite the historical event of the opium war of 1842, in which China in spite of her just cause was defeated by England and compelled to cede to her the port of Hongkong. T. Tanabe took issue with the Viscount and supported his argument by expressing his admiration for a foreigner who was none other than Townsend Harris, the first American Consul-General to Japan. The story of Townsend Harris, narrated by Tanabe, was a revelation to the Viscount, and from that moment he became not only an extreme admirer of Townsend Harris, but also a staunch friend of the United States of America. Thus at the very start of his foreign trip, the fortress of anti-foreignism constructed by the hands of ignorance and prejudice in the heart of the Viscount was shattered by the explosive power of knowledge and enlightenment. The far reaching influence upon the Viscount of the impressions he received from the story of Townsend Harris as told by Tanabe, can be estimated as almost equal

to all the other influences he came under during the
rest of his journey. For the Viscount's contributions
to the promotion of healthy and lasting friendly relations
between Japan and America fill a large part of his
long career and can be traced back to that hour of il-
lumination. This is no place to discuss the Viscount's
relation with Townsend Harris. But as his unreserved
admiration for the character and deeds of Townsend Harris purified his whole attitude toward America, and as
his relation to America constitutes the major part of his
international activity, the author feels justified in giving
in advance a glimpse of the life of Townsend Harris by
quoting the words of the Viscount. The reader may
construe these words as the Viscount's version of the
story told by Tanabe. The quotation is taken from the
Viscount's inscription on the back of the monument
dedicated to the memory of Townsend Harris, in the
premises of Gyokusenji, Shimoda, Idzu, dedicated on the
12th of October, 1927.

"Townsend Harris, the first Consul-General of the United
States of America to reside in Japan, arrived at Shimoda, Idzu,
in August 1856. In those days, our people of all classes were
poorly informed about the World's affairs, and most of them
took it for granted that all foreign Powers were insatiably greedy
and aggressive. Nothing daunted by this unfavorable atmosphere,
he spared no pains to point out to our authorities the advantage
of starting commercial connection with foreign nations, and explained to them the established usages and conventions of international intercourse. His painstaking efforts at enlightening
the minds of the officials of the Shogunate, were finally crowned
with success in concluding a commercial treaty between Japan
and America. This formed a model for the treaties which the
Shogunate subsequently negotiated with other Powers. As a

matter of fact, however, there were not wanting among our countrymen people who entertained toward Mr. Harris a deep feeling of indignation, because they thought that the treaty which he had succeeded in arranging was won by intrigue and chicanery on his part.

In the meantime, Mr. Harris was promoted to the post of Minister Plenipotentiary and his official residence was moved to Edo. The Shogunate was then increasingly involved in difficulties, domestic as well as foreign. To add to its troubles, the Representatives of the Powers, generally lacking proper understanding of Japan and of things Japanese, not infrequently acted in an arbitrary and arrogant manner, thereby aggravating the public agitation against the Government. But so far as Mr. Harris was concerned, he always conducted himself fairly and squarely, constantly showing his sympathy to Japan. His honorable attitude was most strikingly demonstrated in connection with the death of Mr. Henry C. J. Heusken, his official interpreter, who was assasinated in January 1861 by rowdies on the bank of the Furukawa in Azabu. All the foreign Ministers, with one exception, were highly wrought up by the incident, and blaming the Shogunate for its incompetency to protect them, they closed their legations at Edo and withdrew to Kanagawa. But the American Minister who happened to be the one most intimately concerned, did not approve the step taken by his colleagues of the other Powers. He refused to stir from his official quarters at the Zempukuji Temple, but calmly attended to his duties as usual as if wholly unconcerned about his own safety. The courageous and magnanimous attitude taken by Mr. Harris on this critical occasion made a strong appeal to the imagination of our people, who were now convinced of the genuineness of his sentiment toward them, and who from that moment began to put trust in America as a true friend of Japan. Japan and America owe a heavy debt of gratitude to Mr. Harris whose noble personality thus initiated the relationship of mutual friendship which has happily united the two nations during these seventy years."

The Viscount kept diaries covering his entire journey, which he published under the title of the " Kosei Nikki " (Diary of the Western Journey). Every thing in the steamer was to him an object of curiosity. He writes : " A stuff made by coagulating the milk of cows was put on the bread and it was delicious." " Drank a hot drink prepared by boiling beans called coffee." " Regular meal was given twice a day, but tiffin was served three times." " The gong was sounded twice before meal time. The first one was to call attention to the hour and the second one to enter into the dining room." " If a guest does not take his seat around the table, the physician calls upon him. If nesessary, medicine is prescribed for him." " These are trifles to write down, but they go far to comfort us and make our life enjoyable." The steamer soon reached Shanghai. There for the first time, the Viscount witnessed street gas lamps and telegraph wires. In Hongkong the Prince and his party embarked on the steamer Impératrice. When the steamer reached Suez, the Viscount made a careful study of the plan for the construction of the Canal.

The most impressive lesson he learned from this gigantic enterprise was the public-spiritedness of the Western man. He writes : " Generally speaking, the Western man does not undertake to do a thing for his own sake alone. He aims at the public welfare of his country or community. The magnitude of his schemes and the audacity of his purposes deserve high admiration." Before he arrived at this conclusion, he writes :

" The Western part of the Red Sea is separated from the Mediterranean by land which joins together Arabia and Africa, and its width is about 150 miles. Because of the existence of this strip of land the war ships and merchant vessels of the West must sail around the Cape of Good Hope in order to travel to the East, thus incurring an enormous expense and great inconvenience. To overcome this barrier a French Company undertook to construct the Suez Canal on a huge scale, beginning the work in 1865 and planning to complete it within three or four years. Along the railway many tents have been put up for the laborers. When it is completed direct contact of the West with the East will be established, and undreamed commercial facilities be enjoyed by the peoples of the two hemispheres."

Whether or not, the Viscount knew that this French Company was organized " with the capital £ 8,000,000 in 400,000 shares of £ 20 each " is not mentioned in his record. But he might have felt that such a gigantic undertaking could not have been carried on by private capital. Hence it may not be wide of the mark to suppose that the Viscount's insistence on the importance of the collective or cooperative system for business enterprise received a subconsicous stimulus from his observation of the work of the Suez Canal. He also had the first experience of riding on railway trains about this time. The Prince and his party took the steamer Saida at Alexandria on the 27th of March, 1867 and crossed the Mediterranean. On the 3rd of April the steamer arrived at Marseilles. There the Prince and his suite were welcomed by the salute of 21 guns. They were met by Flury-Herald the honorary Consul for the Shogunate. Then under the escort of troops of cavalry the party entered the Hotel Marseilles. The firing of 21 guns in honor of the Prince meant to place him in Imperial or Royal rank. The party spent a few days in Marseilles for sight-seeing. They were

invited to witness a military review and to inspect
schools. In the port of Toulon, they inspected battle-
ships, an iron factory, smelting-furnaces, reverberatory,
and various machinery. On their way to Paris they stopped at Lyons and visited a silk spinning factory, where
several thousand girls were working. At last they
reached Paris and registered their names at the Grand
Hotel. The chief affair for the Prince on arrival was to
have an audience with Emperor Napoleon. A few days
were spent in preparation and on April 28 the Emperor granted audience to Prince Mimbu. The creden-
tials of the Shogun were delivered to the Emperor and
the written acknowledgement of its receipt was handed
to the Prince. The Viscount was not present at this
ceremony, as the Prince was attended only by his officers for foreign affairs, but he learned all about it from
his colleagues.

Beginning with this introduction Prince Mimbu's
status as a royal visitor to France became widely known.
Invitations from Emperor Napoleon III to theatre
parties and from high Government officials to brilliant
balls followed one after another. The Prince and his
party were dazzled and intoxicated by the magic of the
material civilization. They visited the botanical and
zoological gardens, hospitals, the water works, reservoir,
and institutions which they could not help but covet
for their own country. Needless to say that they visited
the Exposition over and over again. Then came the
red letter day when Emperor Napoleon III, surrounded
by the Imperial and Royal visitors of different nations
as well as by high dignitaries of fame, faced an
immense audience in the Exposition ground to conduct

the public ceremony of awarding prizes to those who had helped the exposition to achieve a grand success. The Emperor delivered His Imperial address in a most elaborate and impressive manner. The Viscount took down the speech a part of which is worth translating here.

"——In the olden time, the Greek poets sang about the great horse races as if they demonstrated the highest peak of their civilization. But this International Exposition includes the best of the arts of different countries. It may be an exaggeration to say that this display of the world's finest products is an indication that the world's culture has reached its highest point, but it can be said that we are moving to that climax. I wonder how those Greek poets would sing if they were to come back to life and witness this scene. The best artists, mechanics, and inventors of the different parts of our mighty globe have attended this Exposition. Moreover, Emperors and Kings have paid their visits and cooperated to make this enterprise successful. The Exposition as such may be temporal and material, but its influence is permanent and spiritual, for it has brought men from all over the world to sit together as friends, prefering one another in honor and forgetting enmities. The participants in the Exposition have contributed their natural and artificial exhibits with the altruistic motive to contribute to mutual enrichment. Certainly this Exposition of 1867 is an enterprise for the universal good.——Your Majesties, Emperors and Kings of the different countries of Europe and other parts of the world, ladies and gentlemen, I congratulate myself on the high honor Your Majesties and all of you present have been pleased to confer upon me by your presence. I take pride in the thought that this splendid opportunity of showing my honored visitors the prosperity, civilization, and culture of my country has been afforded me."

The ceremony lasted nearly four hours, beginning at one o'clock in the afternoon. Prince Mimbu performed his duty to his credit, thus fulfilling his mission to France. Between this and September 3, when the Prince and his small party started on an inspection tour of other European countries, they were kept busy in sight-seeing and social functions. The Prince and his party were invited by Ministers of different countries stationed in France to banquets, balls, and theatres. The first other country the Prince and his party visited was Switzerland. There he was received by the President of the Republic at the city of Bern. On the 13th of September, the party left Switzerland and arrived at The Hague on the evening of the 15th. They were welcomed by the Government officers and taken to the Belevue Hotel in a state carriage. The next day they inspected the Parliament building and on the evening of the 17th, they were escorted by the cavalry troops to the Palace where they were received by the King. While staying there they visited the arsenal, the shipyard, barracks, and the gun factory. The Prince formed an acquaintance with the Crown Prince, the brother of the King. From The Hague the party went to Brussels. Here too the party was welcomed by the civil and military officers. They were taken in a state carriage and presented to the King for an audience. In the evening, the party was invited by the King to a theatre party. While in the city, they inspected the Military Academy, shooting ground, chemical factory, barracks, the fortress of Anvers, the gun factory of Liege, the iron and gun factory of Seraing, the glass factory of Sainte-Marie-d'Oignies. Also they were invited to inspect a military review and to banquets and hunting parties.

On the 19th of December, 1929, H. M. the Present

Emperor of Japan was exceedingly gracious to invite the Viscount to an informal luncheon specially planned in his honor. On that occasion the Viscount touched upon an incident which happened 62 years ago, when the King of Belgium granted an audience to Prince Mimbu. The story runs in this fashion :

"King Leopold thus spoke to the prince, 'A nation which uses iron is strong, and a nation which produces iron is wealthy. It is necessary for Japan to become powerful by using iron. This means that Japan should import iron from a foreign country, and I hope that that foreign country will be no other than Belgium.' The King presented the case in an interesting manner. But to me, who was raised according to the teachings of Confucius and Mencius and in the atmosphere thick with *Bushido* spirit which scorns material interests the King's words appeared very strange, and made me question in my mind whether is it kingly for a royal personage to act like a merchant."

The Viscount adds that H. M. the Emperor seemed to have taken a fancy to the story. Surprising as was this Belgian experience to the Viscount, nevertheless it was a precious lesson which taught him the sanctity of industry. The party returned to Paris at the end of their visit to Belgium. After a few days they proceeded to Italy where the reception was nearly the same, including an audience with the King, sightseeing, and inspections. When the party came to Florence, the British Minister to Italy called on the Prince and transmitted to the latter a message from the Queen of England extending an invitation to the Prince to inspect the fortifications of the island of Malta. The party accepted the invitation and embarking on a British cruiser, they left Livorno on the 3rd of November and reached Malta on

The Viscount ready to Start for France.

Flury-Herald.

Prince Mimbu.

the 6th. Twenty-one salutes were fired from the fortress in welcome. On landing they made inspections of the dockyard, factories, and an iron foundry. They were invited to an evening party. On the 11th they left Malta for Marseilles on board the British cruiser Indemion. But at the distance of about one hundred miles from Malta an accident happened in the cruiser at night. It was a damage to the crank-shaft. A great stir was made in the ship and the captain approached the Prince to apologize for the mishap. However the captain's visit to the Prince was more than a mere expression of apology. The object was to obtain a decision as to whether or not the Prince and the party would prefer to return for repairs to Malta one hundred miles back, or go on by using sails, in which case it would take much longer to arrive at the destination. By this time all members of the party had gathered together around the Prince. The dilemma in which the captain was caught was that even if he did sail back to Malta, he could not guarantee the complete repair of the boat, and that if the voyage was to be continued, a considerable delay must be expected as the wind might change its course at any moment. At a time like that the Viscount's counsel was always sought as his ability to cut the Gordian Knot was famous among his colleagues. The Viscount made a simple recommendation to the Prince which the Prince approved. "The best thing for us to do is to give full power to the captain and stop talking." The Viscount was chosen to confer with the captain and addressed him through an interpreter: "Placing full confidence in the captain we have entrusted our lives into his hands. He has a full right to do as he pleases, whether to let the boat go on or turn back." The captain, an English officer, who placed faith above life itself, was highly delighted in this expression of confidence. Here it is not difficult for us to imagine that the captain and his crew took fresh courage and put new enthusiasm into the manoeuvering of the boat. The boat arrived at Marseilles on the 16th, but on account of the stormy weather, all the passengers stayed in it till the next morning. They spent one day in Marseilles and arrived at Paris on the 19th. Having spent ten days in resting, the party started for England on the first day of December. They were welcomed at Dover with the salute of 21 guns and by many civil and military officials. They proceeded to London where the Prince and his suite were received with military ceremony. The arrangement for the audience with Queen Victoria was made through the Department of Foreign Affairs on the 3rd of December and the next day the Queen received the Prince at Windsor Palace. During the visit to England the party inspected the London Times, the Bank of England, the Mint, shipyards, armories, barracks, the Military Academy, Portsmouth Naval Station, and the Crystal Palace. Besides, they were invited to evening parties and military reviews. They returned to Paris on the 17th of December. This concluded the European itinerary of the Prince and his suite. Henceforth a new program began for the Prince. It was the taking up of the study to which the Prince and his advisers had been looking forward.

Almost within a fortnight after the study question was settled, the news of the political change in Japan

reached France. The first news of the change was mentioned in the daily papers of Paris on the 2nd of January, 1868. From that day on the papers reported what
was transpiring in the political field at home. A paper of
the date of the 25th of February mentioned the fight
between the Imperial army and that of the Tokugawa
regime at Toba and Fushimi. The Prince and those
around him were painfully stirred by the news,
even though they were skeptical about the truthfulness
of the reports. But to the mind of the Viscount
the news of the political reformation in Japan was
no surprise. His farsightedness was keen enough to
diagnose the ailment of the Tokugawa regime so that
he knew its days were numbered. Therefore, he held
himself calm and undisturbed in the midst of the con-
sternation and confusion which took hold of the minds
of Minister Kurimoto and others. In the reminiscences
of the Viscount, a glimpse of the mood into which most
of his colleagues were thrown is given in the following words :

"Beginning with the report that the Shogun returned his
governing power to the Emperor, similar reports were mentioned
in the Parisian papers from day to day. But the Japanese surrounding the Prince and his French tutors condemned them as
propaganda, and were loathe to believe them. But remembering as I did what was going on in Kyoto, it had been a fore-
gone conclusion with me that a great political change would
sooner or later take place. I spoke of it more than once. So
at this time I argued with my colleagues and upheld the cred-
ibility of the newspaper reports. The first information from
home reached us in the early part of January. It said that on
the 14th of October the Shogun returned the governing right
to the Imperial Court and that it was accepted; and that the two

Clans of Satsuma and Choshu had allied themselves to fight the Shogunate. When we read this information we naturally anticipated that there would take place a rapid change in the political field. Toward the beginning of April we received further information that the forces of the Shogunate and those of the two Clans above mentioned had clashed at Toba early in January; that the Shogun's army was defeated, as a result of which the Shogun himself was obliged to give up the Osaka Castle and to return to Yedo on board a ship; and that in Yedo he issued a proclamation to his Clansmen to surrender themselves to the Emperor, the Shogun himself retiring to Mito. It is needless to say that every bit of this information overwhelmed us, living in a far away foreign land, with indescribable bewilderment and nerve-racking anxiety.......But what is done cannot be undone, even though we gnash our teeth and tighten our folded arms. Not the slightest good comes from crying over spilled milk."

Now that the Shogunate had fallen an important question was raised with reference to the present status of Prince Mimbu in France. The question was whether he would immediately return home or remain for study. The Viscount upheld the latter plan and his views prevailed. But Minister Kurimoto was stationed in France by the Shogunate and it was only proper that he should resign his post. Thus on the 24th of April, 1868, he left Paris for home. The Viscount conferred with the Minister about the future support of the Prince. A perfect understanding was reached between the two gentlemen, so that there could rise no embarrassment even if the Shogunate had lost its power. Yet the Viscount felt the need of preparing for the worst. He wanted to save money enough to support the Prince for the next two or three years.

The first move he made was to dismiss the Prince's private tutors. The next was to give up the expensive "Temporary Residence at Paris" at No. 53 Pergolèse St. and to register the Prince's name in a school. The third was to reach an understanding with his father in Japan that he would render financial assistance in case the Viscount might be in need. These plans of the Viscount seemed the wisest thing to do and he committed himself to them. But on the 20th of July the Prince received an official letter from the local government of the Mito Clan. It read: "By the order of the new Government the Mito government urges the Prince's return. S. Isaka and J. Hattori have been despatched to escort the Prince back." At this time Prince Yoshinobu was residing in Mito and the message from Mito was construed as his own. Hence the order was final and irresistible. The Prince must give up his intended study and return. A message of the same nature was addressed to the Prince from the foreign office of the new Government and it read : " The Restoration has been achieved and the Prince should return home." The Viscount in conference with Minister S. Kurimoto discussed steps to be taken to bring to an end the Prince's stay in Paris. The first thing to do was to ascertain the attitude of Emperor Napoleon III and his Government with regard to the Prince's return. The reply of the Goverment to the Prince was : " We have done our best to make the sojourn of Your Highness in this country profitable as well as pleasant in conformity with the wish of the last Shogun. But now that the new Government has been established, we are under obligation to ascertain its idea in regard to the return of Your Highness. So we have already sent an official communication to it requesting a definite reply. We shall lose no time in communicating to Your Highness the reply from Your Highness' Government." Although the return of the Prince was a settled question, yet in deference to the request of the French Government the Prince decided to remain in France until he heard from that Government. In the meantime, the Prince was urged by his French tutor to make an inspection tour. In response to this suggestion, the Prince with a small party left Paris on August 2. They visited an iron foundry, the reverberatory, and the fortress at Cherbourg; saw a bronze statue of the great Napoleon at Place d'Armes; inspected fortresses on the mountains and the sea coast at Roule ; also inspected the iron foundry, the shipyard, and the armory at Brest; studied the trade and marine industry at Nantes and Saint Nazaire ; and visited the iron foundry at Basse-Indre. The party returned to Paris on the 11th of August. On the 24th of August the Prince and party started on another inspection trip. Near Rouen they inspected cotton spinning factories, dyeing and printing works. At Le Havre they visited the Exposition of naval armaments and machineries and inspected the fortress. On August 27th they came back to Paris.

On the 9th of September Minister Roches, who had just returned from Japan to France, called on the Prince and told him minutely what had happened in Japan since the Restoration. The minister paid a further visit to the Prince on the following day and gave his judgment to the Prince as follows : " I believe the commotion in Japan will not cease for sometime. Nay, the nation will suffer from increasing confusion. Facing such a situation it will be unwise for Your Highness to give up your study just begun and return. It is highly desirable that Your Highness complete your study and increase your knowledge about politics and military tactics, thus enriching your experience and broadening your views." The Prince expressed his hearty appreciation to the minister for the courteous advice and yet told him that it was impossible for him to conform to it. The Prince's reply was as follows: "The ex-Shogun retired to Mito at the behest of the new Government. Moreover, there came an official note from Mito urging my return. It amounts to a command from the last Shogun to which there is no way open for me but to obey. Your Excellency's timely suggestion is deeply appreciated, although I profoundly regret my inability to accede to it." The Minister was disappointed not a little, but the argument was too obvious for him to refute. On the 22nd of September the two men Isaka and Hattori, who had been despatched to escort the Prince back home, arrived at Paris and the conditions at home were minutely explained to the Prince. From then on the Viscount's time was occupied by the preparation for the departure. Various items had to be attended to. The first one was to confer with the French Government on behalf of the Prince. Emperor Napoleon III had pursued the policy of promoting cordial relations with Japan, and purposed to strengthen this policy by keeping the Prince in France as long as possible. The Emperor and his Government seemed to have been in perfect harmony in such a policy. The conference was a delicate one, but the Viscount succeeded in making his point clear in regard to the immediate return of the Prince. Other items discussed were the dismissal of the Prince's tutors; the financial preparation for the homeward journey of the Prince and his party; and the account with the owner of the "temporary residence" for which the Prince had paid rent in advance covering three years. Every thing having been satisfactorily settled, the Prince made his farewell call on the Emperor and the high officials of his Government, and he and his suite left France on board an English steamer in the middle part of October 1868. This concludes the colorful journey of Prince Mimbu and his suite.

But before we conclude this chapter, it is highly important to sum up the influences that moulded the life of the Viscount during his French and European trip, as they had vital bearings on his career from thenceforth to the end of his life. The most important factor in Viscount Shibusawa's life was of course his extraordinary natural ability. He came in to this world with a soul endowed with an ever-expanding capacity for things true, good, and beautiful, and he jealously kept that capacity pure and undefiled. His was a soul healthy, vigorous, and powerful, scrupulously following the leading of the inner light. His nature was profoundly ethical. In this respect he is beyond emulation, and this may very likely discourage many seriously minded youths who carefully study his life instead of encouraging them. Nevertheless, a soul like his has an inestimable educational value. The Viscount's trip to France served first to vitalize his innate force of character and to make him wake into a strong self-consciousness, so that his personality became social, national, international, and universal. The trip made him a magnetic personality and gave him fine social adaptability.

The fact that the Viscount visited Europe not in an individual capacity, but as an attendant on Prince Mimbu gave him a splendid opportunity to enter the most refined and highly cultured circles in Europe. He came into close contact with Napoleon III, a strong champion of human rights and liberty, and with other rulers and dignitaries of Europe. He inspected many industrial plants; naval and military forces; and educational, religious, and social institutions. He saw the panorama of modern civilization.

There were two Europeans who exerted permanent influence upon the Viscount. One of them was Flury-Herald, an honorary Consul-General for the Shogunate. Flury-Herald was an experienced banker. He often took the Viscount to the *Bourse* to explain its activities in the buying and selling of securities. All this was a living education for the Viscount whose assimilative mind did not allow anything worth remembering to pass by unnoticed.

Another man was Colonel Willette. The status of the Colonel can be judged from the fact that he was made an advisor or tutor to the Prince. Emperor Napoleon III ordered the Minister of War to select a military officer and recommend him to the Prince as his tutor. The choice fell upon Colonel Willette. The Viscount was trained in fencing, as we already have seen, and had had much experience in demonstrating his ability. He was by no means a mere amateur in that art. This manly spirit of the Viscount found a congenial response in the heart of the Colonel, and the Viscount became his fast friend. He must have influenced the Viscount in understanding the patriotic and noble spirit of the high military officers of the French nation.

The friendly and democratic relationship existing between the Consul-General and the Colonel was something new and highly suggestive to the Viscount. Colonel Willette as a military officer represented to the mind of the Viscount the class of *samurai*, and Flury-Herald as a banker, the class of businessmen or merchants. To him, the difference between the two classes was almost irreconcilable, because Feudal Japan divided her people into four classes—*Samurai, Farmers, Artisans,* and *Mer--chants*. To the Japanese mind of the Viscount it was condescension on the part of Colonel Willette to put himself on the same level with Flury-Herald, a business man, while it was unpardonable presumption on the part Flury-Herald to step up into the circle where the Colonel moved. But in France the two men mingled freely and talked pleasantly as if they were brothers. Here in this relationship, the Viscount for the first time saw the possibility of doing away with class distinctions and with the superiority-complex of officials in their attitude to the people. Viscount Shibusawa broke down the tradition which divided people into classes and gave preference to military officers over the people because he combined in his own person *Samurai* and *Chonin*. The Viscount speaking about the relationship of the two men said:

" There exists no class distinction between these two gentlemen. They are perfectly equal. One is an officer and the other a banker, but the way they deal with each other is enviably friendly in

the eyes of Japanese grown up in the air of officialism. They
frankly exchange arguments. This their friendliness gave me
a deep impression, and from that day I made up my mind to
surrender my political career to the work of developing commerce,
through which the destruction of officialism can be achieved."

CHAPTER V

GOVERNMENT OFFICER

THE unseen hand of Destiny has more than once interfered with the personal intention or determination of Viscount Shibusawa overruling him in spite of his powerful remonstrance. Each time he yielded to it, not because it threatened him with the weapon of tyranny, but because it waved over him its magic wand of humanity and friendliness. The full-orbed common sense of the Viscount always left a flexible margin in his bosom to reconsider or even to change if necessary his preconceived plans in deference to one who offered a substitute, so long as it did not infringe upon his sense of justice and fairness. This was true when he yielded to the persuasion of Ranko Odaka to give up the rebellious movement described in an earlier chapter, and to Yenshiro Hiraoka to become a retainer to Prince Yoshinobu Tokugawa, a representative of the Hitotsubashi Branch of the great Tokugawa Family, whose regime the Viscount had wanted to destroy; and when he kept up his relationship with Prince Tokugawa as his Lord, even after the Viscount's opposition to the Prince's accepting the office of the Shogun was ignored. The office which he now came to hold was forced upon him much against his convictions. Here again the invisible hand of Destiny, through the powerful personality of Marquis Okuma, presented strong arguments why the Viscount should join the group of men who were to shoulder the responsibility of the national welfare. But before we listen to the Marquis, we shall briefly describe the movements of the Viscount after his return to Japan.

To begin with, Viscount Shibusawa was a typical loyalist who despised the duplicity of serving two masters.

He cast in his lot with the Tokugawa regime and with the fall of that regime he closed his career as an official. However, he would serve the deposed Lord as his loyal servant as heretofore. The Viscount's actual Lord was Prince Mimbu, whom he served nearly two years as a close attendant, and there is room for speculation whether the Viscount might not have continued his service with Prince Mimbu instead of returning to the ex-Shogun, the elder brother. If the Viscount had served Prince Mimbu for the rest of his life, he could not have been blamed as a betrayer of the principle he advocated—loyalty to one master. Staying with the Prince might have more deeply satisfied the demand of his conscience, because he had gladly accepted the appointment to accompany the Prince to France and grew in favor with the Prince during that most interesting and inspiring journey, while he was sorely disappointed even to resigning his office, when his serious recommendation to Prince Yoshinobu Tokugawa not to accept the office of the Shogun was apparently ignored, and thus the spiritual relationship between the master and the servant had been broken. Moreover, the transfer of loyalty from one master to another in this case was from brother to brother.

The Viscount on his return home visited his family who had missed him for a long time and whom the Viscount was very glad to see again. Then he came to Tokyo to attend to the business of the Prince who was living at the mansion of the Mito Clan at Koishikawa. The Viscount was asked to go to Shizuoka, where the ex-Shogun was then living in voluntary confinement. The Prince handed him a letter addressed to the Shogun and commanded him as follows:

"Carry this letter to the ex-Shogun and tell him about events and matters as they have so far transpired. I have written in the letter how grateful I have been for the treatment accorded to me while I was staying in Kyoto; how I had to give up my intended study in France when the great change at home took place; and how discretely I am withholding my visit to him, closing with the statement that he would learn more fully from Shibusawa. Keep this in your mind when you address him. When you have finished your audience with the Shogun, you must return to Mito and tell me your impressions. As I have repeatedly told you lately, Mito is a place full of trouble and the future is uncertain. The worst is that I have very few to depend upon. Come back as quickly as possible."

Thus the young Prince, whom the Viscount has accompanied nearly two years and served under manifold circumstances, speaks to him with the utmost confidence and trust. Can any one imagine that the Viscount with his cultured sensibility failed to catch the full meaning of the concluding remarks of the Prince: "Come back as quickly as possible" He must have journeyed toward Shizuoka with these words ringing in his ears. It was toward the close of December of 1868 that he arrived there.

There in Shizuoka, Ichiō Okubo was the chief minister of the Shizuoka Clan. To him the Viscount delivered the message entrusted to him and requested the minister to hand the Prince's letter to the ex-Shogun. The Viscount also requested the minister to arrange an audience with the Shogun. At the same time, the Viscount presented to J. Hiraoka, the Treasurer of the Clan, the financial reports covering the entire journey of the Prince to France. Two or three days after the Viscount had closed the business transaction with the treasurer, an announcement reached him that the ex-Shogun would grant him an audience. The ex-Shogun was virtually under a ban and dared not receive any one of social distinction. But it was different with the Viscount, as he was an attendant to the brother of the Shogun and was not conspicuous in his official status. The hour for the audience came. To one over whom the memory of the life in the " Temporary Residence " of the Prince in France was still hovering, the reception room where the ex-Shogun was to condescend to meet his faithful servant was modest and shabby. The Shogun appeared. The young Shibusawa could not suppress his emotion and addressed his Lord : " I never dreamed to be received in audience in such a place. It overwhelms my heart." The ex-Shogun responded most serenely; "I came to meet you in order that I may hear about Mimbu, and that is all. You must not depart from the business at hand." This response from the Lord sounded austere and cold to the Viscount. But at second thought he felt that the Lord was right as the mission entrusted to him was not to bewail over the past, but to make full report about Prince Mimbu. So he went on to minutely tell about the European tour of the Prince. At the conclusion of his narration, the Shogun said :

" When you heard of the great change which had taken place at home, you must have been greatly surprised and it must have caused you numerous difficulties. I cannot be too grateful to you for the labour you underwent for the welfare of Mimbu who has safely come back from his extended journey. Unexpected changes take place in human affairs. It is useless to bewail the past. The fact that you came back home in good health is a matter of sincere congratulation."

With mingled emotions of joy, pain, and sorrow, the Viscount bade farewell to the ex-Shogun. He waited for a few days for the ex-Shogun's written reply to the Prince, but could not obtain it. His patience was sorely tried almost to the breaking point. Then he received a written appointment as the chief Treasurer of the Shizuoka Clan instead of a letter of reply! The Viscount, somewhat indignant, insisted that he must deliver the ex-Shogun's reply to the Prince before he could consider any offer in regard to himself. Then it was revealed that it was the will of the ex-Shogun to have the reply to the Prince taken by some one else, keeping the Viscount in Shizuoka. The ex-Shogun's words are worth quoting :

" Shibusawa need not go back to Mito. A special messenger should be sent there. If Shibusawa returns to Mito, Mimbu will surely promote him to a high official position as he is fond of Shibusawa. The Mito officers would not tolerate this, and there is no telling what danger Shibusawa might not be exposed to. Even if the matter might not be as bad as that, yet his usefulness would be hampered to a great extent. Better to employ him here. If Shibusawa takes my reply to Mito and stays there a while, there would surely spring up an affectionate sentiment between Mimbu and Shibusawa hard to break. Send some one else by all means !"

Marquis Okuma.

This revelation of the ex-Shogun's thoughtfulness for the Viscount swept away misunderstandings on his part and made him bow in profound humility before the towering virtue of his Lord. Henceforth forevermore the Viscount vowed to be faithful and loyal to the ex-Shogun. He came to Shizuoka because he wanted to live close to the ex-Shogun. He did not dream of an official life. His heart was set on the promotion of commerce and industry. He soon turned his attention to that work and organized a commercial institution there. The stage upon which the Viscount was to play his leading role was prepared and the hour to demonstrate his newly acquired ability came. Just at this time, however, an unexpected call came to the Viscount. It was a call from the Premier of the Cabinet of the Meiji Government in Tokyo through the Governor of Shizuoka—the Government which the Viscount would not care to serve. It was very difficult for the Viscount to give up the local stage where his debut as a Prince of industry was to be made. Therefore he stoutly declined to accept the call. But the Governor could not ignore the message from the Premier, and insisted that the Viscount go up to Tokyo. Though a lover of human right and liberty the Viscount was always ready to give due regard to the higher authorities.

The Viscount had to come to Tokyo and reached that city the first part of November, 1869. In Tokyo he found that he was already appointed as Head of the Bureau of Taxation—an office of national significance. He acknowledged the receipt of the written appointment, but did not accept it at once. He wanted to confer with some prominent man before he decided to accept or decline. The Viscount was introduced to Marquis Okuma who was a leading member of the Cabinet and who produced convincing arguments why the Viscount should serve the new Government in spite of his firm determination never more to participate in political affairs.

The first point was that the Viscount could not serve the new Government in deference to Prince Tokugawa, his Lord. The Marquis refuted this point by arguing that the Viscount's stand on the matter would place the ex-Shogun in an exceedingly awkward position for if one, whom the Goverment wished to appoint as the right man, refused to accept the appointment on account of the ex-Shogun, the latter might be suspected of blocking the way and indirectly opposing the authorities of the central Government. But if the Viscount accepted the appointment and demonstrated his ability as an officer, he would honor and glorify the name of the ex-Shogun, from whose jurisdiction the Viscount came. This would mean that the ex-Shogun was rendering the nation a useful service through his retainer. Moreover the Viscount's service in the new Government and his acquaintance with its high officials might create an opportunity whereby the real motives of the ex-Shogun as a genuine patriot and an ardent royalist could be demonstrated, thus dissipating the clouds of misunderstanding on the part of the leaders of the new Government. This would redound to the glorious recovery of the lost reputation of the ex-Shogun. In no profounder or more permanent way could the Viscount repay his debt of gratitude to his Lord. The second point was on the ground of ignorance. The Marquis argued that ignorance in the present case at least constituted no ground for refusal. A revolution in any country produces a great change in personnel. Revolutionists are generally amateurs in everything. They come together and discuss the nation's policy. They investigate all kinds of administrative measures. Through them long existing abuses and prejudices are swept away. No one of us really knows how to conduct the affairs of the government. We are all unexperienced. We must start anew on all points, the taxation problem especially.

The third point was that he had already started an institution such as a Chamber of Commerce in Shizuoka, the seat of the ex-Shogun. The Marquis' view on this point was that the Viscount not only could do a larger good for the country by taking an office in the central Government, but also it would not be too late for the Viscount to enter into business life, even after the country was better organized. His experience as government officer would constitute a valuable asset to his future career. At any rate, the present situation is critical in all directions. This is the time when the country needs men of talent and brains. It is no time for the Viscount to hesitate to accept the appointment.

The Viscount promised the Marquis a prompt reply. Quietly thinking over what had transpired he was persuaded in his mind to respond to the Marquis affirmatively, but with this significant reservation: "Please remember that I may resign my office at an opportune hour." Marquis Okuma was greatly pleased with the outcome saying: "It will be commendable to try to carry out your original plans by resigning the office at a proper time."

When Viscount Shibusawa went into his office for the

first time, the impression he received was that everything was in a chaotic state. There was no system, no order, and no law. The young officers who helped achieve the Meiji Restoration were little more than talkative braggarts, arguing back and forth over current topics. They were busy in self-exaltation over past merits and the office hours were soon exhausted without bringing any fruits of labour. It was totally contrary to the disposition of the Viscount to pass days in such a wasteful manner. So he called on Marquis Okuma and conferred with him on the policy to systematize and unify the affairs of the Government. The result was the creation of a "Bureau of Reorganization." The main officials of the Bureau consisted of the high officials of the Departments of the Interior and the Treasury, and the Head of the Bureau. Prince Date was the Minister in charge of these two Departments. Marquis Okuma and Prince Itō were under Prince Date. Next to them came Viscount Shibusawa. Through these leaders many reformations and innovations were brought about. The first was the revision of the tax system and the survey of the entire country. The idea of survey at once suggests measurement. Hence the system of weights and measures must be included in this first item of revision. The Viscount as the head of the Bureau of Reorganization had to take up many practical matters. For instance, the Viscount found a man named Y. Sato, a surveyor, who studied the method of T. Inō, a born genius in the science of surveying. Satō was employed by the Bureau. Laws of transportation, census registration, decoration, trading companies, and exchange were introduced and put into operation.

Prince Itō, then the vice-minister of the Treasury Department, made various recommendations such as regarding the coinage system and public loans, to the Bureau of Reorganization. The Bureau took up these recommendations and systematized them, including the two subjects of " Business Organization " and " Banking," and presented them to the Cabinet which adopted the plans as presented. Immediately after this Prince Ito was ordered to go to America for study. This was in October, 1870. The trip of Prince Itō to America meant a great deal for the future welfare of Japan, because it proved to be a contribution to the establishment of the future financial system of the nation. The Prince took with him A. Yoshikawa, J. Yoshida, and G. Fukuchi a well known writer by the pen name " Ochi-koji." The subjects the Prince was to investigate in America were :

(1) Reformation of the Treasury Department, including its administration ;

(2) Banking system (the so-called National Bank system) ;

(3) Currency system (gold standard) ;

(4) Organization of companies ; and

(5) Method of receipts and disbursements, (revision of book-keeping)

Not long after his arrival in America Prince Itō presented to his Government a written proposal concerning financial subjects—namely to adopt the gold standard in the currency system; to issue public bonds convertible in gold coin ; and to establish a bank to issue paper money. Moreover, the Prince investigated the office routine of the different Departments of the American

Government and sent reports to the home Government. All these documents from the Prince were handled by the Bureau of Reorganization whose head was the Viscount. Not only the correspondence between Prince Itō and the Bureau, but also the drafting of regulations based on the results of the Prince's investigations were carried on by the Viscount. A busier man than the Viscount, in the Bureau as well as in the Treasury Department, could not be seen. While he was thus busily engaged another serious question confronted the Bureau. It was the question of raw silk.

Raw silk is the staple of Japan's exports. It was so in the beginning of Meiji era, though the amount of export then was small. The rise or fall of this trade affects the nation's finance. For this reason the Treasury Department had constantly watched this industry. Marquis Okuma turned his attention to this subject. Just about this time an export merchant of raw silk, a foreigner living in Yokohama, complained about the inferior quality of the raw silk. Alarmed by this criticism the authorities in the Treasury Department went even so far as to employ an expert from a foreign country. Viscount Shibusawa who had had long experience in this work could not remain indifferent to this most important subject, and it was very natural for the Bureau of Reorganization to interest itself in the question, even though it was so fully occupied with other activities. The Bureau at once set up machinery for investigation of this industry. The results of the investigation were formulated and recommended to the Department which in turn put them into practice. All the details were superintended and directed by the Viscount, as chief of the Bureau of Reorganization. In connection with this, mention should be made that the Viscount had the rare honor to serve as a counsellor to three Empress Dowagers who have taken a deep interest in the whole process of the silk industry.

We saw that it was Marquis Okuma who persuaded Viscount Shibusawa to take up a position in the new Government. Also we saw that Marquis Okuma was the virtual head of the amalgamated Department of the Interior and the Treasury. The Marquis was progressive in his policy and wide awake to the new situation. He knew how to pick up able men to work with him. Once he was accused because of his choice of officers from among the retainers of the Shogun who was then labelled as an enemy to the new Government. Disregarding such criticism and opposition the Marquis acted according to his own convictions. Conservatives were greatly displeased with the way the Marquis was acting in his Department, and pressure to remove him was brought to bear by a superior official whose political background was more powerful and influential than that of the Marquis. The Marquis was entrapped and a change in the Treasury Department was brought about. Marquis K. Inouye became the successor to Marquis Okuma. The Viscount who knew the ugly course of the political struggles staged on account of personal enmity and jealousy among the high officials, must have been disgusted with political life as poisonous and detrimental to moral and honest living. He might have gone even so far as to seriously consider that, if those high officials were eager to gratify their own political ambition, the promise of a political career for those of

Shizuoka who were stigmatised as traitors might be exceedingly slim. Hence it would not be amiss for us to conjecture that the Viscount might have felt the hour had now come for him to give up the post as he had spoken to Marquis Okuma at the time he accepted the appointment so much against his desire. But the Viscount found Marquis Inouye to be an able man who pursued the policy Marquis Okuma had inaugurated, and they worked together in perfect harmony.

The most important and difficult task they confronted was how to unify the national finances as the loosely federated Clan system was replaced by the unified prefectural system under the Central Government. Some of the Clans issued within their jurisdictions paper money convertible with the Government coin then in currency. But the abuse of the privilege created the situation that the enormous increase of paper money far exceeded the point of convertibility, and at the beginning of the Meiji Era the value of the paper money became as worthless as waste paper. The new Government felt the necessity of dealing with this problem at once, and in December, 1869 issued a proclamation: " No Clan shall be allowed to increase its paper money issued at the permission of the Shogunate. Every Clan shall report to the Treasury Department by February, 1870 the amount of the currency it has. The use of any paper money issued by a Clan or Prefecture after the Restoration shall be stopped." The manufacture and issuance of the paper money and the consequent responsibility and liability rested upon the shoulders of the several Clan Governments. But in order to unify the national finances, the whole question and its settlement were now to be handled by the new Government. This complicated work it now faced, and the decision to abolish the Clans and establish the Prefectures in the year 1871 precipitated the officers in the Treasury Department into a whirlpool of activity. One of the most vexing questions which taxed the brain of Marquis Inouye was the problem of disposing of the currencies of different types and values. But to his credit as a financier of unusual sagacity, he steadily prepared a plan of solving the problem. This plan was made public in the form of a proclamation of the Cabinet on the very day when the Imperial Edict of the abolition of the Clan system was proclaimed, July 14th, 1871. The proclamation reads as follows : " The currency should have uniform value throughout the entire country, but so far, the different Clans have issued paper money of varying prices creating much confusion. Now that the Clan system is abolished, the rate of exchange current on the day of July the 14th, 1871 shall hereafter determine all exchange." Then on the next day—the 15th, the Department of the Treasury sent out notice to all the Prefectures on the following points :

" (1) Send in as early as possible a written statement about the rate of exchange current on the 14th day of July, 1871 as the paper money issued before and after the Restoration shall be exchanged according to the rate of exchange of that day ; (2) The determination of the quotation shall be made according to that of July the 14th in the places where it was customary to conduct such business of exchange ; (3) The quotation shall be determined by taking the average rate from three to five main exchanges if there existed that many ; (4) The community being small and only one exchange existing, the quotation of that place shall determine the rate; (5) If there were no definite place for exchange, the merchants in the community shall confer and determine the rate ;   (6) When the quotation is determined by taking the average rate, the places and quotations of the constituents shall be reported ; if there is only one place, its quotation shall determine all the rest; and if the quotation is determined by the conference of merchants, the place of meeting, and the names of conferees and the details pertaining to the transaction shall be reported;   (7) As soon as the quotation is determined, that fact shall be made known to the people within the jurisdiction, so that there may be no misunderstanding among them about the matter ; and (8) How much of the original reserve for the exchange with the paper money is left over shall also be reported."

These orders were issued from the Department of the Treasury, but it was a well known fact that all these plans and drafts for the plans were prepared by Viscount Shibusawa, no less clear headed and energetic than Marquis Inouye his Chief. The work of the Treasury Department was not finished with this, but only began. Under the old Shogunate regime, each Clan enjoyed the liberty of raising its own loans and meeting its own financial exigencies. Thus some of the Clans issued their own currencies ; raised public loans ; and ordered payment of taxes in advance. And they incurred debts with foreigners by buying from them guns, ammunitions, cruisers, and steamships. The demand for the payment of these debts by the new Government through the foreign ministers was urgent. The Treasury Department handled all these problems. The Viscount and his colleagues were worried not a little about these foreign loans and in September, 1871, they created a Bureau in the Department to investigate the details and formulate a scheme to promptly meet whatever necessity might arise. That they came to the conclusion to pay all the foreign debts in cash was significant and praiseworthy.

The next problem which the Treasury Department was to tackle was the reformation of the tax system. The Viscount accepted the government office as the head of the Bureau of Taxation, and there was no question that he had some ideas about this work although he was modest enough to confess his ignorance on the subject. At this time Marquis Inouye was the virtual Minister for the Department of the Treasury and the Viscount the vice-Minister. Count Mutsu was the head of the Taxation Bureau and Marquis Matsukata the assistant. They were the most conspicuous figures in bringing about the reformation of the old system.

Just about this time the Viscount was appointed to visit the mint at Osaka in his official capacity. He was holding an additional office in the Bureau of Commerce created within the Department of the Treasury at the beginning of the Meiji era, and it was quite natural for him to come in contact with leading business men in Osaka and Kobe. His impression of the status of the average business man was exceedingly discouraging. He keenly felt that unless the education of business men was improved, no regulations or institutions for business would amount to much. But the very discouragement of the Viscount over the inability and servility of business men before the presence of the government officer spurred him to give up his present official position and to plunge into business life himself. No man of small calibre and of limited vision could have scanned the situation as the Viscount did. It takes a man of vision to sacrifice his personal comfort, convenience, interest, and ambition for a cause which the average man may scorn as worthless, but which potentially promises a great future. Business in terms of commerce and industry, though poorly manned at present, was the greatest and highest thing in the eyes of the Viscount because he saw in it, when it was developed, a mighty factor to civilize and strengthen the country which he so intensely loved. Therefore, even in the midst of the most intense labor during his official activities, the Viscount never forgot to look for the first chance to resign office and to enter into a business career.

The conflict between Prince Okubo and Viscount Shibusawa on the budgetary question almost brought a rupture, as the result of which the Viscount might have resigned his office. The Prince presented before the budgetary conference the budgets of the Army and Navy. Marquis Inouye happened to be absent from this conference. The Viscount was astounded by the absurd proposition of the Prince and could not keep silence. Thoroughly understanding the financial condition of the Department of the Treasury and being no respecter of persons he squarely opposed the proposition of the Prince. The point the Viscount made was that it should be the unalterable rule of the Department to balance expenditures with income. The proposition of the Prince ignored this rule and could not be tolerated. At this stage of transition the financial outlook of the Department was in a nebulous state and the exact statement of the income could not be formulated, but about forty million Yen (¥ 40,000,000) was the amount according to the latest investigation of the Department. But over against the total income of ¥ 40,000,000,

Prince Okubo submitted a budget of ¥ 8,000,000 for the Army and ¥ 2,500,000 for the Navy, a total of ¥ 10,500,000. The Viscount felt that this proposition, if carried through, would upset the whole scheme of the Department. Some of his colleagues were better posted in financial matters than Prince Okubo, but none opened his mouth to back up the view propounded by the Viscount, possibly being awed by the authority of the Prince. It was different with the Viscount. He was straightforward and fearless. Devotion to duty eclipsed all other considerations. Prince Okubo had anticipated not the slightest opposition to his motion, but the voice of antagonism was raised from an unexpected quarter and the Prince was disturbed. He spoke to the Viscount, saying : " Do you mean to say that the Army and Navy are no concern to us ?" To this the Viscount quickly responded ; " Though my knowledge about military matters may be meagre, yet I am second to none in advocating the importance of the army for the country. What I object to is the absurd demand upon the Treasury while the financial status is still in the process of making. Such a demand is highly dangerous at this stage." Prince Okubo and Viscount Shibusawa were the only speakers in this conference, and the motion of the Prince carried the day. The result was highly unsatisfactory to the Viscount, because he thought that the financial system could never be soundly established, so long as a high official like Prince Okubo controlled the Treasury. Here again the Viscount's desire to resign his office arose in his bosom. He appealed to Marquis Inouye, stating how difficult and even impossible it would be to build up the financial system of the nation on a sound basis, if the present staff of the officials of the Department of the Treasury continued to conduct its affairs. Marquis Inouye was in hearty sympathy with the Viscount and poured oil upon the troubled waters and made a secret promise.

How fondly and earnestly Viscount Shibusawa was looking forward to the day when he could stimulate the business world could be seen from the publication of two books, the one being his own work and the other a translation. The former might be termed Rules for Business Management, and the latter the Banking System. The translation was accomplished by G. Fukuchi under the auspices of the Viscount. Busy as the Viscount was during the tenure of his office in the Department of the Treasury, yet availing himself of fragmentary moments, he gave these books to the business world for its guide. The books were widely circulated all over the country and greatly contributed to the promotion and unification of business methods in general.

We saw that Marquis Inouye succeeded in persuading the Viscount not to resign his office by making a secret promise. Its discloure gives us knowledge of an event of national significance and it would not be out of place to give it our passing notice. The event was the dispatch of the Iwakura Mission to America and Europe in November of 1871. Marquis Inouye told the Viscount that Prince Okubo would be included in this mission and be away from his present office and so would no more interfere with the affairs of the Department of the Treasury. The Marquis' prediction came true, Prince Okubo being made one of the vice-envoys with Prince Iwakura, the Ambassador Extraordinary and Plenipotentiary. The mission consisted of 48 high officials of the government. Miss Ume Tsuda, later the founder of Tsuda College, Count K. Kaneko, now a veteran member of the Privy Council, and Baron T. Dan, later the Director-in-Chief of Mitsui Company accompanied the Party.

Another question which embarrassed the authorities of the Department of the Treasury was the agitation to send an expeditional army to Formosa. Loo Choo islanders had drifted to Formosa. Fifty-four of them were murdered and twelve returned in safety. This was the cause of the agitation, in which the militarist leaders like the Great Saigo were firm to adopt strong measures. This trouble occurred in November of 1871, the month the Iwakura Mission started for the West. Prince Sanjo, the Premier, invited to his official residence all the heads of the Departments to discuss the question. Marquis Inouye the head of the Department of the Treasury should have been present on the occasion but the mourning on account of his mother's death kept him away. At this time Viscount Shibusawa's position corresponded to that of vice-Minister, and it was natural that the Viscount should represent the Department of the Treasury. The Viscount produced an argument against the Formosan Expedition from the standpoint of the Department. The gist of his contention was that although the grand work of the Meiji Restoration had been inaugurated by great leaders, yet in reality the work was still in process, demanding every care and attention for the readjustment of internal affairs, and leaving no room to divide our energies in foreign affairs; that the national finance was in a sad plight, the people in general suffering from heavy taxation; that at present it was not enough even to meet the domestic needs; and that it was desirable to avoid any radical move, even though we may seem to take a backward step in the matter. The Premier who had been paying breathless attention to the words of the Viscount rose and confirmed the statement by saying: "Am I right in understanding that the Department of the Treasury is opposed to the Formosan Expedition?" To this, the Viscount made a decisive reply: "Yes, Your Excellency, the Department is opposed to the new departure." The ground of the opposition was made clearer than ever, when a shortage of ¥6,000,000 was publicly declared in the budget for the year 1871–1872 for domestic expenditures.

On the 22nd of February 1872, the Viscount was promoted to be vice-Minister of the Treasury Department. On the 26th of the same month a big fire took place in Tokyo. An extensive area was devastated by it. This calamity caused the Viscount to think seriously regarding the prevention of the recurrence of such disasters, and he was reminded of his French life, when he slept in a fire-proof building and learned about the institution of fire insurance companies. He at once felt that there was no more opportune hour than this to advocate the adoption of the plan to build brick buildings and to organize fire insurance companies. Proper steps were taken to obtain an official recognition of the scheme. The Viscount prepared a draft of a statement of how important it is to build fire-proof buildings, when new buildings were put up in devastated sections, and to adopt a system of permanently preserv-

Prince Ito.

Marquis Inouye.

ing those buildings with very small cost. The citizens of Tokyo, especially the "Edokko" (sons and daughters of Edo), who had from time immemorial been accustomed to think of fires as "the flowers of Edo" could not be awakened to the necessity of adopting such new methods. But leaders were quick to see it. The Tokyo Prefecture and the Interior Department co-operated in the new scheme and the far reaching result was the creation of the Ginza street, on both sides of which long rows of brick buildings were built.

The organization of the National Bank; the adoption of its regulations and rules ; the issuance of paper money of different classes, of postal stamps, and of revenue stamps; the inception of the system of the stock exchange, shares, and stocks; these were all due to the energetic and progressive activities of the Viscount, who had learned of all these institutions during his French life. Thus the Viscount contributed to his government and to his country in an extraordinary manner. So far as devices and suggestions were concerned he had put into operation all his resourceful brain had devised, and it seemed as though the day of liberation from official life to which he was eagerly looking forward had now come. The final resignation of the Viscount was precipitated by that of Marquis Inouye, with whom the Viscount had assiduously labored in the Treasury Department, sometime even continuing "to prepare drafts without resting or sleeping for two or three days and nights "

The Viscount entered into the government service in November of 1869 and retired in May of 1873, covering a period of less than four years. But his achievements during this brief period were amazing and he was only 34 years old when he tendered his resignation. First Marquis Ōkuma and then Marquis Inouye gave Viscount Shibusawa a large opportunity to realize his potential powers and abilities, as the two Marquises gave the Viscount a free hand to deliberate on the affairs of state. But the fact that he was an under-officer or an employee must at times have hampered the free exercises of his creative genius, as for instance in the conflict between him and Prince Ōkubo on the budgetary question, and between him and the militarists on the question of the Formosan expedition. Now that he was perfectly free from any handicap and was his own master, with his intuitive and acquired abilities awakened through his varied and colorful experiences, he was sure to promise the world achievements before which it would stand in awed admiration. Brilliant as was the official career of the Viscount, yet it was no more than one phase of the panorama of his entire life. The dictum of Mr. K. Shiraishi, the author of the book entitled " Eiichi Shibusawa the Grand Old Man," characterizing the career of the Viscount in connection with the Treasury Department, is worth quoting. He says: "The Viscount's term of office in the Treasury Department, in which he made achievements which an ordinary person could not have achieved in a whole life-time, passed away. One cannot help but think of it as a brilliant period and an exciting one too. Such a period would be the proudest hour in the life of any ordinary man to be enjoyed once for all. But it was only a tiny fraction of the totality of the life of the Viscount. In his later larger life we see the real Viscount."

CHAPTER VI

FOUNDER OF DAI ICHI GINKO

IN the preceding chapter, we saw how eloquently and tactfully Marquis Ōkuma refuted the arguments of Viscount Shibusawa in his conviction not to serve the new Government as one of its officers and how finally the Marquis prevailed over the Viscount. Perhaps neither the Marquis nor the Viscount could foresee at the time the full force and the deep significance of the former's argument that the office would help prepare the Viscount for a larger efficiency and a wider usefulness instead of hampering him in his life work.

We cannot fail to catch the firm determination of the Marquis to win over the Viscount to his side. Yet the argument does not seem to be entirely free from a selfish tinge and it makes the Marquis appear like a miller who draws water to his own mill at the expense of others. On the other hand, the Viscount, one of whose characteristics was always to seek to see the better and brighter side of any man and who was, on that very account, often erroneously criticised as a man of loose toleration promiscuously swallowing both the good and the bad, was greatly moved by the enthusiasm and earnestness of the Marquis, and out of grateful appreciation of his friendly attitude consented to accept the offer with this reservation: " Please remember that I may resign my office at some opportune time." The Marquis was anxious to bring the Viscount into his political fold, while the Viscount was equally anxious to get out of it at the earliest opportunity. The whole game between the two heroes seems to have been confined to the needs of an emergency with no far reaching outlook. This is the reason why we asserted that neither gentleman could have foreseen the full significance of the argument advanced by the Marquis. No sooner had the Viscount plunged into the whirlpool of his office in the Department of the Treasury, than torrential responsibilities pressed and beat down upon him. During the nearly four years of his work in positions in an ascending scale in the Treasury Department, the responsibilities were not only continuous but cumulative. They were merciless and cruel to the young official. But he was dauntless and fearless, because of the inexhaustible physical, mental, and ethical resources stored in him by natural endowment and deliberate acquisition, and he came out on almost every occasion as conqueror. In other words, the hand of Destiny which had thus far directed and guided the Viscount in the various crises he had encountered, put him to this final test to prepare him for a great work. That work was the founding of Dai Ichi Ginkō (the first bank in Japan)—the bank which is a huge monument and an everlasting tribute to the real worth of the Prince of Industry, Viscount Shibusawa.

It is worth pausing for a time to trace the steps up which the Viscount climbed to the summit of his life, that is to say, to the founding of Dai Ichi Ginkō. When we speak of the " founding ", we do not mean a mere starting or beginning. Rather, we mean both starting and completing the institution in the sense that it was put on a firm and sound basis for performing all the functions it claimed to perform to meet the de-

mands of the public as a financial institution. Viewing
the existence of Dai Ichi Ginkō in this light and also
viewing the Viscount's relation to it as its founder and
builder, the author feels fully justified in designating
Dai Ichi Ginkō as the summit of the life of the Viscount. There are at least two reasons for the justification.
The first is that Viscount Shibusawa from his early days
was looking forward to this kind of life and later looked
back to it during more than half a century. The second
is that Dai Ichi Ginkō was no isolated institution for the
Viscount, but was the power house from which he
directed and manoeuvred all his activities. It was the
headquarters where the Viscount, the generalissimo of
the huge industrial army, commanded the creative and
constructive forces for building up the industrial civilization of modern Japan. Mr. T. Watanabe gives a
graphic account of the Viscount's activities as a leader
in the business world in the booklet "Viscount Shibusawa," and his account corroborates the assertion we
have just made. Mr. Watanabe says :

"Viscount Shibusawa, together with Marquis Inouye, resigned
office in the year 1873 as their financial program had been rejected. From that day the Viscount firmly set his mind to
the task of industrial development. He was then at the age
of 34. His vigorous movements as an authority and leader of the
industrial world were amazing. Beginning with the founding of the
First National Bank (now Dai Ichi Ginkō), the paper mill (now,
Ōji Seishi Kaisha), the bureau of the Tōkyō-fu Gas Co. (now Tokyo
Gasu Kaisha), the Osaka Spinning Company (now Tōyō Bōseki
Kaisha), nearly all branches of industry were created and fostered
by the powerful and zealous work of the Viscount. He directed
and guided 250 industrial companies such as banking, cotton
spinning, paper manufacturing, making of artificial fertilizer,

brewery, shipping, railways, gas, electricity, iron manufacturing, ship-building, textiles, hemp-dressing, steel manufacturing, coal mining, hotels, brick making, cement factory, making of hats, sugar manufacturing, harbour construction, insurance, stock exchange, warehouses, reclamation, cattle breeding, emigration, wireless telegraphy, aircraft, etc. Of all these, the Viscount gave his longest and best effort to Dai Ichi Ginkō as its highest executive. How one person could take up so many enterprises is a colossal mystery. In this connection, we recall what he used to say about himself. ' I was a Jack of all trades born in a dilapidated village. In order to develop Japan in those days one had to touch every thing in a general way.' "

The accuracy of Viscount Shibusawa in financial matters was early demonstrated in the days of his farm life. His book keeping in balancing profit and loss was clean and straight to the last penny. This habit of accuracy grew with him as the circle of his life was enlarged.

Under Prince Yoshinobu Tokugawa in Kyoto, the Viscount made a recommendation to strengthen the financial position of the Prince and was successful. He was financial secretary to Prince Mimbu during the Prince's French tour ; kept up the details of minute accounts as the private treasurer of the Prince ; and carefully formed the budget for the expenditures of the Prince during his study in France. He also endeavored to increase the revenues of the Prince by exploiting the financial machinery in operation in Paris. When the return of the Prince was ordered by the new Government, in spite of the fact that the Prince had settled down to remain in Paris for study, the Viscount attended to the settlement of various financial matters such as the cancellation of the contract of the rented house; the discharge of the private tutors; and the selling of bonds and securities which the Viscount had bought on the advice of Flury-Herald, the counsellor to the Prince. On his return home, the Viscount submitted the full report of the finances from the beginning of the journey to its close to the treasurer of the ex-Shogun. Then came the period of his four years service in the Treasury Department, beginning his official career as the head of the Bureau of Taxation and closing it with the office corresponding to that of vice-Minister. Four years in government office was but a short span in the long life of the Viscount, but it was a period in which he was subjected to severest tests and to the hardest discipline. Marquis Ōkuma tells us that Viscount Shibusawa worked on the preparation of the drafts of rules and regulations through whole nights, and that because of his youth sleepless work for a week did not seem to make him tired. Marquis Inouye speaks of the Viscount's diligence through "three days and nights without rest and sleep." The Viscount's ability and his energetic application of it made him a victim of jealousy among his colleagues. Marquis Ōkuma, who singled out the Viscount and placed him in the office, had to bear the brunt of this jealousy. But all this worked out for the highest possible development of the Viscount bringing out into his conscious realization his dormant and potential power. Mencius says:

"Thus, when Heaven is about to confer a great office on any man, it first exercises his mind with suffering, and his sinews and bones with toil. It exposes his body to hunger, and subjects him to extreme poverty. It confounds his undertakings. By all these methods it stimulates his mind, hardens his nature, and supplies his incompetencies."

Then, there is another factor which prepared the Viscount for his peerless career as a Prince of industry. Think of the leaders the Viscount met and associated with during this brief period of less than four years. Actually he knew, and was known by, every great leader in the Government such as Prince Sanjo, Prince Iwakura, Prince Matsukata, Prince Ito, greater Saigō, Marquis (lesser) Saigō, Marquis Okubo, Marquis Kido, Marquis Ōkuma, Marquis Inouye, Count Mutsu, and Count Yoshikawa. The Viscount's acquaintance with those great statesmen, financiers, and warriors was by no means a formal and perfunctory one. It was a friendly one on which he could avail himself in case of necessity for advice or actual assistance. It was afterward an invisible but an invaluable asset both to the Viscount and to the bank, as the success of business transactions in those early days much depended on the credit and support of the leaders in the Government. There can be no question that it was the Viscount's native ability which made him the organizer and officer of 250 industrial organizations during the period of his activity as the President of Dai Ichi Ginkō. But it is doubtful whether the Viscount could have played such a brilliant and magnificent role on the stage of industry, without the rich background of the unique prestige he established during the incumbency of his office in the Treasury Department.

Now, fully equipped for any emergency or crisis, Viscount Shibusawa, as a far-sighted statesman, challenged the industrial world with a platform involving three principles—namely those of enriching and strengthening the nation; of organizing and conducting business on the basis of the collective and cooperative system; and of elevating and stabilizing the status of business men in general. Carrying with him the "National Banking Laws" which he framed while serving in the Treasury Department, the Viscount undertook to organize the First National Bank. The system was totally new to business men at that time. The Viscount, the organizer, had to encounter numerous difficulties from the very start of the enterprise. The Banking Laws had been framed, but very few business men of the day understood the laws. Even if they understood them, they did not have ability and power to put the machinery of a bank into operation. Marquis Inouye and the Viscount were anxious to organize a bank while they were still in the Treasury Department and had their eyes on three companies then in existence. They were the Mitsui, the Ono, and the Shimada. As the Shimada company failed not long after, the other two were counted as the possible nuclei for a new bank. The Viscount conferred with Marquis Inouye over a preliminary step to be taken for its organization, and the result was the call of an informal conference at the residence of the Marquis in the month of May, 1872, in which the Marquis, the Viscount, and the representatives of the two companies were present. In this conference the Viscount gave a warning to the representatives of the two companies, saying:

"There is a rumour that the Mitsui and the Ono Gumi companies are not on good terms. If the rumour be true, it is regretable indeed, as both companies are doing the same business of the Government. They should not be prey to the spirit of rivalry and jealousy. As to the organization of a new bank, they should freely and frankly exchange their views in a friendly manner, aiming at cooperation. The most important thing is to bring the enterprise to a grand success."

The spirit of rivalry between the two companies was more than a mere rumour. It was a reality and could not be got rid of easily. Thus the authorities of the Treasury Department were obliged to bring pressure to bear upon them, threatening them with the deprivation of the Government business, if they did not take heed to the warning. The Government pressure and the Viscount's determined persuasion bore fruit and finally the main representatives of the two companies agreed to form a bank under the name of Dai Ichi Kokuritsu Ginkō (The First National Bank).

The regulations of the First National Bank, originally drafted by the Viscount on the model of the American national bank laws and finally adopted, were proclaimed as the laws of the nation on the 15th day of November, 1872. On the 22nd the promoters five in number representing the two companies published an advertisement in the *Tokyo Nichi Nichi* for the issuance of 30,000 shares, the face value of each share being ¥100. The two companies were responsible for 20,000 shares equally divided. The remaining 10,000 shares were to be raised from the public. But the public was rather apathetic to the appeal as they did not quite understand the nature of the enterprise. The utmost number of the applicants who responded to the invita-

on was a little over 30 and the amount raised was
440,800. This left a shortage of ¥559,200 to make
p the third ¥1,000,000, and it was hopeless to expect
) complete the proposed amount. Therefore, they
stablished the First National Bank with a capital of
he odd amount of ¥2,440,800. The first general meet-
ng of the share holders was held at the assembly hall
f the Mitsui Company at No. 1, Kabutocho, Nihonbashi-
u on the 11th of June, 1873. Thirty four persons were
resent. R. Minomura of the Mitsui, one of the pro-
noters, presided at the meeting. Thus he addressed the
neeting : " Gentlemen, we are gathered together here
o-day to elect the Directors and to deliberate concern-
ng the policy and management of the bank. Please feel
'ree to speak frankly on these questions." The share
iolders present were unanimous in the wish that the
bank should conduct its business on a most sound basis,
strictly observing the regulations laid down in the
national bank laws. Next, Viscount Shibusawa who,
though he had tendered his resignation and it had been
accepted yet was not wholly relieved of his office, rose
and addressed the meeting, narrating how the national
bank laws came to be framed and what was the purpose
of the Government authorities in introducing such laws
to the public. Then he made a motion to the effect that
the business of this bank should be conducted according to the bank laws and regulations ; that the Directors should be chosen from among the leading members
of the Mitsui and the Ono Gumi companies, omitting
the formality of election, as the bank was organized on
the basis of their cooperation ; and that, besides the
Directors, a general superintendent should be elected

from among the share holders to supervise all the details of the business of the bank, as there would exist for the two firms the risk of confounding their private business with that of the bank, owing to the fact that the same Directors will attend to the business of their firms and of the bank, and read the by-laws which would regulate the official duties. The motion was unanimously adopted and the Directors eight in number were elected. The Viscount was honored with the position of the General Superintendent whose duties and responsibilities are thus specified in the articles of the by-laws:

"In order that all the officers may bring about the best possible results in working together in harmony and in coordinating the various activities a General Superintendent shall be elected from among the leading share holders, who shall assist and inspect the work of the President, the Directors, and the Managers; shall control all the legislative and administrative activities of the bank and prepare drafts; and shall direct and admonish the President and all the under-officers. The said General Superintendent, by always maintaining an impartial and fair attitude, shall supervise the actual activities of all the officers of the bank from the President, Directors, Managers down to the under officers; and shall fully investigate and reprimand any who may either disobey the provisions of the laws, regulations, by-laws, and the supplements of the by-laws, or break promises. He shall have the right to act as the Chairman of the conference of the President and Directors and decide all questions arising in the conference. He shall endeavor gradually to bring up the business of the bank into a sound and prosperous condition by promoting the welfare of the bank, counselling with experts of banking either native or foreign concerning methods and regulations of various kinds and applying them to the present situation, besides superintending the actual work of the bank."

The question may arise in the mind of the reader why it was necessary to create the office of General Superintendent above that of the President. This is a pertinent question and needs to be explained. We saw that the Mitsui and the Ono Gumi companies were the two main share holders holding an equal number of shares. This situation necessitated giving the representatives of the two firms equal rights and powers in the bank, electing two Presidents, two Vice-Presidents, and two Managing Directors, etc. It was a thorough-going arrangement of equalization worthy of admiration, but utterly impracticable in that the system lacked a unifying and controlling agency. In order to save the bank from this predicament, the office of General Superintendent was created. The provisions which minutely regulated the contract between the bank and the Viscount, as its General Superintendent, were signed by the parties concerned and the Viscount started his business career as the virtual President of the First National Bank of Japan. Thus the banking business was started on the 20th of July, 1873. During the next three years, the bank carried on its business, dividing it into two departments—namely the business of the Government revenue and the ordinary banking business. The regulations and rules for transacting the business both for the Government and the general public were carefully prepared. Looked at from the present day knowledge of the banking system they may not seem new or extraordinary. But in those remote days of the inceptional stage they must have taken a tremendous amount of energy and brain power on the part of the responsible party. We have already seen that the bank was organized with a capital of the odd amount of ¥2,440,800 in November of 1872, but it was increased to the amount of ¥2,500,000 in January of 1874, which fact indicates that the bank was making steady progress. Indeed, the bank's prospect was bright and promising if only its progress were not arrested. But as we Japanese often say whenever we are beset with adversity : " The moon has its clouds and the flowers their storms." This three year old fledgeling received a severe blow almost fatal to its life. It was the sudden failure of the Ono Gumi Company. In regard to this, "The History of Half a Century of Dai Ichi Ginkō" tells us the following story :

" The failure of the Ono Gumi Company gave an almost fatal blow to our bank, because, although the bank was organized under the share system, yet in reality it was not only a joint enterprise between the Mitsui and the Ono Gumi companies, but it had loaned the Ono Gumi Company more than ¥1,380,000. General Superintendent Shibusawa, who was then managing the affairs of the bank, sensed the ominous situation and made a desperate effort to save the bank in its terrible plight. The result was that the Ono Gumi Company had to deliver to the bank all the share-certificates which the members of the company held to the value of ¥830,000 ; more than 49,756 *koku* of rice ; ¥13,500 of the new public securities ; the two mines of Ani and Innai with their buildings, machines, and copper. On the other hand, the bank presented to the Treasury Department all the documents relative to the loan to the Ono Gumi Company, requesting instruction to be given for a proper settlement of the case. On the receipt of the order from the Department the bank attended to the disposition of the proffered articles. The share-certificates were forfeited and the other materials were sold. Thus the bank emerged from its crisis, suffering a loss to the extent of only a little over ¥19,300."

In this connection, a few words should be said to the credit of the Ono Gumi Company, especially to that of I. Furukawa, the manager of the Tokyo branch of the company. Of Furukawa, the Viscount gives the following account: " Dai Ichi Ginkō which loaned the Ono Gumi Company one million and several hundred thousand yen was threatened with a great financial loss. As I trusted Mr. Furukawa, I loaned him money to carry on the business of rice, mining, and yarn without a mortgage. If Mr. Furukawa were a dishonest person and evaded the payment of the loan, taking advantage of the unmortgaged loan, Dai Ichi Ginkō might have gone to ruin as the Ono Gumi Company did. But Mr. Furukawa was an honest and straightforward man. He offered to Dai Ichi Ginkō everything then in the possession of the Ono Gumi Company, including the last bushel of rice in the go-down and the mines with all their accessories. Nothing was hidden or withheld. In this way, Dai Ichi Ginkō escaped even the slightest loss. On the other hand, Mr. Furukawa lost everything. When the Ono Gumi Company was bankrupt, Mr. Furukawa offered to the company his salary and all his savings which he had earned by his hard work for many years to help pay off its debts. He left the company with only the suit of clothes he was then wearing. Such was the type of man Mr. Furukawa was, and having known him well, I trusted him......"

This Gordian Knot could never have been so cleanly cut by any other person than by the Viscount, who had had ample training in the days gone by to cope with such a grave situation. After the Viscount had recovered from the shock he suffered, he calmly inspected the effects the trouble left behind and thereby enriched his experience to forearm himself against future contingencies in the banking business. He at once entered into the work of forming new regulations and rules to preserve the safety of the bank under his care. For instance, the prohibition of loans without mortgage and the limitation of an individual loan to the amount of ¥150,000 were some of the lessons taught by the highly bought experience. Marquis Ōkuma was the Minister of the Treasury at that time and must have felt proud of the Viscount's statesmanlike disposition of the whole matter. The Marquis was ready to recommend the Viscount to the office of President of the bank and an order was issued from the Government to that effect in June, 1875. An extraordinary general meeting of the share holders of the bank was convened on the first day of August, 1875 and the Viscount was elected a Director by the votes of a large majority. Then at the Directors' meeting, the Viscount was elected President by unanimous vote.

While the Viscount was still an officer in the Treasury Department, the necessity of employing a foreign expert in banking was felt by the authorities of the Department. The result was the employment of a young banker in the Department in October, 1872, who was then a member of the Oriental Bank of Yokohama. His name was Allan Shand, an Englishman. Urgent need for instruction was felt, as about this time the Viscount was drafting the national bank laws which were to be published soon and there was

Dai Ichi Ginko.

Four Presidents of Dai Ichi Ginko.

Viscount Shibusawa.
1875—1916

Mr. Y. Sasaki.
1916—1931

Mr. K. Ishii.
1931—1935

Mr. T. Akashi.
1935—

Allan Shand.

hardly any one who knew anything about banking business. The Viscount kept up his intercourse with Mr. Shand right along during his Presidency of Dai Ichi Ginkō. Mr. Shand's contribution to the banking world of modern Japan was immense, because he was the banker who not only taught future bankers like Mr. Y. Sasaki, who became the second President of Dai Ichi Ginkō, but wrote books relative to banking business. As we already have seen, the banking system of Japan was copied after the national bank system of the United States of America introduced by Prince Itō, but it was later entirely changed to the methods practiced in England. Shand's influence played a most important part in bringing about this change. Shand's vital contribution to Dai Ichi Ginkō was the fact that he persuaded the Viscount, its President, to abstain from creating an exchange department in the bank by opening a branch office in Shanghai. The ground for Shand's contention was that it would be too risky for an ordinary commercial bank of only a few years experience to undertake to carry on an exchange business. Long afterward the Viscount made a confession that if he had not heeded the warning given by Shand regarding the plan to start an exchange bank in Shanghai, Dai Ichi Ginkō would not have achieved the success it did. Thus the bank which had escaped the disaster caused by the failure of the Ono Gumi Company was again saved from the calamitous menace of the Shanghai enterprise.

What might be called a third calamity to Dai Ichi Ginkō took place in the year 1875. The President of Dai Ichi Ginkō had hardly recovered from the blow received from the bankruptcy of the Ono Company, when he had to face another menace. It was the announcement from the Government that it would no longer allow Dai Ichi Ginkō to handle the Government revenue. One can easily see why the Government came to adopt this drastic measure. It was because of the threatened loss of credit brought upon Dai Ichi Ginkō by the failure of the Ono Company, its powerful co-partner. The Viscount, a man of fair play and square deal, must have understood quicker than any other person the reasonableness of the action of the Government in this case. But as the President of the Bank, he must find the way out of the critical situation, because the greater part of the bank's deposits then consisted of the Government moneys. The sudden withdrawal of the deposits amounted to a run on the bank. The President at once prepared a written protest and presented it to the authorities. Marquis Ōkuma was the Finance Minister. The protest was well received and the withdrawal of the total amount was postponed for a few months. In addition the Treasury Department granted to the bank a loan of ¥750,000. When the time for the return of the total deposit to the Treasury Department came, the bank fulfilled its obligation. But the deposits of the Departments of the Interior and Communications, and also those of local governments, were handled by the bank. Thus it was that all the Government deposits were not withdrawn at once. Nevertheless it was a painful blow to the bank, as the amount of ¥9,900,000 of the bank deposits, according to the report of the first half year of 1874, was reduced to

¥2,200,000 in the report of the last half year of 1876.

The concern of the new Government ever since the Meiji Restoration had been how to straighten out and readjust the nation's finances. The Government had changed the system of the hereditary pensions of the *Daimyo* and *Shizoku* into that of bonds and the bonds issued for the pensions amounted to the sum of one hundred and seventy four million yen. This new system became a source of almost endless financial disturbance. In order to meet the need, the Government granted the privilege to the existing national banks to issue national bank paper currency. At the same time the Government made an official proclamation that the national bank paper currency will be honored just as the regular currency for tax payments, for other public or private uses, and in conversion with specie. Quite a large amount of national bank paper currency was distributed to the banks.

This caused inflation, and the value of the currency went down, drawing gold out of the banks at the same time. The time soon came when the national banks could not meet the demands of the public for the exchange of specie with the bank currency. So the Viscount conceived the idea that, instead of meeting the demand of the public with specie for the national bank currency, Government paper currency should take the place of the specie, and he recommended the adoption of the plan to the Government. The recommendation was accepted and put into force. At first, the Government gave a certain amount of the regular paper currency to the national banks, requiring of them to return to the Government the amount of the national bank currency for the value received from it. In course of time, this arrangement took out of the national banks all their paper currency and supplied them with the Government paper currency. This process made the national banks to lose the privilege of issuing their national bank paper currency. Thus the necessity of revising the National Bank Laws was felt by the authorities of the Government. The revision was achieved and the application of the revised bank laws opened the door wide for many national banks to spring up. Within less than four years namely from 1876 to 1879, more than one hundred and fifty national banks were organized. Two provisions in the revised laws were accountable for this rapid growth. One was a method whereby the Government allowed the national bankers to issue national bank currency on the mortgage of its bonds, and the other was the provision whereby the national banks could convert their paper currency into the Government currency instead of specie. This seemed to be a happy solution of the existing financial perplexity. But another inflation took place, so that a device known as "The Voluntary Abandonment of the Privilege of National Banks" and a twenty percent reduction of the national bank currency, both of which were conceived by the Viscount, were effected. Such measures were unwelcome to the average banker. But to the Viscount, who had never entertained any selfish desire except to enrich the public and the country, they were most feasible plans.

A large number of the national banks were rapidly organized, and yet very few businessmen knew even the rudiments of the banking system. The Viscount had to teach them. President Sasaki, right hand man and successor of the Viscount, tells us : " The founders of national banks in different parts of the country in those days knew nothing about the management of their banks. Therefore a host of men gathered round the Viscount for instruction." There is a paragraph worth quoting in the book entitled " The Review of the History of the Banks of the Meiji Era." It reads : " Especially the national banks were well organized in different parts of the country, and the management was left mostly in the hands of the *Shizoku* (Samurai) superior in rank to the farmers, artisans, and merchants. The fact that the national banks had played an important role as champions for the development of commerce and industry may be due to the qualities of the leaders. This precedent will long influence the moral status of the coming bankers." By placing this remark side by side with that of President Sasaki we will be able to see in a bold relief what a banker of bankers Viscount Shibusawa was, who had in season and out of season preached and practiced the doctrine of the harmonization of morality and economy.

Directly related to the banking activity of the Viscount there is a matter which should not be overlooked. It is the organization of the Taku Zen Kai and the Tokyo Bankers' Association. The name Taku Zen Kai needs explanation for it bears a mark quite characteristic of the Viscount. *Taku* means choose, *Zen* good, and *Kai* society. The two words *Taku* and *Zen* were taken from the Confucian Analects, his Bible. In that book a sentence " Choose good and obey it " is found. This Taku Zen Kai contributed a great deal to the development of the banking business among bankers. It became a medium through which the knowledge of banking operation in foreign countries was spread among the members of the society and by which the members exchanged their views aud opinions. As the membership grew larger and stronger, it was reorganized under the name of the Tokyo Ginkō Association in 1880.

The time came when the First National Bank (Dai Ichi Kokuritsu Ginkō) was to be transformed into the First Bank (Dai Ichi Ginkō). In March of 1896, the Government made public the laws dealing with the national banks whose business terms had expired. The President of Dai Ichi Kokuritsu Ginkō called an extraordinary general meeting of the share holders on the 17th of May, 1896. The meeting decided that the banking activity should be continued as a private bank under such and such regulations. On the 26th of June, it obtained permission from the Government to continue its business. On the 19th of July, the President called again the extraordinary general meeting of the share holders for the election of the officers who would become the Directors when the formal declaration for the continuance of its existence had been decided. Thus the Dai Ichi Kokuritsu Ginkō was dissolved at the completion of its term and Dai Ichi Ginkō was established on the 29th of September, 1896. The Viscount was elected its President.

We remember that the Dai Ichi Kokuritsu Ginkō was organized with the capital of two million four hundred forty thousand and eight hundred yen in November of 1872, and that it was reduced to the capital of one million and five hundred thousand yen on account of the failure of the Ono Gumi Company, three years later. Up to the time of its dissolution in 1896, the capital amounted to two million two hundred and fifty thousand yen. To this an equal amount taken from the reserves was added, and the capital was doubled, amounting to four million and four hundred fifty thousand yen. In 1899, five hundred thousand yen were added to the capital, making its total five million yen.

Looking at the business end of the bank, we find the following figures: The deposits in 1892 amounted to seven million and four hundred thousand yen, which had increased to over eleven million yen in 1897; in 1902, to over twenty million and seven hundred thousand yen; and in 1907 to forty nine million yen. The loans in the corresponding years increased in the following rates; eight million yen, twelve million yen, twenty six million yen, and forty eight million yen.

The activity of Dai Ichi Ginkō was not confined to Japan alone. It early began work in Korea. It was in the year 1878 that it created its branch office in Fusan. Within thirteen years beginning from 1896, Dai Ichi Ginkō established eighteen new branch offices, of which twelve branches were established in different parts of Korea. About the currency system of Korea much can be said, but suffice it to say that Dai Ichi Ginkō greatly contributed in the stabilization of the money market there by issuing the Dai Ichi Ginkō paper currency of ten, five, and one yen denominations, convertible with the Japanese Government currency. Now and then the old ten yen bill with the image of Viscount Shibusawa can be seen.

Dai Ichi Ginkō of today is one of the six largest

financial institutions under the management of private citizens. Recently it built a ten million yen structure solid, dignified, roomy, and beautiful in the most strategic place in Tokyo. It is far more than a mere institution. It is a kingdom, spreading its financial net all over Japan and in important cities of Chosen. It has a capital of fifty seven million and five hundred thousand yen and the reserve of sixty six million and three hundred thousand yen, making the total fund of one hundred twenty three million and eight hundred thousand yen. Mr. T. Akashi, a son-in-law of the Viscount is its President, and Viscount K. Shibusawa, a grandson and heir of the Viscount, one of the managing Directors.

CHAPTER VII

BUSINESS ACTIVITIES

THE Viscount's business activities viewed from their results, or as phenomena, are amazing both in quantity and quality. No one who rightly reads the history of the industry and commerce of modern Japan would dare deny the fact that the Viscount was the first and the last leader in the domain of Japan's industry and commerce. Here again some may argue that the Viscount was a favorite of Heaven or a pet of Destiny. But Heaven is no respecter of persons. Heaven has nothing to do with caprice, prejudice, and partiality. If it favors a man and prefers him above others, it has a sound moral reason for doing so. Heaven does not pick a favorite first and then make a hero out of him. The reverse is its method. A potential hero is born and struggles for his existence. Heaven extends its helping hand to him because he is a potential hero to guard, guide and direct, so that he may later become a real hero. Therefore in the last analysis to call a man "Heaven's favorite" means that he is really a great man.

Others may contend that the Viscount's environment was peculiarly conducive to make him a unique person. The fact that environment has much to do with human destiny is an axiomatic truth. But environment does not create a hero or a great man out of the average man. It only furnishes an opportunity for a potential hero to become conscious of his own power and to avail himself of it.

In the transition stage of the Meiji Restoration, there

were quite a number of young patriots who lived in a similar environment with the Viscount, but only one Viscount Shibusawa came out. To-day, thousands of students upon thousands are graduated from their universities under the unified system of education, and yet their mental and moral inclinations differ from each other as their faces do. We do not find many heroes among them either.

It is beyond contradiction that Heaven, Destiny, or Environment played a very important part in bringing the Viscount to the unique position as the captain of industry of Modern Japan, but without his own power of selection and appropriation of the influences momentarily shed upon him by Heaven, Destiny, or Environment, the result would have been quite different from what was actually achieved. The Viscount's insistence on the cooperative principle seems to have been extended beyond the human relationship. He cooperated with Heaven, Destiny or Environment. And as we shall see later, he would have had one nation cooperate with another nation, thus harmonizing nationalism with internationalism.

In order that we may understand the business activities of the Viscount, we shall take up some typical cases—as for instance—his relations with the Mitsui, the Mitsubishi, and a few other outstanding companies. The Mitsui and Mitsubishi are the most powerful financial firms in Japan. The Mitsui has a much longer history than the Mitsubishi. The former was already in existence during the Tokugawa regime, while the latter was a product of the Meiji Restoration.

The relationship between the Viscount and the Mitsui

began, when the Viscount organized the First National Bank on the basis of the collective or share system in the year, 1873. R. Minomura was the representative of the Mitsui. Minomura had long maintained an enviable position in the Mitsui firm. In fact, it was said that it was by his keen business sagacity that the Mitsui could safely pull through the financial crisis during the transition period of the Meiji Restoration. Minomura was a progressive businessman and entertained the idea that the secret of success in this world rests upon the search for new knowledge. The Mitsui seemed to have had an eye on the Viscount to invite him as a chief officer of the firm as soon as he resigned his Government position. This plan was undoubtedly formed by Minomura, for it was he who later approached the Viscount with the offer. The Viscount gives a bit of his reminiscences on this point ; " Mr. Minomura of the Mitsui desiring to make me his successor, one day called on me and gave me a suit of clothes with the family crest of the Mitsui. But I told him that I would be pleased to serve the Mitsui as an adviser, but not as its employee. I felt that I could be of some help to the firm. This incident was the origin of the friendship between the Mitsui and myself."

Minomura was the number one man in the Mitsui concern, and the Mitsui as a business concern was the biggest firm in all Japan in those days, with the possible exception of the then rising Mitsubishi. How important a man Minomura was for the Mitsui could be ascertained from the fact that he was made vice-President of the Mitsui Ginkō, when it was formed in the year 1876, and that he had been trusted in a special way by Marquis Inouye, a staunch supporter of the Mitsui until his death. Minomura's invitation to the Viscount was that of the Mitsui itself, of which firm the Viscount would have become the Director-in-Chief, if only he had accepted the invitation. A greater enticement to any ambitious business man could not have come to him for a life time, and he might easily have been tempted to yield to it.

It was a rare chance for him to kill the two birds of wealth and fame with the one stone of " Yes ". But his reply was " No " when he told Minomura that he would be willing to help the Mitsui as its adviser and not as its employee. The sensitive and appreciative nature of the Viscount would not allow him coldly to turn his back to such a flattering offer, and undoubtedly he must have tried hard to show his true appreciation. So he pledged the Mitsui his faith as an adviser. He could go no further because his mind was filled with bigger questions and higher dreams. To promote the development of commerce and industry ; to elevate the status of the businessman ; and to spread the " collective " system throughout the country with the view of enriching and strengthening the nation—these were his passionate desires. No wonder then that a single business firm, no matter how big and promising it might be, could not allure him from the course he had mapped out for his career. If the Mitsui had been successful in winning the Viscount, that firm would have attained a greater success than it has already achieved. But the nation on the whole would have been poorer, for it would have been impossible for the Viscount to make himself so universally useful as he did make himself, if he were bound to one particular firm as its employee.

This episode between Minomura and the Viscount reminds the author of another interesting story, which he heard a long time ago, but which remains in his memory as fresh as that of yesterday. Leland Stanford, a pioneer California multimillionaire and a statesman of great vision, founded Stanford University in memory of his only son Leland Stanford, Jr. The early death of this son had brought upon him such profound sorrow that no mortal physician could heal the wound. The great wealth and the magnificent mansion without his loving son stood before him as a mockery. Hence he concentrated his whole attention on the creation of a memorial through which he might in the best and highest way cherish the memory of his son. He made up his mind to build the greatest university in America and find for it the perfect President. The cost of the buildings or the amount of salary for the President were no concern to him. So he looked around for such a President throughout America and Europe. Herbert Spencer was at the zenith of his scholarly fame at that time and strongly appealed to the imagination of Stanford. Stanford approached him with the invitation to become the President of Leland Stanford Jr. University, offering the British scholar and educator a fabulous amount of salary. The proud scholar replied to the American magnate that Herbert Spencer of England could neither be bought nor sold for money, but that he would be pleased to recommend the kind of scholar Stanford was searching for. Dr. David Starr Jordan who became the first President of Stanford

University was the choice,

In the world of glaring materialism it is highly refreshing to be able occasionally to find men like Viscount Shibusawa and Herbert Spencer who are firmly fixed in their moral conviction that there are men and things in this world that cannot be bought with money.

What Spencer told Stanford was of a similar nature to that which the Viscount told Minomura. Spencer said that he could not be President or employee of Stanford University, but would help the institution to the best of his ability. The result was the finding of of President Jordan, a great scholar and administrator. The Viscount promised Minomura to help the Mitsui in the capacity of an adviser, but not as an an employee. What was then the help the Viscount offered to the Mitsui?

We have already noted that the Mitsui had had a long career and had established a prestige as a solid financial agency. Hence it might not have needed any help from outside so far as the ordinary routine duties in dealing with the money market were concerned. But certainly it needed leaders whose vision and executive ability would enable the firm not only to keep up with the progress of the nation, but occupy a place of leadership in the van of civilization. That the Mitsui had entertained this sort of ambition can be seen from the fact that it dared to dispatch the five young members of the family to the United States of America to study the banking system in that country as early as February, 1872. They were Benzo, 22 years old, Teijiro, 21, Takenosuke, 18, Choshiro, 16 (Baron Mitsui), and Yonosuke, 17, accompanied by the two employees, Shyukichiro Noyori, 28 and Tsunetaro Yoshioka, 20.

The progressive spirit of the Mitsui is again demonstrated in the public statement signed by Minomura, the representative of the entire Mitsui firm on the occasion of founding the Mitsui Ginko in March, 1876. Minomura after having touched upon the unstable condition of human affairs, alternating success and failure, puts this question; how can we best insure our safety? Then in answer to the question, the following statement is made:

" To insure our security is to adopt a cooperative system in business. There are several forms of such a system, but the best of them all is an anonymous company, by which it is meant that the company is named after the work it aims to carry on, instead of having the names of the persons involved in it. The transaction of business and the performance of duty are decided by conference according to the laws and regulations recognized by the government of the country. The whole procedure precludes privacy and guarantees fairness. This is the best procedure and to adopt the best is to keep up with the march of time. Therefore, we now drop the name of Mitsui Gumi and change it to Mitsui Ginko. Moreover, the relationship between the employer and the employee should be changed to that of partnership, aiming at co-existence and co-prosperity—namely to let all the members share profits as well as happiness. Such is the outline of the prospectus for founding Mitsui Ginko."

To idolize Viscount Shibusawa as the only businessman ahead of the time in those early days would harm both the admired and the admirer. One would incur a severe reprimand from the Mitsui firm if one held that the sending of those five young men of the Mitsui to America in such an early period for the study of the banking system and the forming of such a wonderful and radically progressive prospectus in founding Mitsui Ginko might not have been realized if Viscount Shibusawa had not been present as a powerful factor in such innovations. But after all, his conclusion would not be considered so absurd when we carefully trace the course through which such a conclusion might be reached. Let us think of the Viscount as the Superintendent of the First National Bank of which Minomura was a Director; of the common traits of statesmanship and business policy between the two men; of the mutual trust and admiration that had existed between them as we have already seen; and then think of the organization of Mitsui Ginko of which Minomura was made the vice-President, the highest position an outsider of the Mitsui family could occupy in the organization.

How much was due to Minomura and how much to the Viscount would be hard to tell. But it is an open fact that the insistence in applying the collective system to Japan's industry was first made by the Viscount. As Minomura was surrounded by powerful constituents and the material to work with in building up a company on the basis of collectivism, the Viscount must have preached the doctrine to him and converted him, and finally through him the Mitsui.

In this sense, the Viscount's promise to his close friend Minomura to assist the Mitsui was amply fulfilled.

The other way whereby the Viscount helped to benefit the Mitsui was by inviting the Mitsui to join in the organization of various industrial companies.

The former Baron T. Masuda had occupied an important position in the Mitsui firm for a long time and had been a very close friend of the Viscount. Baron Masuda represented the Mitsui in several companies in which the Viscount occupied central positions.

Next we shall observe the relationship between the Viscount and the Mitsubishi concern.

The name of Mitsubishi at once suggests other names, the name of Yataro Iwasaki, the founder of the Mitsubishi concern, and the name of Nippon Yusen Kaisha. Iwasaki, the sole ruler of the Mitsubishi kingdom, which could be said to have risen into power within a day compared with the long history of the Mitsui and to have become so powerful as to stand a rival to it, was an adventurer of a rare type. Like Minomura of the Mitsui, Iwasaki of the Mitsubishi had his eye upon the Viscount and desired to take the latter into partnership in his business enterprise.

Iwasaki's success in business was largely through his own strength and activity. His experience made him a believer in autocratic self-determination. He believed that the collective system in business retards or obstructs achievements. He was essentially an autocrat, dictator, or dogmatist. In this sense Iwasaki radically differed from the Viscount, and the two men could not be reconciled so far as their attitude toward business enterprises was concerned any more than oil and water. But Iwasaki saw in the Viscount ability, wisdom, and resourcefulness. He felt that he could make the Mitsubishi the greatest financial power of Japan, if he and the Viscount could work hand in hand. So one day Iwasaki approached the Viscount with a far-reaching proposition, and the two met together only to bring out into sharp contrast their business policies. The Viscount was strongly intrenched in his collectivism, while Iwasaki was equally firm in his individualism. Finally they agreed to disagree and parted company with one another.

Where then can we find any part played by the Viscount in his relation with the Mitsubishi firm? To answer this question would mean a discussion of the history of Japan's marine transportation enterprise, culminating in the formation of the present N. Y. K., one of the world's greatest marine transportation companies, and we shall very briefly review the general aspects of this work.

Although there were not wanting some foreign styled steamships in Japan at the time of the Meiji Restoration, yet most marine transportation was carried on by native boats. The American Pacific Steamship Company monopolized transportation between Yokohama, Kobe, Nagasaki, and Shanghai. The Meiji Government wanted to let native businessmen handle this work. This resulted in the rise of the Japan Mail Steamship Company in the year 1871. The Viscount was serving the Treasury Department then and rendered considerable assistance in promoting the industry.

On the other hand, Yataro Iwasaki, who had supervised the shipping business of his clan, borrowed three ships from the clan government and conducted regular transportation work between the ports of Tokyo, Osaka, and Kochi, under the agreement that he would offer his services to the local government in case of any emergency. He formed a company of semi-government

nature. In the year 1873, the name of the company
was changed to Mitsubishi. At this time, the entire
concern fell into the control of Iwasaki—the first step
in his autocratic move. In the following year, what
is known as the Saga rebellion took place. Still later
the Formosan expedition was carried on. These emer-
gencies forced the Government to buy thirteen ships from
a foreign country at the cost of over a million five
hundred thousand dollars to transport military officers,
soldiers, goods, food, and ammunition. The management
of these ships should have been entrusted to the hands
of the Mail Steamship Company, but that company was
so badly dilapidated that it was far from being able to
meet the order of the Government. This state of affairs placed the Government in an embarrassing position.
Just at this time, Iwasaki made a proposal to the
Government that he would offer all the ships belonging to the Mitsubishi Company for the services of the
Government. This offer was welcomed by the high
authorities which granted Iwasaki the privilege of ma-
noevering the thirteen ships just bought. The Mitsubishi Company made a phenomenal success in managing the affair to its high credit. The Mail Steamship
Company also was given a part of the work, but could
not show any success.

At the close of the Formosan Expedition, the Government had turned its attention to the development of
marine industry and gave free hand to the Mitsubishi
Company to attend to this work. Another object of
the Government was to buy off the right of navigation
from the American Pacific Steamship Company. Thus
in September, 1875 the Government gave its first or-

dinance to the Mitsubishi Company under the following specifications : The Government would unconditionally cede to the Mitsubishi Company the thirteen ships bought for the use of the Formosan Expedition ; make an annual grant of two hundred and fifty thousand yen for the aid of navigation ; and grant eleven thousand yen annually for the next fifteen years to help the work of the mercantile marine school of the company and also to educate crews and workmen. The obligations on the part of the Mitsubishi in response to these privileges were that, in peace time the company should carry on regular voyages to Shanghai and various home ports ; that it should undertake mail transportation free of charge ; and that it should meet the requisition of ships in war time. At this time the name of the company was changed again and was called Yubin Kisen Mitsubishi Kaisha (Mail Steamship Mitsubishi Co.). The Government gave twelve ships to this newly named company, taking them out of the old Mail Steamship Company. This addition greatly strengthened the marine power of the new Mitsubishi, making it the owner of thirty three steamers with the tonnage of thirty thousand one hundred fifty, besides many sail boats.

One reason why the Government so generously subsidized the Mitsubishi was because it wanted to defeat in competition the American Pacific Steamship Co. Hence the Mitsubishi commenced to compete with the American Pacific Steamship Co. in May, 1875. The fight was intense and after a severe struggle on both sides for a few months, the former practically defeated the latter, which was obliged to sell its steamship lines and four steamers to the former. This victory meant for the Mitsubishi the monopoly of navigation along the coast lines of Japan. But in 1876, a formidable rival appeared in the P. & O. Company of England, which opened a line between Yokohama and Shanghai. The Mitsubishi, the recent victor over the American Pacific Steamship Co., challenged the P. & O. and vanquished it. Next a Chinese Steamship Co. was ousted from Japan. Thus all trace of the influence of foreign companies was swept away from the coast line of Japan.

Hence the Government issued a second ordinance to the Mitsubishi to grant a subsidy of two hundred and fifty thousand yen to assist the six mail lines conducted by the company. By this time, not only transportation along the home coast lines, but those of China and Korea, came under the control of the Mitsubishi. During the Satsuma Rebellion, the Mitsubishi offered to the Government all its ships for its service, except those which were sailing between Shanghai and Japan. But this being still insufficient, the Mitsubishi, adding its own funds to what it borrowed from the Government, bought ten more new steamships to meet the emergency.

After the suppression of the rebellion, the Mitsubishi vigorously pushed the work of its expansion. From 1878 its regular lines had been extended to Ogasawara Islands, Loo Choo Islands, Vladivostock, and special lines to various ports of Hokkaido and to Hongkong.

The Mitsubishi had received an enormous amount of subsidy from the Government for various purposes, amounting to nine million and two hundred fifty thousand yen. This support coupled with the extraordinary ability of Iwasaki made the Mitsubishi what it was then. Stimulated by this wonderful success in the marine industry, Iwasaki turned his attention toward the enterprises of mines, banks, marine insurance, and storage, etc.

With the increase of wealth, the power of Iwasaki had grown. There is nothing wrong for a man to be wealthy and powerful, provided that he makes good use of his wealth and power. Danger lies in a monopolistic use of these forces for personal gratification or selfishness. And the type of man who is liable to fall into this sort of danger is a man, autocratic, dictatorial, or despotic, for he will increasingly strengthen himself with egoism and absolutism against altruism and collectivism until he wields the sceptre of "A monopoly of unlimited power."

The rapid growth of the Mitsubishi in economic power and the strong support it received from the Government caused the Mitsubishi to exercise its arbitrary power. Its menace began to be felt in the economic circle of Japan which was yet in an adolescent and formative stage. Public spirited men also came to feel the necessity of checking the aggressive movement of the Mitsubishi. Viscount Shibusawa was one of them. Why the Viscount wanted to put a brake upon the Mitsubishi must be obvious to the reader for he has already seen how radically business principles advocated by him and Iwasaki differed. By this time, the collective system has been adopted and the number of cooperative companies under the leadership of the Viscount had been increasing. If the opposing principle of Iwasaki's should prevail, the outcome would be easy to be foreseen. Some kind of adjustment or understanding between the Viscount and Iwasaki was necessary, and a conference between the two captains of industry was arranged. They met in a conference which resulted in making clearer than ever the existence of a wide chasm between their business convictions.

The Viscount finally resolved to fight the Mitsubishi Company by creating a rival company. He appealed to the Mitsui which was only too anxious to stop the Mitsubishi's arbitrary move, and to a few local magnates. The former Baron T. Masuda who was holding an influential position in the Mitsui highly approved the plan conceived by the Viscount. Thus what was known as Tokyo Fuuhansen Kaisha (Tokyo Sailingship Co.) was organized in the year 1880 with the capital of three hundred thousand yen. Later, the Viscount augmented the company by uniting with it two existing transportation firms, and called the newly organized machinery Kyodo Unyu Gaisha (United Transportation Co.). This was achieved on the 14th of July, 1882. In the year 1881, there took place a change among the cabinet officials, Marquis Ōkuma, a patron of the Mitsubishi, resigning his office and from that year on the Government stopped the subsidy to the Mitsubishi Co., thus creating a turning point in the industry of marine transportation. Not only the subsidy to the Mitsubishi was stopped, but requirements and restrictions were placed upon the company by the third ordinance of the Government, issued in February, 1882, which reads : " The province of a marine transportation company is simply to transport goods. It should never conduct the business of selling and buying them. The ships it owns should be solid and secure, maintaining a certain rate of speed and with the total tonnage

registration of not less than twenty two thousand tons."
In addition certain regulations were given concerning the
points of supplementing and repairing the ships. A
restriction was placed on the rate of fares. The Government brought pressure to bear on the Mitsubishi on one
hand, and on the other rendered assistance to a company coping with the Mitsubishi—namely the subsidiza-
tion of the United Transportation Co. At this time, the
administrative work of the marine transportation industry came under the Department of Agriculture and Commerce. The minister of the Department was the lesser
Saigo—Marquis Jūdo Saigo and the vice-Minister was
Viscount Yajiro Shinagawa who was highly displeased
over the tyranny of the Mitsubishi. Viscount Shibusawa did his utmost to hold the Mitsubishi down while
he extended his hearty assistance to the United Transportation Co. Under the support of the Government
the United Transportation Co. was organized as a
cooperative enterprise between the Government and the
people with the capital of three million yen. However,
this was altogether too small a company to cope with
the Mitsubishi, and therefore the company's capital was
increased up to six million yen.

Necessary preparation for competition being completed
the gauntlet was thrown down. The competition first
took place along the regular routes in Hokkaido, in
different parts of Japan Proper, and between Kobe and
Shanghai. The public seemed to have welcomed the
debut of the United Transportation Co. as it had been
abused by the monopoly of the Mitsubishi. But there
was a political party which disliked the United Transportation Co. The party was known as *Kaishin To*

(the Reform Party), and was led by Marquis Ōkuma. All the papers patronized by this party were against the company.

Over against this opposition, *Jiyu To* (the Liberal Party) led by Count Itagaki took the side of the United Transportation Co., and ruthlessly attacked the Reform Party as well as the Mitsubishi. The stand the Government took in the midst of a fierce competition between the two marine powers was firm. Then Viscount Shibusawa, though he was not organically connected with the United Transportation Co., was a hidden power supporting it from the standpoint of his principles. This competition was a fight between collectivism and individualism; between Viscount Shibusawa and Y. Iwasaki; and politically speaking a fight between the Government and the Reform Party; and between the Liberal Party and the Reform Party. It was by no means a skirmish which took place in a hidden corner.

In a way, all Japan was involved in this struggle. Whether Japan would become an industrial nation under the collective system as the Viscount would have it so, or under the monopolistic scheme as was advocated by Iwasaki, was forever to be decided by the outcome of this fight.

In the meantime, the competitive actitivity had been going on from bad to worse for nearly three years. How intense the fight between the two rival companies was could be shown from the fact that the normal fare of ¥5.50 for third class passage between Yokohama and Kobe had gradually fallen down to the absurd price of less than one yen. This was the extreme limit they could go. So they competed in speed. This meant an enormous use of coal and a risk for the passengers. The financial statistics of the two companies showed huge losses. All through this fight the Liberal Party had kept up its attack on the Mitsubishi Co., and the United Transportation had received moral support in an indirect way. But still the financial loss of the company was glaringly big, so much so that there was raised a voice of complaint in the Government quarters against Viscount Shinagawa. This complaint cast a shade upon the relationship between the Government and the United Transportation Co., and caused the shares of the company to fall to two-thirds of the paid up value. Thus the management of the company had become hopelessly difficult. Seizing upon this pitiful state of the company, the Mitsubishi conceived the idea of a union, and presented its argument in favor of union to some influential officials in the Government. It also bought a majority of the shares of the United Transportation Co., placing the latter in a very unfavorable position for a union on equal footing. The Government tried to arbitrate between the two companies for the purpose of saving both, but they were hopelessly irreconcilable, the Mitsubishi remaining the stronger of the two. The Government sized up the situation and saw it was hardly possible to outdo the Mitsubishi. Moreover, the public began to clamour against the Government's attitude toward the Mitsubishi, in earlier days first encouraging it, and now becoming so powerless to control it as to try to offset its dictatorial waywardness by helping organize the United Transportation Co. The latter if allowed to grow strong by outdoing the Mitsubishi, might become a second Mitsubishi to play its predecessor's game. On the other hand, if the competition continued to be carried on, both might be ruined, in which case the marine transportation industry of the country would be ruined. The only way out was to form a union. The Mitsubishi was favorably inclined to see the plan carried out as we have already seen.

Political elements entered into the union movement, and finally the union between the Mitsubishi and the United Transportation was consummated, on the first day of October in the year 1885. This was the birth of Nippon Yusen Kaisha. An observer of the financial world of Japan in those early days thus gives his opinion on the creation of N. Y. K.:

"Here a big monster called Nippon Yusen Kabushiki Kaisha (N.Y.K., Ltd), full of mystery made a spectacular debut under the hue and cry of the majority of the people. This took place on the first day of October, 1885. The Government urged Mr. Yanosuke Iwasaki (a younger brother of Yataro), to be the new president of N.Y.K., but he strongly declined to accept the offer. Thus Mr. Masazumi Morioka, then the President of the United Transportation, became the first president of N.Y.K. This arrangement gives the appearance that the United Transportation received a beautiful bouquet, but in reality Mr. Yanosuke Iwasaki was the President. If the United Transportation had united with the Mitsubishi on the basis of parity, either Viscount Shinagawa, by resigning his official position, or either Mr. Eiichi Shibusawa or Mr. Takashi Masuda should have been made the first president of N.Y.K.—The fact that the name of Mr. Eiichi Shibusawa was not included among the directors of N. Y. K. at its organization exposes two things. The one is how hard the Satsuma clique in the Government, which had worked behind the scene in the union movement, endeavored to stamp out the Mitsui influence from the

newly organized Company. The other is that we can imagine
how badly Messrs. Shibusawa and Masuda were mortified by
looking at the outcome. As Mr. Masuda represented the Mitsui
openly, his partisanship was very distinct, and on that account
he might not have been able to obtain any official seat in the new
Company. But though Mr. Shibusawa's relation with the Mitsui
was quite close, yet his standing as a great leader in the business
world was altogether unique, and for the Mitsubushi to have
left him out from the official group was an irreparable loss and
a poor policy to resort to from the standpoint of business
strategy."

The fact that about seven years later, N. Y. K.
invited Viscount Shibusawa to become a director proves
the correctness of the view held by this observer, both
as to the importance and worth of the Viscount in his
relation to N. Y. K. The Viscount might have resented
the offer from N. Y. K. as an affront had the company
followed the beaten path of autocracy of the old Mitsubishi, but as N. Y. K. had become one of the strongest
companies organized on the cooperative basis, for the
realization of which he had directed his campaign from
his headquarters of Dai Ichi Ginko, he was only too
glad to forgive and forget the past wrongs connected
with it, pledging to it his ever unwavering patronage.

While we are still on the subject of the marine transportation industry, we may mention why and how
the Viscount poured his energy into this industry in
those days.

China's pressure upon the peninsular of Korea was
becoming threatening and the national feeling of Japan
with reference to China was getting tense. The Viscount was beginning to feel the imperative need of fully

preparing the power and scope of marine transportation.

He also felt the necessity of opening fixed lines between Bombay, Australia, America, and Europe. He urged N. Y. K. to open up the Bombay line and succeeded. He and his colleagues of the Tokyo Chamber of Commerce proposed to the authorities of the Government to subsidize the Bombay line and the proposition was accepted. It is needless to say that he worked hard along these lines because he wanted to extend Japan's industry in various spheres and to enrich the nation.

We already saw that the Viscount organized some two hundred and fifty companies in which he took a leading part. Not all of them survived him. Some died in the midst of the process of organization. But there are many strong companies which have weathered storms and come out triumphant because a right kind of leader piloted the way in the right direction.

There are strong testimonies borne by able junior businessmen to the business activity of Viscount Shibusawa, and we shall bring this chapter to its close with a few quotations.

Mr. Y. Sasaki, the second president of Dai Ichi Ginkō who succeeded the Viscount says :

" Viscount Shibusawa flung himself into the promotion of the the industrial welfare of Japan from the very beginning of the Meiji Restoration. It can justly be said that there was hardly one among various enterprises of commerce and industry which did not receive direction and guidance from him. It will be impossible to write the history of the development of industry of Japan apart from the biography of Viscount Shibusawa."

Mr. Eihachiro Tanaka, President of Dai Nippon Jinzo

Hiryo Kabushiki Kaisha (Artificial Fertilizer Manufacturing Company of Great Japan, Ltd.) says :

" Farmers of the country in those days knew hardly anything
about the value of chemical fertilizers. Their general knowledge
was low. No farmer bought the chemicals. The company could
hardly make anything. This made its management exceedingly
difficult. Moreover, the factory took fire in the year 1893 and
nearly half of it was destroyed. The company was almost defeated. The Directors fell into deep pessimism and some of them
moved for dissolution, but the Viscount who believed in the
bright future of this enterprise rejected such a gloomy proposal
saying ' This enterprise should not be looked upon from the mere
angle of profit making. If the majority of the shareholders
desire dissolution, I shall for the sake of the good of the
country manage the affairs of the company by buying all the
shares left : ' This powerful utterance of the Viscount made it
possible for the company to survive the crisis."

Mr. R. Fujiyama, President of Dai Nippon Seito
Kabushiki Kaisha (Sugar Manufacturing Company of
Great Japan, Ltd.) for a quarter of a century, in his
address to the extraordinary general meeting of the
shareholders of the company held on the day of the
25th anniversary of his presidency (April 27, 1909–
April 27, 1934) has these words :

" —Attacked by the tidal wave of the financial fluctuation
soon after the Russo-Japanese war, our company suffered a severe
set back. This misfortune was not confined to the company. It
disturbed the political and social equilibrium of the time, creating the wide spread sensation known as the Japan Sugar Company
case. Viscount Shibusawa was then the adviser of the company
with power above its President. He said: 'The president has committed suicide,and influential statesmen are suffering from dis-
honor because of their relation to the company. The company

itself is gasping its life away. I dare not let it die, but I am now seventy years old. I need most urgently some one as its new president to resuscitate the life of the company.' The Viscount agonized over the situation. I had no special relation with the company at that time, but the Viscount was the President of the Oji Papar Mill then and I the managing Director. Finally he almost forced me to assume the presidency which I accepted with fear and trembling, simply because he urged me and promised to support me."

The late Mr. K. Makoshi, President of Dai Nippon Biiru Kabushiki Kaisha (The Beer Company of Great Japan, Ltd.) over a quarter of a century says :

" It is no exaggeration to say that there was hardly any business enterprise worthy of the name which was not fostered by Viscount Shibusawa. Indeed, he was a great benefactor of our industrial world. This our company came to its existence as the result of the union of the three companies of the Sapporo Beer, Ebisu Beer, and Asahi Beer in the year 1906. Up to the time of the union, these three companies fiercely competed almost to the point of their self-destruction and to the detriment of the nation's economic life. The best remedy was in the consummation of union. The representatives of the three companies agreed in principle to unite, but in practice many difficulties confronted them. It was finally accomplished only through the Viscount's sincere and unselfish efforts. Really, he should have been made the first president of the present company, but he insisted that I should fill the position."

Mr. K. Kagami, President of Tokyo Kaijo Kasai Hoken Kaisha (Tokyo Marine Fire Insurance Company, Ltd.) says :

" That we young officers of the company could have pulled it through its life and death struggle in early days with un-

wavering determination and confidence was because the presence
of Viscount Shibusawa with us steadied our nerves, giving us
a deep sense of security. When I looked at the Viscount in
his calm posture listening to what we young people were deliberating, I felt that the Tokyo Marine Fire Insurance Company had
a strong pillar in him. I believe even now that the company
might have gone to pieces if Viscount Shibusawa had not been
with us then. The fact that the Viscount organized this
company and brought it to a grand success is his imperishable
merit to be mentioned in the economic history of Japan."

CHAPTER VIII

WITHDRAWAL FROM THE BUSINESS WORLD

IT might be asked why one chapter should be devoted to the simple subject of "Withdrawal from the Business World." "Withdrawal" is usually a single act. Nothing much can be involved in such an act. Here the critic falls into error. He has forgotten that a great figure, active and energetic, is involved in this act of "Withdrawal," as its dominant center. He has also forgotten that this seemingly instantaneous act is the effect of the long considered decision of that extraordinary personality whose presence in, or absence from, the field with which he was vitally connected would mean prosperity or depression, as the presence or absence of the sun produces light or darkness in the world. Hence the motive, purpose, and circumstances of his withdrawal from business activity should be brought into light. In other words, the why, how, and when of the withdrawal from business activity of the late Viscount Shibusawa is a study frought with instruction and suggestion for the rising generations of public spirited men.

Viscount Shibusawa repeatedly said on different occasions that his activity in the industrial world was not caused by the slightest desire to make himself wealthy, powerful, and famous, but that the country and people in general should be made rich and strong. As a means to attain to this end, he firmly adhered to the collective system of share holding. From the day he organized the First National Bank in the year 1873 to the time he withdrew from many companies in the year 1909, and from almost all the others in 1916, he had devoted his time and energy to organize and foster various kinds of industry. This means that the Viscount entered into business life at the age of thirty-three; and partially withdrew from it at seventy; and almost entirely at seventy-seven. In Japan, the age of a man at sixty, seventy, seventy-seven, and eighty-eight are regarded as epochal in his life. They are called "Kanreki," "Koki," "Kiju," and "Beiju" respectively. He receives congratulations from his friends at such times, and makes important decisions either for concluding his accustomed course of life or starting a new course. The Viscount followed this time-honored custom and at the age of seventy announced an important alteration in his career. Mr. Shiraishi makes this observation on the change of the course of the Viscount's activity— namely that up to the age of seventy the ratio between his business relations and those of public work was seven to three, while after seventy, the ratio was reversed and was three to seven.

Viscount Shibusawa experienced severe illness three times during his life, succumbing to the last in the year 1931. Between 1903 and 1904, he suffered from influenza, tympanitis, and pneumonia. The attack of pneumonia was quite serious. Even after its cure it left a permanent weakness in the Viscount in the form of chronic asthma. How seriously he was ill can be learned from the following record :

"The physicians in charge at the time were Dr. Kenkan Takagi and Dr. Baelz. The Viscount was prepared for the worst, and wanted to obtain permission from the doctors to invite

Prince Matsukata and Marquis Inouye to come to see him because he desired to confer with them concerning the future of the
industrial situation. Dr. Takagi hearing the request of the Viscount said : ' It sounds as though you were going to speak your
last words. Inasmuch as I am your physician, please have confidence in your recovery. Moreover, it is unadvisable to enter
into such a conversation as you contemplate at this critical time
when a slight excitement may cause fever to rise. Please postpone the attempt. Now is the hour you should give complete
rest to your nerves. We two will guarantee your perfect recovery.' "

Nearly three months were spent in his recovery.
Japanese and Chinese poems were composed during his
convalescence. Thus his mind was occupied with different scenes and no doubt complete rest was given to
it.

The great mind, alert, resourceful, and highly retentive, was, for the time being, emancipated from the whirl
and pressure of intensive and extensive business activity,
and an ample opportunity for meditation in the form
of introspection and retrospection was given to it. The
Viscount, a typical pioneer of unusual foresight, must
have gone over his achievements in the field of industry and seen that the ideas and principles whereby
he wanted to conduct business operations—namely the
application of the collective system—were quite widely
understood and extensively adopted through his efforts.
He must have been satisfied in having seen that the
effort of his labour extending over a period of more than
thirty years was yielding abundant fruit in large cities and
throughout all Japan. He clearly saw that his associates
and junior business men could carry on their business
activities according to the most advanced system of co-

operation, no longer needing his paternal care or direction. Thus it was that he turned his attention to a different field of activity—public service along the lines of educational, social, and international relations.

There can be no doubt that the serious illness of the Viscount at the age of sixty-five became a pivotal point when his life's activity took a new turn. In calmer moments, he scanned the business field and saw how widely and completely he had been identified with it. He wondered how he could have shouldered so heavy responsibilities in the days gone by. As he had entertained no ambition to make himself a multimillionaire nor an autocrat famous in the business world, it was quite natural for the Viscount to look for an unexplored field which, when explored, might contribute to the promotion of the national welfare of Japan in no less degree than wealth does. So out of the Viscount's illness, a new line of activity arose which became the model of an unselfish life for public service. In this sense his illness was a blessing in disguise for him and the Japanese people. The vast results of his public service from the time of his retirement from the business world to his death, numbering over four hundred separate items according to Mr. Watanabe, were all of them creative of goodness and helpfulness to humanity in general. Regarding the public service of the Viscount, this fact must be kept in mind that not all of it began from the time of his retirement from business activity, but that much of it had been carried on by him along with his business activity. His fifty years presidency of the Tokyo City Poor House, a typical institution of philanthropy, is a good illustration.

But was it easy for Viscount Shibusawa to give up his complicated business relations all at once ? So far as his own preference or determination was concerned, it would have been an easy matter to cut loose from the established relations, as he had expected little from those relations in the way of personal gain. But as it is always the case with a great and influential man, the Viscount's life was no longer his own or his family's. He belonged to Japan, or more particularly he was the Viscount of the business world. To have or not to have him meant its life or death.

That there must have taken place this kind of a struggle in the business field can be seen from the circumstances at that time :   (1) The Viscount made his decision of withdrawal from business life during his convalescence which fell within the year 1904, but his actual withdrawal did not take place till the year 1909, five years after his decison was made ; (2) There were business relations which he could not give up if he would, or he would not give up if he could. The inter-relations between the Viscount and some of the business firms were such that the historical relation and actual situation could not permit him to leave them at a moment's notice. In some, the very honor and chival-rous loyalty of the Viscount were involved. Then there is another consideration which might be regarded more or less speculative, but not wholly groundless, and that is the postponement of his withdrawal to a much later date, if the illness had not befallen him in the year 1904. The Viscount's idea about the limit of posses-sion of one's personal wealth was that one should pos-sess wealth sufficiently to lead a decent life in the community, providing for himself and his family. Beyond that, one should work for the public welfare. What kind of life the Viscount meant by the " decent life" we cannot tell, but as he used to call himself a middle class man, while in reality he was a millionaire, approaching the class of multimillionaire, his conception of the decent life must have been very high. At any rate it was axiomatic with the Viscount that he never intended to accumulate wealth for his personal gratification.

Why then would the Viscount linger on in lucrative business life ? Unlike the average *Samurai* of a conservative type who took pride in despising material possessions, the Viscount cherished a high idea concerning wealth. One of the convicitons the Viscount wanted to instil into the minds of the public and the coming generations was the harmonization or reconciliation of morality and economics. First of all he demonstrated this truth in his own life. Then he spoke, and put it into phonograph records. For the Viscount moral life and business life were one and not two. For him there was no need to give up the one in order to retain the other. He was never ashamed of the fact that he was a businessman. Nay rather he gloried in it. As no one else did, the Viscount elevated the status of the businessman in the eyes of the public. K. Makoshi, a business colleague of the Viscount, aptly remarked that the Viscount reversed the social orders of Japan from *Shi* (samurai), *No* (farmer), *Ko* (artisan), and *Sho* (businessman) into *Sho* (businessman), *Ko* (artisan), *No* (farmer), and *Shi* (samurai). Legally speaking there no longer exists any such distinction in Japan. We are all one people.

When we think and ponder over this phenomenal change wrought out in the industrial world by a man like the Viscount, we would wish to have him remain in that relation as long as possible and he too would have staid on in the high place which he had won for himself through his own creative power, and where the host of his admirers would have him comfortably and securely stationed as a prince of industry. He thoroughly identified himself with businessmen and they with him.

Among the last words he uttered a few days before he breathed his last as a message to a large group of businessmen then gathered together at his home, there are these significant expressions, which give us the sense of his absolute devotion to the cause he had espoused and to the class of businessmen : " Though I may be removed into another world, yet I would be with you and guard your health and work. Please do not think of me otherwise than I have been with you in the past." He preferred to be treated by the coming generations of businessmen as one of them, sitting and talking with them in the capacity of President, Chairman, Auditor, Director, Advisor, or Councillor.

We have already seen how scrupulously the Viscount guarded himself, so as to avoid misunderstanding on the part of the public regarding his attitude toward wealth. He was constantly exposed to a danger of misapprehension on account of his seemingly contradictory life, in that on the one hand he openly avowed his unselfishness, and on the other was entering into an ever widening state of material prosperity. The judgment which

the public passes upon its leader or public man is
generally fair and just as far as it goes, but it is narrow, superficial, and partial. It fails to enter into his
motives, purposes, and intention—the elusive part of a
man to be sure, but at the same time most essential in
rightly understanding him.

About the year 1907, which was three years after the
time the Viscount made public his intention to withdraw from the business world on account of his health
and two years preceeding the time he carried out his
decision, a young journalist full of fighting spirit criticized him in the presence of a friend of the Viscount.
The journalist thought that the Viscount was involved
in many business activities because of his selfishness.
The friend of the Viscount felt sorry that the young
writer was so mistaken and wanted to dispel this misunderstanding from his mind. This resulted in an interview
between the Viscount and the journalist. The following is the account which the Viscount reproduced as
the words he addressed to the critic :

" The cause which led me into business life was neither a
desire to increase my own wealth nor to attain to pomp or glory.
Although it might have been egotistic on my part, yet I felt
that Japan should abandon conditions existing previous to the
Meiji Restoration and thoroughly awake, if she expected to carry
on commerce with foreign countries. It was this belief of mine
that induced me to throw in my lot with the business world
and the slightest idea of fame and wealth did not enter my mind.
Motivated by this belief, I organized Dai Ichi Ginko in the year
1873 based on the " share " system. It goes without saying that
confidence or credit is most essential for business transactions, but
it is equally true that business could not be carried on without
adequate funds. Hence I bought shares or stocks and re-

ceived salaries. In this way my fortune increased, but that
was not my real purpose. You say that one man should stick
to one vocation. That depends upon circumstances.

"Suppose that you are going to open up a store in a region
newly opened. You cannot conduct your business according to
the system of division of labour. You will have to have all
sorts of goods in your store, groceries, dry-goods, and hardware,
etc. The industrial world of Japan was primitive, and very much
like a new settlement. Commerce, transportation, insurance, and
industry which is again subdivided into silk and hemp, etc.,
all demanded my attention and care. There may come a time
to straighten out my relations with these various lines of business, and I am waiting for it. Then you tell me that I could
not have made a fortune like mine simply from my salaries.
But for instance, I buy shares with one hundred thousand yen.
Times being favorable, they may increase to two hundred thousand
or three hundred thousand yen. My object does not lie in the
increase of wealth, but from the nature of the business it so
happens. That is all. Never for a moment did I aim at my
own profit...."

In this conversation, the Viscount repeatedly asserted
that it was not his object to make himself rich and
famous, but that he had a larger and higher idea to serve
the country and that the people urged him to enter into
business life. The same idea permeates all his public
and private utterances.

In the year 1892—that is to say—fifteen years before
this incident took place, the Viscount was assailed by
ruffians as he was riding in a carriage. This is known
as the Water Works Iron Pipe Case of the City of
Tokyo. Fortunately the Viscount was not hurt but
a great sensation was created. The host of friends of
the Viscount were shocked by the event. This mur-

derous plot broke out on the eleventh of December, 1892. On the twenty-fourth of the same month the bankers of Tokyo and Yokohama united together to hold a congratulatory meeting for the Viscount because of his safe deliverance from the hands of the assassins.

Baron K. Sonoda, the President of Yokohama Specie Bank, presided over the meeting delivering the address of felicitation. In the response of the Viscount, we find the same sentiment which was expressed by him fifteen years later. After having expressed his deep appreciation of the sympathy and kindness of his colleagues, the Viscount said :

" It was in the year 1872 that I cast in my lot with the business world. From that time on, I have undividedly devoted my energy to promote the welfare of the public, and not the slightest consideration for my own profit has entered into my mind. In planning and managing the various kinds of public enterprise, I am far from being able to say that I have been faultless, but I can swear by heaven and earth that I have never deliberately cheated others, betrayed my pledge, or played a hypocrite."

In the year 1915, the Viscount organized a family trust company, known as Shibusawa Dozoku Kabushiki Kaisha, the first of the kind ever created in Japan. Commenting upon this new device, the Viscount gives the following account :

" I have organized Shibusawa Dozoku Kabushiki Kaisha (Shibusawa Family Trust Company, Ltd.) for the sake of my family, and regret that it may appear as if this project contradicts my well-known principles. My determination at the time I resigned my office in 1872 was that I should devote my whole life to the development of industry since I chose business as my life-time profession. During the last forty-two years, I can say that I have uninterruptedly carried out this intention....Through industry I thought I could discharge my obligation to my country. My personal fame and my family's wealth have never entered into my thought from the very start of my career. My burning desire was to promote through the application of the collective system the welfare of the country ; the development of Japan's industry ; the increaae of the public wealth ; and to elevate the status of merchants and businessmen so that they could be placed on an equal footing with those of Europe and America. With an eye single to this objcet, I have chosen business as my life work.

" In the world there are persons who believe that the end justifies the means, but I cannot agree with them. Needless to say, the end must be right. In the same way, the means also must be right. However much the end may be good and right, if the means used is wrong, it would spoil the end."

" Likewise though the means be right, if the end is unreasonable, wholesome success cannot be achieved. Therefore, I have made it my life-long creed that in order to do anything both the end and the means must be good and right. Inasmuch as I faced the world claiming that I was going to manage companies according to the cooperative system, there remained nothing for me but to do my utmost in supporting my family with the remuneration I received. To go beyond this limitation was to me an abuse of the means. As I made up my mind never to depart from the path of duty once I chose it, I have held myself close to it. I was determined to let nothing but death separate me from the service which I assumed at Dai Ichi Ginko in 1873. From that time on, I have entered into relations with many business enterprises which have sprung up in the progress of human affairs. This was inevitable for the promotion of the national welfare, but through it all I absolutely withheld from planning anything for my private interest. I caused the organization of my family trust company on the basis of the " share " system, but was far from aiming at the promotion of personal interest. As I had a large family, I felt it my duty to plan for their safe and impartial support by appropriating what little I have been able to save. Apprehensive of misunderstanding, I wanted the actual organization of the company to take place after I had passed away, but the majority of the members of the family insisted that it should be formed in my life-time. I yielded to their persuasion and allowed it to be organized. I sent notices to my close friends as to the motives and reason in creating this trust company by fully explaining to them the circumstances which led me to adopt this method."

In gathering up the statements made by the Viscount in different stages of his life, we can clearly see that he completely won the confidence of the contemporary leaders in the business world and that therefore they felt safe in relying upon his advice or council. This prestige and worth of the Viscount made him the leader of leaders, being sought by innumerable business organizations simply to identify himself with them. His voice of yes or no carried with it a tremendous weight in organizing a new company or in preventing it. Thus it was that he became involved in so many business concerns which would have him remain with them indefinitely. Superficial onlookers were dazed with the rapidity whereby the Viscount had increased his business relations with many and strong companies, and falsely concluded that the Viscount was making himself busy blinded by his selfish interest. His clean and clear conscience could well afford to ignore those false accusations, so far as his personal justification was concerned, but as a social being he had to protect his honor before the public. Hence his frequent allusions to his integrity were necessary. At any rate, it was no easy thing for him to sever his deep rooted relations with the business world which had claimed his life-time service, unless he was persuaded to see that a still higher and nobler service was beckoning him.

The late S. Ebara, an educator, statesman, and a member of the House of Peers, once told his pupils at a large gathering that the greatness of Viscount Shibusawa lay in the fact that the Viscount deliberately sacrificed his economic ambitions for non-profit making social services, while it was fully possible for him to make himself one of the biggest multimillionaires of Japan.

CHAPTER IX

SOCIAL, EDUCATIONAL, AND
OTHER PUBLIC ACTIVITIES

VISCOUNT Shibusawa gave his time and energy
to the service of about four hundred organizations, large and small, permanent and temporary,
under the heading of the present chapter. The major
part of this service was rendered during the last fifteen
years of his life, although, as we have already seen,
much of his philanthropic work had been carried on
along with his lucrative activities.

"The Tokyo City Poor House" at Itabashi, Tokyo,
to which the Viscount had devoted his service as its
President for almost sixty years, can be taken as typical
of his work.

Before we enter into the discussion of the Tokyo City
Poor House, we need to know, as a sort of introduction, the nature of the savings known as the "Common Fund." Toward the close of the Feudal System,
Yedo (present Tokyo) was governed by an able statesman, Prince Sadanobu Matsudaira, whose office corresponded to that of Premier. He is well known as Prince
Rakuo Shirakawa. During his administration he had
saved money by reforming the municipal policy and
added to it a Government contribution. These savings
were to be increased yearly and to be used in an emergency. After the Meiji Restoration, the fund was transferred to the hands of the Tokyo Prefecture. The
prefecture was to take charge of it as a Common Fund,
and at the same time could use it for the promo-

tion of public works in the city of Tokyo, such as the repair of bridges, the management of the union cemetery, and the establishment of a gas factory, etc. Among these public works, one which was later developed into the Tokyo City Poor House was included. In November, a year and a half after the Viscount had organized the First National Bank, he was appointed a custodian of the Common Fund by I. Okubo, the Governor of Tokyo Prefecture. Here, for the first time, the Tokyo City Poor House was introduced to a big hearted philanthropist who took care of it through the vicissitudes of sixty long years, at last putting it not only on a solid foundation, but making it a model for all the other social service organizations in Japan.

The origin of the Tokyo City Poor House dates back to 1870, when an Imperial Prince of Russia paid his visit to Japan. In those days beggars infested various parts of the city, and they had to be interned in a special quarter in order to clean up the city where the distinguished guest of the nation would spend most of his time during his sojourn. The expense for the work was to be met out of this Common Fund as an emergency measure.

Two years later a definite location was chosen near Uyeno Park for paupers of both sexes, crippled and sick children, numbering over one hundred and forty, and the place was named the Tokyo-fu Poor House.

The expenditure for the up-keep of the Tokyo-fu Poor House was to be defrayed from the Common Fund, but the budget was quite inadequate fully to meet the need of the House, and in the year 1879, the prefecture assembly just organized voted aid for the institution. The Governor of Tokyo-fu at the time was Masataka Kusumoto. Among the members of the assembly were Yukichi Fukuzawa, a great educator and Genichiro Fukuchi, a famous writer. The following reminiscent accounts of the Viscount are interesting, giving the picture of the political and social conditions of the day :

" If I remember correctly, it was about the year 1882 that strong opposition was launched against the maintenance of the Poor House. A member of the Assembly, Mr. S. Numa, argued saying 'A man should not receive help from outside. The idea that some one may help him will cause him to fall into laziness. He will soon cease to toil. This is bad enough. We must lead men not to have the idea of dependence. To rescue is to weaken them. We must not assist people. To others we should be austere and cold.' Such an idea was quite generally entertained in those days, but I radically disagreed with it and argued that we must extend our helping hand to the helpless. We should never be heartless and cold to them. The opponents turned their deaf ears to my argument and the support of the Tokyo-fu to the Poor House was stopped. Although Mr. Numa and I exchanged sharp arguments, yet personally we were good friends. Mr. T. Sudo, his elder brother, was one of the Directors of Dai Ichi Ginko and a close friend of mine.

" The Poor House, thus thrown overboard by the assembly, had to resort to a negative measure by ceasing to take in any new applicant, and thus bringing the institution gradually to a close. But I felt it my duty to endeavor to maintain it. The institution was abandoned by the assembly in 1885 and its maintenance was provided by contributions from my associates and the Women's Aid Society organized by my wife and her friends. In this manner it was supported for five years—namely until 1889. At that time the Poor House was located in the street called Nagaoka, in the Honjo ward. In

1889, a local change of administration took place, and autonomy
was granted to the city of Tokyo. The change of public sentiment during these five years was quite phenomenal. The attitude
of the public toward the Poor House also had changed. The
cold arguments produced by Mr. Numa were no longer heard,
and an opposite attitude came to be entertained everywhere.
But the question of what should be done with the Poor House
was yet to be solved. Just at this critical moment, the Department of Home Affairs issued a proclamation to the effect that
if the city thought the institution to be necessary and its operation proper, it might take over the management of the institution.
Thus Tokyo City decided to take charge of the Poor House.
In others words, the management of the Poor House was transferred from private hands to Tokyo City, which has continued
since then to maintain and support the institution."

When the institution fell into the hands of the
private management of Viscount Shibusawa and his
friends, its immates did not exceed three hundred in
number. But soon after, sick wanderers and orphans
increased, and at the end of 1890, the number of inmates exceeded four hundred. With this pressure upon
the management, numerous problems confronted the
authorities of the institution. The building was old.
Extensive repairing was needed. The location was in a
low part of the city, and not infrequently floods inundated the place. All these unsatisfactory conditions called
for the immediate attention of the authorities. In 1891
the standing committee was authorized to find a new
place, high, healthful, spacious, and open. After careful
investigation a new location was found. The next
question was how to put up adequate buildings. Plans
were decided upon and the construction began in December 1894. The work was completed in June of

the next year. The entire institution was moved to the new quarters in March, 1896. Otsuka was the name of the place. Here the authorities of the institution carried on the growing work, until again it had to be removed to still larger quarters in 1923—the year the great earthquake and fire devastated Tokyo and Yokohama.

In the years 1894 and 1895, Japan fought China in the war known as the Sino-Japanese war in the world's history. Judging from the size and population of the two countries, the warfare between them was like that of David against Goliath. Consequently the entire people of Japan strained every nerve to the highest pitch. Such being the mood of the nation many abnormal phenomena, caused by stress, fear, and suspicion occurred in the highways and byways of the country. The increase of young loafers in the streets of Tokyo was one. They were picked up and interned in the Poor House. This influx of street arabs soon created a problem which had to be solved as soon as possible. The problem was the bad influence of the new tough inmates over the orphans previously taken in. The Viscount was the first officer in the institution seriously to think the question over. He and subordinates discussed it carefully, and reached the conclusion to establish a reformatory school, at the same time forming a plan for public subscriptions.

In January of the year 1897, the Empress Dowager Eisho passed away, and in commemoration of Her Majesty's demise a large amount was granted to the charity organizations throughout the country for their endowment. Tokyo Prefecture was to receive a part of the gift. This was a favorable wind for the sails of the new enterprise. In May of the same year, the Viscount presented two motions before the council of Tokyo City. One was to decide upon the establishment of the Poor House. The other was that a part of the Empress Dowager's gift appropriated to the city of Tokyo should be turned over to the Poor House as an endowment fund for the reformatory department. Both motions were passed. Around the nucleus of the Imperial grant enough public subscriptions were soon made to begin the construction of the building. It was started in the year 1899 and completed the next year. In July the educational work was started, and the experimentation went on nearly one year, at the end of which the authorities concerned found the result to be a sad failure. Then they carefully investigated the causes of the failure, and came to the conclusion that although separate buildings had been erected for the unruly youngsters, yet their presence on the same grounds was the sole cause of the trouble.

In order to remedy this defect, the Viscount and his associates hunted up a suitable location for a separate institution. A new site was obtained, and in 1904 the construction of new buildings was begun. It was completed in March of the next year, and in July the whole reformatory school moved into the new quarters. Today it is known as the Inokashira School of the Reformatory Department of the Tokyo City Poor House.

The next question which confronted the authorities of the Poor House was how to separate the old inmates from the young ones. As the incorrigible young inmates had a bad influence over the comparatively innocent ones, just so the old, worn out, and emaciated inmates tended to demoralize the younger ones. Another separation or shifting was necessary for the sake of the proper education of the younger inmates. This meant the provision of land and buildings. A committee was formed for the purpose of finding a proper location. They found just the place, and buildings on it for sale. The plans of the Poor House to buy the whole concern progressed favorably. The necessary amount was to be raised by subscriptions. The Viscount again appealed to the public as well as to the City Assembly. Everything came about satisfactorily, and what is known as the Sugamo Branch of the Poor House was created.

This, however, did not end the administrative troubles of the authorities of the Poor House. The teachers of the Sugamo Branch school soon found that there were children of feeble health. The head physician of the Poor House was consulted and asked to submit his recommendation for dealing with the case. The result was to experiment in seashore life for the pupils of weak health. The experiment was carried out and the effect of the seashore life was remarkably helpful. Encouraged by this method, the Viscount again stirred up the sympathy of the city authorities and the public to rally to his project to build a school on the seashore. The appeal found a ready response and another branch of the Poor House was created. This is known as the Awa Branch of the Tokyo City Poor House.

Now we see that the Tokyo City Poor House consists of four departments: the headquarters at Itabashi; the reformatory school at Inokashira; the ordinary school at Sugamo; and the seashore school at Funakata in Awa.   As we have seen the headquarters were built in 1923.   The area covers 27,011 *tsubo* (a tsubo being six feet square).   The entire building area consists of 5,490 tsubo.   This improvement cost the authorities of the Poor House 1,461,763 yen, and the cost was met in the following manner :   One million yen accrued from the sale of a part of the old property at Otsuka ; 128,532 yen from public contributions ; 149,200 yen transferred from the endowment fund, and 94,031 yen surplus income for the year.   In this way the Tokyo City Poor House inclusive of all its branches showed in 1931—the year the Viscount passed away, the following figures : the total area of land, 87,217 *tsubo* ; the total building area, 10,211 *tsubo* ; the total amount of current expense 537,876 yen.   The inmates at the close of the year 1931 numbered 2,369 persons.

Mr. Shiraishi concludes his chapter on the Tokyo City Poor House with the following words :   " Does the Viscount belong to the Poor House or the House to the Viscount ?   Anyhow, it is a crystallization of the Viscount's sixty years of effort and a living monument to him promising an ever expanding future."

The Viscount used to take great pride in showing this institution to interested visitors from abroad, such as General William Booth and Dr. Labindranath Tagore. Foreign newspaper men and distinguished social workers were welcomed by him there.

Alongside this great work of Viscount Shibusawa we would look into his efforts for the improvement of institutions for lepers.   In this connection, nothing will give a more satisfactory description of the spirit and

intent of Viscount Shibusawa concerning the problem
of leprosy than the words he spoke with deep feeling
at the time when he heard that an association for the
prevention of leprosy had been organized on a national
scale. He spoke thus:

" Nothing gives me a greater joy than to hear the news that
the Association for the Prevention of Leprosy has been organized on a national scale. I have long cherished the desire of
helping to prevent leprosy, of providing living quarters for lepers,
where they can spend their lives safely and comfortably, and
of saving their families and relatives from unreasonable and merciless disdain. I feel now as if my object was attained.

" When I look back to the long past, 1 can see how I came
to take a deep interest in the subject of leprosy. In that dear
old home where I was born and reared I imbibed a sympathetic
feeling toward this unfortunate class of people. There lived a
family very close to our house. I had a friend in that family—
a boy one year younger than I. His mother was a leper and
none of the villagers would approach her. But my mother who
was exceedingly humane continued her intercourse with the
suffering woman. Influenced by my mother, I played with the
boy not infrequently, but with a mixed feeling of hatred and
pity. In the meantime, the boy's mother was shut in hardly
ever to be seen by her neighbors, and it was rumored that the
boy too was to be confined at home. When I heard this, my
heart was filled with sorrow and compassion. This deep impression I received in my boyhood days was revived in me long
after when I faced pitiful lepers brought into the Tokyo City
Poor House. I was struck by the thought that the community
must from the standpoint of humanity wake up to look after
these unfortunate people.

" By unappointed and spontaneous contacts with some of
them, I came to learn their mental condition in which was disclosed their attitude of revolt and cursing toward the community

wherein they lived. They entertained desperate destructive ideas against the general public. I found painful reasons why they could not be in a wholesale manner dismissed as social outcasts when I heard the story of their experiences. Hence an additional reason why something must be done from the standpoint of social welfare took hold of me.

"One day this incident occurred. A lovely boy-servant of a wine shop keeper became ill, and was brought into the House. He was a leper and the pity for the boy was that the disease was incurred by contagion from his master. The doctor then in charge of the House carefully explained to me and the Secretary that leprosy is not a hereditary disease, but a contagious one. The doctor's view about it was so convincing that the Secretary and I were deeply stirred, so much that we were moved to believe in the necessity of the segregation of the inflicted ones. This was a serious question which should receive immediate attention from the viewpoint of the national health.

"Not long after the Russo-Japanese war I, in cooperation with businessmen representing different parts of Japan, went to America as the goodwill messengers of the peoples' diplomacy. Japan's victory over the great nation of Russia made her highly elated, but there were some foreigners who were somewhat loath to admit that Japan was a nation of honor and culture. They made this criticism. 'Japan claims that she has risen to the rank of a first class nation. Yes she is strong in fighting, but she is not yet able to control the terrible disease of leprosy, which cannot be seen to-day in any other civilized nation on earth.'

"On my way home I stopped at Hawaii and visited the asylum for lepers in the island of Molokai. There I was amazed to see the gigantic scale in which the American people were trying to exterminate this disease. On my return home, once more I carefully examined our national policy toward leprosy and the method of dealing with lepers. It only deepened my surprise and sorrow.

"In those days lepers resorted to shrines and temples, begging for mercy from pilgrims and worshippers. Leper quarters were conducted in only a few places in the country, and most of the organizations for their relief were carried on by foreign missionaries.

"I have frequently called on the authorities of the Government to call their attention to the case of leprosy. The head of the Bureau of Sanitation of the Government was Dr. Kubota, who later became the vice-President of the Central Social Work Society. He deeply sympathized with me and by his effort the laws for the prevention of leprosy were proclaimed. As the result of this measure federated leprosy quarters were opened in five places in the main cities of Japan. Here the sufferers were compulsorily taken in, thus reducing the number of the wandering lepers to be seen in the streets.

"That much improvement was made but not all the lepers were properly cared for and protected. A large majority of the afflicted ones were confined in their own homes or were quartered in poorly equipped places.

"In the Central Social Work Society, which was formed not long after the laws for the prevention of leprosy were enacted, Dr. Kubota and I often met in the capacity of vice-President and President respectively.

"It was quite natural that the two of us should exchange our views about the subject and plan a board of investigation; and again to confer with the Government authorities concerning a project for the prevention and extermination of leprosy. Two years ago this summer, I together with vice-President Kubota and the General Secretary of the Central Social Work Society, called on Mr. Adachi who was just installed as the Minister for Home Affairs in his official residence and explained to him our plan. The Minister not only showed his profound sympathy with our work but told us that he would do his utmost in cooperation with us."

The dark clouds of depression over-hung the financial world of Japan at the time, and the appeal for subscriptions to help this cause was coldly received. But there was a rift in the clouds through which the sunshine of encouragement fell upon the disconcerted hearts of the promoters.

An announcement was made through the Home Minister that the Empress Dowager had graciously granted a gift to promote the cause. It was indeed glad tidings to those who were puzzled for the time being. At the same time appeal after appeal came to the Viscount from different parts of Japan to do something for the pitiful creatures scattered all over the country. Letters of sympathy and encouragement came to him. A contribution together with a letter couched with rhetorical persuasion reached him. The Viscount, who was always quick rightly to diagnose a situation, felt that the opportunity for action had arrived though he might have to encounter minor difficulties. Thus on the 21st of October, 1930, the Home Minister and the Viscount invited to the official residence of the Minister twelve leading business men of Tokyo, Baron Goh being one, and conferred with them concerning the organization of an association for the prevention of leprosy. The motion to organize the association was unanimously carried and everybody present consented to become promoters. The Home Minister ; the head of the Bureau of Hygiene in the Department ; Governors of all the prefectures ; the local officers in the charge of health departments; and leaders of local fame all joined in signing their names as organizers. There were six hundred and forty who thus signed their names, and over one hundred persons gathered together in the official residence of the Home Minister. Here the Association for the Prevention of Leprosy was formally organized on the 21st day of January, 1931.

The Viscount's concern over lepers and leprosy was very genuine and personal. He gave not only his money toward the cause but he gave himself. In the year 1922 he invited Dr. A. L. Dean, President of the University of Hawaii, who was the inventor of the chaalmoogra oil for leprosy, to visit the large asylum for lepers in a suburb of Tokyo. The Viscount and Dr. Dean put on the preventive gowns and under the direction of Mr. Mitsuda, the Director of the institution, went into the operation room to watch the epidermic injection of the oil given by Dr. Dean. Then they visited the assembly hall where Dr. Dean gave an interesting and comforting talk to a large audience of men and women. The Viscount was greatly pleased with the visit of Dr. Dean because the visitor did so much good to the lonely group.

Next we shall take up the educational side of the activity of Viscount Shibusawa. The present Tokyo University of Commerce, its origin and development, will bring out many characteristic features manifested in the life of the Viscount.

The reader may recall the Common Fund in connection with our discussion of the history of the Tokyo City Poor House. This Common Fund has much to do with the birth of the Tokyo University of Commerce. Y. Mori, who had early served as a Minister to America, was deeply impressed with the advancement of industrial education there and wanted to see a business school established in Tokyo.

He approached I. Okubo, the Governor of Tokyo Prefecture, for advice on the matter and the Governor favored the plan Mori had conceived. Where could a fund be obtained for the establishment of the school? After careful deliberation the Governor saw a way to take the necessary amount from the Common Fund which had been entrusted to the hands of the Viscount. The Viscount, who too was anxious to have such an institution, welcomed the proposition of Mori endorsed by the Governor. So the Viscount called a meeting of the Board of Trustees of the Common Fund and presented the case to them.

The motion to appropriate a part of the Fund for the purpose was unanimously adopted. Mori also contributed a large amount, and a school named the "Shōhō Kōshū Jo" was established and was directed by him for about one year. At the end of the year he was appointed as Minister to China, and who would take his place was a question that needed immediate attention. The Viscount was consulted. It was decided that the management should fall into the hands of the Prefecture, the necessary expense being met by the appropriation from the Common Fund. This took place about 1875. In 1878 the Tokyo Chamber of Commerce was organized, and while the direct operation of the Shōhō Kōshū Jo was conducted by the Chamber, its general management was left in the hands of Tokyo Prefecture. The financial support was to come from the Common Fund. Under this triple management the school continued its work till about 1882, when the Prefectural Assembly passed a resolution to abolish it. The Governor of Tokyo Prefecture was Count A. Yoshikawa. The policy of the Prefecture for the disposal of the school was to give it to the Mitsubishi

Company. The reader will recall how rapidly the Mitsubishi had emerged as a strong financial organization. It was almost a slogan of those days that the Mitsubishi was the first and the last in all economic affairs. Some of the leaders did not like this and the Viscount was one of them. Therefore he vigorously opposed the proposition that the school should be transferred to the company. He advocated the idea that the school should temporarily be entrusted to the Department of Agriculture and Commerce with the view that it should soon be put on a basis of self support. An appeal for public subscriptions to help promote the school was made, and about thirty thousand yen were raised. Whether or not the Viscount underwent a similar nerve strain in this case, as he did when he shouldered the responsiblity of carrying on the operation of the Tokyo City Poor House abandoned by the City Assembly, does not matter much. But the coincidence tells again how the Viscount was always willing to place himself in the position of a burden-bearer in order to unload or lighten the burdens of other people.

While Shogyo Gakko (Business School) was passing through this somewhat uncertain and insecure course during the years 1888 and 1889, Y. Mori, who had started the school some ten years before, was appointed Minister of Education. Fortune began to smile on the institution anxiously struggling for its existence. The Minister of Education took the matter into his own hands and brought it into the fold of the Department of Education. Then the name of the school was changed from the Shogyo Gakko to the Koto Shogyo Gakko (Higher Commercial School).

Thus it was made just as much a Government school as Dai Gaku (University) was.

If we are to give a summary of the career of the Higher Commercial School it can be stated in the following order: About 1875, Yurei Mori founded the institution as Shoho Koshu Jo. Its management was transferred to Tokyo Prefecture about 1878. The Tokyo Chamber of Commerce took charge of it till about 1882. From about 1884 it came under the control of the Department of Agriculture and Commerce. And it was finally raised into the status of a Government school about 1889 through the efforts of the Department of Education.

Although the old Shoho Koshu Jo steadily progressed and was elevated to the status of a Higher Commercial School in a period of fifteen years, yet this was but a preliminary step to the final goal which it aspired to attain. That goal was to reach University status.

Viscount Shibusawa had identified himself with this school from its very beginning and he was one of its trustees for a long time. It sent out many graduates. They formed an alumni association which in turn created a standing committee. Soon a magazine as an organ of expression was published and distributed among the alumni. From 1899 on bright and promising students or graduates began to continue their studies in Europe and America. Their observations and investigations along this particular line of commercial education were reported back to the school and the alumni through the magazine. The entire school reacted to the reports and were gradually waking up to a vision ahead. On the

first day of July, 1900, a banquet was held in honor of
the Viscount under the auspices of the Alumni Association of the Higher Commercial School. The object of
the banquet was twofold—namely to celebrate his
Kanreki (the completion of his sixty years) and to
congratulate him on his elevation to the peerage as
a Baron.

In the response he made that evening we find a few
sentences, which from that time on served as a great
inspiration to gather and to unify the fragmentary ideas
quietly fermenting in the minds of the faculty, students,
and alumni to transform the school into a University.
The Viscount said: "If we look into the matter of
commercial education we shall find that it has not come
up to par with other branches of education. As I am
a man of no systematic education, I cannot enter into
a scholastic discussion of the question, but I have repeatedly spoken in the past in regard to the necessity
of elevating our school of commerce to the rank of
a University...."

This sounded like a clarion call of a field marshal
to commence a simultaneous charge against an enemy.
The question of making a University out of the Higher
Commercial School was no longer confined to the authorities and students of the school. It became a question for the whole country. The trustees, faculties,
graduates, and members of the Alumni Association began
their activities.

The Viscount during his American and European trip
in 1902, met with groups of the graduates of the school
in different cities in those Western countries. He was
welcomed everywhere and everywhere he talked of the

necessity of having the commercial school elevated into University status. These graduates abroad too were very enthusiastic for the movement.

Through these efforts the possibility of realizing the project for a University of Commerce was becoming positive and concrete, until suddenly the breaking out of the Russo-Japanese War drove this question into abeyance for some time. At the close of the war the question was taken up again and it seemed quite promising. But there was a misunderstanding between the Department of Education and the school authorities—a misunderstanding which hindered the success of this movement of the Higher Commercial School. The crux of the whole trouble was that Tokyo Imperial University and the Department of Education were strongly inclined to make the Higher Commercial School one of the colleges in the University like the Agricultural, Medical, and Law Colleges while the Higher Commercial School, wanting to be true to its tradition and prestige, wished to attain a University status equal to that of the existing Imperial University.

Finally the Higher Commercial School won its case but not without a high cost. A big strike of students was called in the spring of the year 1909. Conferences of various kinds were held. Step by step victory was won by the school, and in April, 1920 the Higher Commercial School was raised to the status of a full fledged University both in name and substance.

Through thick and thin, for fifty years, Viscount Shibusawa had stood by the University. He was its patron of patrons, whom the entire institution held in high admiration with ever increasing appreciation for the valuable services rendered to it. In this connection it is highly significant that one who was educated in this University and often witnessed manifestations of the kindly and unselfish attitude of the Viscount, later became his private Secretary, serving nearly twenty years and writing a voluminous biography of his master, filled with appreciations and admiration. It was as though the Alma Mater chose one of her brightest and worthiest sons and dedicated him to the Viscount in her stead. His name is Mr. Kitaro Shiraishi—a man of many talents and varied tastes.

So far we have followed the deep interest Viscount Shibusawa manifested in the education of young men. Did he show a similar interest in the education of young women ?

A sign of the Viscount's interest in girls' education could be seen in a subscription he made to Meiji Jo Gakko (The Meiji Girls' School) in July, 1885. The next year we see him as one of the members of the Council for Joshi Kyōiku Shōrei Kai (The Society for the Encouragement of Girls' Education). This was the year when the Japanese Government adopted the system of cabinet administration for the first time. Prince H. Ito was the Premier and Marquis K. Inouye the Minister for Foreign Affairs. Both of these high officials were very close friends of the Viscount. The Premier and the Foreign Minister, being progressive in political and social questions, were deeply anxious to westernize Japan so that Japan might be looked upon as a nation of equal civilization with the West. This need opened their eyes to the practical question of how the wives and daughters of high class families should be educated so as to freely mingle with and entertain the ladies in the diplomatic circles and in the foreign business concerns. It was obvious to the minds of these leaders that the traditional education of Japan for women was antiquated and wholly inadequate to meet the demands of the day. Western etiquette and social dancing had to be taught. All this led them to organize the Society for the Encouragement of Girls' Education, and out of this society the Tokyo Jo Gakkan (The Tokyo Girls School) was born. Naturally this school was aristocratic. Its aim was cultural and social trying to educate the pupils to meet the conditions created by the influx of western customs and manners. The foreign teachers of the school were mostly English ladies. There were few Americans in Japan in those days. Most of the foreigners were English and European. Moreover the high minded promoters of the school thought that Anglo-Saxon English was superior by far to American English.

The Viscount gave a great deal of his time and energy to the promotion of this institution. His sense of responsibility for the welfare of the school was of equal vigilance and intensity to that which he sustained toward the Tokyo City Poor House and the Tokyo University of Commerce.

About ten years later, in 1896, the Viscount was brought face to face with a far larger scheme of establishing an institution of learning for young women. The originator of this scheme was Jinzo Naruse who became the first president of Nippon Joshi Dai Gakko (The Japan Women's University). Naruse had had experience in training girls and felt the necessity of establishing a higher grade school for young women.

He broached the plan to Marquis Okuma. The Marquis advised Naruse to go to Viscount Shibusawa, telling him that a plan on such a large scale could not be handled by a person of lesser calibre than Viscount Shibusawa.

Naruse called on the Viscount and made a strong appeal to him to support the plan to establish a university for women. The Viscount saw, through his characteristically clear intuition, the impossibility of establishing the institution Naruse had in mind by private agency. His word to Naruse was that only the Government could carry on such a work. But the Viscount was constrained by the zeal of Naruse to consent to do what was within his power. Still the difficulty of raising subscriptions for the fund was facing the promoter. One day Naruse paid a visit to Baron Morimura and narrated the same story. He came back to the Viscount and requested him to persuade Baron Morimura to contribute a large amount as the Baron had promised Naruse to see the Viscount in regard to the matter. The interview between the Viscount and the Baron resulted in the Baron's consent to give to the cause nearly two hundred thousand yen. Then appeals were made to other magnates such as the Mitsui and the Iwasaki. Thus the start was made for the Japan Women's university.

Marquis Okuma, Viscount Shibusawa, Baron Morimura, and President Naruse made tours to different parts of the country to raise subscriptions for the University and at the same time to inform local people of the importance of women's higher education. It is true that the conviction of the Viscount that a university of this nature and scope should be conducted by the Government in order to realize its ideal remains irrefutable. Still the effort the Viscount made to bring the institution to its present position should not be lost sight of. Mr. Asoh, the immediate successor of President Naruse, has this to say :

" Viscount Shibusawa was never absent from the meetings of the Council and the graduation exercises of the University during the last twenty-seven years since its foundation, except when he was ill or had gone abroad. The Viscount in his modesty attributes the wonderful development of this institution during little over a quarter of a century to (1) the earnest effort and management of President Naruse ; (2) the self-sacrificing help of the members of the Council ; (3) the enthusiastic support of sympathizers ; (4) the harmonious cooperation between teachers and officers ; (5) the loyal services of the graduates ; (6) the pure hearted devotion to the school of the under-graduates ; (7) the demands of the time ; and (8) the geographical advantage of the school. But if the school had not received from the hands of the Viscount unchanging and generous care, it is doubtful whether it could have achieved what it has."

As an example of the cultural activity of Viscount Shibusawa the organization of Kiitsu Kyōkai (the Association Concordia) might be cited. The aim of the organization was an ambitious one in that it sought to create a new religion transcending and unifying all the existing religions under an eclectic and synthetic method. The Viscount entertained deep concern about the governing principle of man's inner life and the thought problem of the day. So far as he himself was concerned he was inclined to believe that Confuciunism expressed in Lun Yu (論語) was sufficient to guide and control the

ethical life of man. But he was not quite convinced
that the teaching of Lun Yu would meet and cover the
the universal needs of the moral life, especially in the
present situation in which Western influence in religion
and science was playing a tremendous role. President
Naruse of Japan Women's University and Baron Morimura were strongly inclined toward the belief that man
needs a certain system of faith to go by. The three
men agreed on the point that there should be a moral
norm, or a guiding principle, for every person, but
what form it should take was a very difficult problem.
In order to tackle this question the Viscount invited a
few scholars and leaders of national reputation to his
home in the summer of 1911. It was quite significant
to notice that there was included in the group a missionary, Dr. Sidney L. Gulick—a broad-minded scholar.
With this beginning meetings were held for discussion.

Opinions and views were exchanged but not a ray
of light for the solution of the problems could pierce
through the maze and confusion of the discussions.
This was characteristic of the association. No special
progress toward the desired goal was being made. Finally the Viscount, whose habit had always been to stand
by whatever plan or organization was once started, lost
patience and was obliged to fall back on his long tried
Confucian method, leaving the Concordia in the care
of the other leaders. In this experiment the Viscount
drank the bitter cup of disappointment. A member of
the association in the midst of a hot discussion in one
of the meetings held later, made a joke to relieve the
meeting in its tense atmosphere, and said : " Our Concordia perfectly concords in the thought that it can

never concord." It was a joke which prophesied the doom of the association.

To one who is acquainted with the history of religions and thought movements in the Western world, the rise and fall of such an attempt as the one made by the Concordia would give no surprise. Therefore the only comfort the promoters could feel in this Concordia movement was that they took part in a world intellectual movement which may in some distant future reach its goal.

In the meantime, we should all be loyal to what we believe to be the ethical or religious criterion in our lives. The confession of the Viscount in this experience may be valuable when we fall into a similar trial. He says :

" But it was no easy task when it was put to a practical test. Hence I shrank back to the old notion that so far as I am concerned I would endeavor to keep myself free from faults."

Before concluding this chapter, one more phase of the public activity of Viscount Shibusawa should be touched upon. This is the organization and activity of " Kyōchō Kai " (the Conciliation Society). The society was organized in the winter of 1919 for the purpose of maintaining healthy and harmonious relations between Capital and Labour. But Viscount Shibusawa had expressed his deep concern over the labour question as early as 1911, three years before Japan joined the allied forces in the World War and six years before the United States did the same.

Under the subject of the " Future Labour Question," he presents his argument roughly as follows :

" We occasionally witness sad events in labour troubles in civilized nations. The trouble begins with a breach of harmony between Capital and Labour. The breach is soon aggravated into ill will and resentment between the two parties. The evil disturbs the good order of society aud threatens the peace of the nation. Such is indeed a deplorable phenomenon produced by the abnormal relation between the rich and the poor.

" Scholars and statesmen of Europe and America early took note of these disturbances and gave close attention to them with the desire that they might bring about happy solutions. From the reason that we have not been long in contact with the Western civilization and because our national habit which controls the labour situation is different from that of the Westerners, our labour question is not yet so acute. We may postpone it if we so desire without much danger. But it is not difficult to foresee that what has happened in Western countries will also happen here sooner or later. Hence to adopt a preventive measure before any beginning of trouble breaks out is most important....

" But the social program set up for the labour movement is susceptible to misunderstanding. Labour is apt to misapprehend and distort what has been stated on its behalf as though it were antagonistic. Lately the Government authorities waking up to the neccessity of controling social and labour movements framed the Factory Act for the protection of labour. The Act limits the hours of labour and forbids child labour. It insists on equipping factories with hygienic apparatus. Labour may resent the enactment of such a law because its application may in the end reduce earnings.

" The law may be necessary for better management. But its enforcement may serve to emphasize the notion of rights and obligations between Capital and Labour, which would tend to lead both parties to a cold and perfunctory relationship destroying the beautiful relations of affection and loyalty long inculcated in the labour life of Japan.

" Instead of the law, Wang Tao (王道) should be practiced by Capital and Labour. If Capital deals with Labour according to " Wang Tao " and vice versa, believing that their interests are common to each other, there will occur no strife. True harmony between them can be fully established. A couple of years ago in my world's tour I visited the Krupp Company in Germany and Waltham Watch Co. in a suburb of Boston. Their systems were based on the family relationship. The atmosphere was most pleasing. Needless to say that I was greatly impressed with such conditions. I call such scenes the perfected form of Wang Tao.

Japan's military prowess and her national strength had steadily been recognized by the Western Powers through the war with China in 1894–5, and the war with Russia in 1904–5. The World War brought Japan into close association with the allied nations, and the formation of the League of Nations in 1919, consisting of 32 States of which Japan was one, made her an actual member of the family of world powers. In other words Japan was internationalized through these contacts as never before. The expansion of foreign trade and the consequent improvement of domestic industry followed the great political and economical change from the national to the international scale. Many large companies were formed. The question of the labour situation was getting acute so as to demand the study of leaders in society for the possible prevention of conflict between Capital and Labour. A question how strikes in the labour circles could be avoided was no longer a theme to be laid on the table for leisurely discussion. Viscount Shibusawa felt the need of a machinery of arbitration which would help settle troubles when they actually took place, but which primarily would study the nature, cause, and preventive measures of strikes. The Reconciliation Society was created for this very purpose.

It has since then averted many threatening troubles between Capital and Labour. What the League of Nations has contributed to the stabilization of European civilization the Reconciliation Society has done for Japan by holding together in many cases Capital and Labour in peace and harmony.

CHAPTER X

INTERNATIONAL ACTIVITIES

DR. I. Nitobe used to say that internationalism does not conflict with nationalism, but that it is cosmopolitanism that tends to destroy nationalism. Having served for more than eight years as an under-Secretary of the League of Nations in Geneva, where internationalism was rife, Dr. Nitobe became so completely acclimated to the atmosphere of Geneva that, on his return to Japan, it was almost curious for him to find people who label internationalism as anti-nationalism or anti-patriotism.

To unravel this tangled notion, he again and again spoke publicly and wrote extensively.

Surely internationalism presupposes the existence of more than one nation. Otherwise no relations can be established. Then admitting the existence of at least two nations, we should naturally find that each nation has its own nationality or principle of national existence, just as an individual has his own individuality. This we call nationalism, and there can be no reason why one nationalism cannot be associated with another thus forming internationalism. With many nations nationalism has been adopted as an exclusive principle—selfishness magnified and exaggerated under the guise of patriotism. But today exclusive nationalism stands judged as a wornout principle and must give way to inclusive or comprehensive nationalism, which is the true internationalism.

"My country right or wrong." "Might is right."

" The strong preys upon the weak." "The end justifies
the means." All these expressions have come down to us,
simply to tell the sad story that in human history gross
materialism and blind force have ignored and defied the
warning and protest of conscience or moral truth. The
principles involved in these traditional expressions are
clearly contradictory to our moral ideals, and yet mankind
as a whole is enslaved to them even in this enlightened
age of the twentieth century. This is a gloomy and
unwelcome reality. Nevertheless it is the grim reality
which must be taken into account in dealing with any
large affairs. It is constantly checking the growth of
the whole ethical nature of the spiritual solidality of
mankind, because our happy and permanent relationships, which are the outcome of faith, confidence, and
mutual trust, can never thrive in such an atmosphere.
A certain far sighted internationalist has said that, before we can have naval disarmament, we must have moral
disarmament. A truer statement could hardly be made.

The idea of internationalism advocated and practiced
by Viscount Shibusawa was exceedingly plain. It was
an application and extention of personal relations based
on the principles of the Chung Shu (忠恕) to international relations. He saw no reason why the principle
that regulates and controls mutual friendship among
individuals cannot do the same among nations. The two
words Chung (忠) and Shu (恕) need to be explained
here as they are understood by scholars and by the
Viscount particularly. James Legge, the author of the
" The Four Books " paraphrases Chung Shu as follows :

" 忠 and 恕, which seem to be two things, are both formed from
心, 'heart'; 忠 being compounded of 中, 'middle,' or 'center, 'and

心; and 恕, of 如 ' as,' and 心. The 'center heart'＝I, the *ego;*
and the ' as heart'＝the I in sympathy with others. 忠 is duty-
doing, on consideration, or from the impulse of one's own self;
恕 is duty-doing, on the principle of reciprocity."

A great Chinese scholar, Chu Tzu (朱子), published
a commentary of the Four Books. His explanation of
Chung Shu is:

內不自欺忠是體
推己及物恕行焉

The Japanese way of reading these sentences is:

" Uchi mizukara azamukazu Chyu (Chung) kore tai
Onore wo oshite mono ni oyobosu Jo (Shu) okonawaru."

The meaning is:

" In the inner life not to deceive the self is Chung, which is
fundamental principle of morality. When one puts himself into
the place of others Shu is accomplished.

The Viscount followed the thoughts expressed by
Legge and by Chu Tzu and made strict honesty, or
integrity, and sympathy the two inviolable rules of his
life. His conscientious observance and deliberate application of these rules made him a stalwart moral man.

The early impressions Viscount Shibusawa received
concerning foreigners and foreign countries were not
very happy. They rather served to create in him
fear, hatred, and revolt. Two historic events entered
into his experience to make him an anti-foreigner.
One was the visit of Commodore Perry to Japan
in the year 1853, when the Viscount was fourteen years old. The other was the opium war fought
between China and England in 1840, in which the

former was defeated and compelled to cede Hongkong to the latter. The complete story of this was given in the book entitled "Shin Ei Kinsei Dan." (Modern Story about China and England).

The sense of justice in the Viscount could not excuse the action of England in waging war against China and later taking Hongkong as a part of war spoils, when he firmly believed that the action of China was perfectly justifiable in throwing overboard the poisonous stuff brought into Chinese ports. He thought that England's attitude toward China in this opium war was nothing but the application of the primitive principle of " the strong preys upon the weak," quite incompatible with the action of an advanced nation like England.

Thus the international concern and reaction of Viscount Shibusawa in his younger days were antagonistic and prejudicial toward foreign countries, and, as we saw in one of the earlier chapters, it was not until he met T. Tanabe in 1867 that the ice of his prejudice against foreigners began to melt. The story Tanabe told the Viscount about the character and deeds of Townsend Harris, the first American Consul-General and later the first American Minister to Japan, made him blush for his ignorance and the false pride born of it. This experience of the Viscount was one of the most significant and far reaching events in his life. It would be no exaggeration to say that the Viscount's progressive and constructive international activities can be traced back to that hour of new awakening. With mind and heart thoroughly cleansed from the deadly poison of intolerance and self-sufficiency, he was now ready to enter into the garden of the Western Civilization for the first time in his life.

Within less than one year, the Viscount as a close attendant to Prince Mimbu, the representative of the Shogun, visited France, Switzerland, Belgium, Italy, and England, everywhere receiving the welcome and treatment which could be accorded only the highest representative of any nation.

Such was the back ground of the Viscount's efforts in his later years to build up international friendship and world peace.

Viscount Shibusawa touched nearly all nations in his international activities and contributed something to each country. But his largest and most systematic activity was confined to the promotion of better understanding and good will between Japan and the United States of America; and between Japan and China. Other international efforts were more or less fragmentary, sporadic, and temporary.

We will begin with China. No intelligent Japanese will deny Japan's indebtedness to China for the promotion of her culture. The Japanese and the Chinese belong to the same race. They use a common written language, although differently pronounced. The Chinese classics are the basis of Japanese literature. The best literary scholars in Japan are without exception profound students of the Chinese classics.

Then we are close neighbors. Apart from politics and diplomatic relations, the peoples of the two countries have most friendly feelings with this deep rooted historic background.

If political stability and internal order can be secured in China throughout the breadth and length of the nation, the result will be of inestimable benefit to both countries.

It was the burning desire of Viscount Shibusawa to bring about the closest friendship between the two countries. The fact that Confucius, who gave Lun Yu (論語) to Japan, was a Chinese was a sufficient reason to the Viscount why in and through him Japan and China can be bound together in peace and harmony. Being a business man, the Viscount felt that the bond which would bind the two countries in a close relation would be in the form of an international economic organization between them.

He and Mr. T. Masuda visited Shanghai to negotiate a loan for China in the year 1877. Also an attempt was made by the Viscount to establish a branch of Dai Ichi Kokuritsu Ginko in Shanghai. Neither of these attempts came to realization perhaps due to the prematurity of surrounding conditions.

However the Viscount never dropped out of his mind his primary desire to unite the two countries in friendly relations, and kept the fire of vigilance burning in him. In 1894 the Sino-Japanese war broke out which further postponed the opportunity to do anything for the promotion of trade or industrial cooperation. It was not until 1904 that the Viscount could, for the first time, thrust in an opening wedge to open up the dormant and clogged situation existing between the two countries. He assisted in the organization of the Konan Kisen Kaisha (Honan Steamship Company) in the same year. In March 1907, the Nisshin Kisen Kaisha (Japan-China Steamship Company) with its capital of one million and one hundred thousand yen was organized under the chairmanship of the Viscount. The object of the organization was to promote trade between Japan and China by unifying the routes which *Osaka Shosen Kaisha*, *Nippon Yusen Kaisha*, *Konan Kisen Kaisha*, and *Daito Kisen Kaisha* severally controlled in China. In the realization of this enterprise, the Viscount's long cherished purpose was fulfilled.

The Nisshin Kisen Kaisha was organized on the solicitation and promise of subsidy from the Government. The personnel of the organizing committee was virtually selected by the Government. How intensely interested and deeply concerned the Viscount was in the creation of this company could be seen from the fact that he not only accepted the position of chairmanship, but later on identified himself with it as its director, even though he was then on the verge of withdrawal from the major part of his business relations. With this beginning to increase the neighborly feeling between the two countries, the Viscount entered into a deeper relation with China through the formation of the *To-A Kogyo Kaisha* (East Asia Enterprise Company) in 1909, and of the *Chyu Nichi Jitsugyo Kaisha* (China-Japan Industry Company) in 1913.

The process through which the *To-A Kogyo Kaisha* came to be formed needs a brief mention as it reveals the thoroughness and determination of the Viscount to make this company a permanent organ to bind Japan and China in an economic bond. As a preparation to the organization of this company, the Viscount proposed to form the Nisshin Kigyo Chosa Kai (the Fact Finding Association for the Japan-China Enterprise). Baron R. Kondo, Baron K. Okura, and Baron Masuda were the members of the association. Mr. R. Shiraiwa was the Executive Secretary—a very important person in the association because he is a rare student of Chinese affairs. In all the dealings of the Viscount with Chinese matters, Mr. Shiraiwa was his right hand man.

What was the work of this association? It was to study, confer, report, and negotiate on such enterprises as a contract for railway construction and a loan for electric railway and telephone projects in China. But nothing concrete resulted from this endeavor until the authorities of the Government strongly urged the parties concerned to push the work. It was in June of 1909 that a conference of the parties was held to thoroughly investigate possible methods to establish business relations with China.

The conference passed a strong resolution to the effect that, as there is a need of creating a syndicate for the purpose of financing and supplying materials for various kinds of enterprises in China, a conference of business leaders of large cities should be held. In July thirty business men met in the Mitsui Assembly Hall and decided to organize a company. A committee was appointed to frame the regulations of such a company. The promoters were nominated and they arranged to convene the first general meeting at the Bankers' Association in August. The assembly adopted the motion to organize a company. The new company was registered on the last day of the same month. The capital of the company at the time of its organization was one million yen. Later it was increased to three million yen, and still later to twenty million yen. The amount invested through this company in China reached the sum of

Townsend Harris.

sixty million yen. The object for all this was nothing but to help develop China, to promote a better understanding between the two countries, and mutually to enjoy the happy outcome of co-existence and co-prosperity.

In all these dealings it is needless to say that Viscount Shibusawa was the master figure.

The Chyunichi Jitsugyo Kaisha was organized with a similar purpose to that of the To-A Kogyo Kaisha. The striking difference between the two companies was that the Chyunichi Jitsugyo Kaisha was composed of mixed officers of Japanese and Chinese, while the To-A Kogyo Kaisha was purely Japanese so far as the constituents of the company were concerned. The origin of the Chyunichi Jitsugyo Kaisha can be traced to the conversation between the Viscount and Sun Yat Sen, the founder of the Chinese Republic, at the Mitsui Assembly Hall on the eleventh of August 1913.

Sun said that as he was a politician and not a business man he would decline to become one of the promoters of this enterprise. So Yuan Se Kai stepped in to promote this work. This was rather unfortunate, because Yuan's attitude toward the company was a treacherous one.

He was a very unscrupulous politician and was suspected of squandering the half of the shares of the company which belonged to the Chinese side for his own political purpose. In the meantime the great European War broke out, and during the war the industrial world boomed. This company became an important medium to promote industrial enterprises in both countries. Bankers and business men vied with each other to make investments in China, and an enormous amount of money

was put up for China through this company. Finally
the armistice was declared and the great World War
ceased. The cessation of the monstrous war began to
upset industrial activity all over the world. Japan and
China equally suffered from the financial disturbance
and the huge amount of investment in China was simply
lost. The Chyunichi Jitsugyo Kaisha from its beginning met severe trials and passed through a miserable
experience. This state of affairs of the company
racked the Viscount's brain and demanded his most
strenuous efforts.

The Viscount made his trip to China in 1914 and
at the age of 75. He had two things in his mind to
accomplish on this journey. One was to satisfy his
longing to visit the mausoleum of Confucius the great
teacher and the author of the Confucian Analects, which
was the book of books for the Viscount, and to take in
the scenic beauties of the famous places described in
those immortal Chinese classics which he repeatedly read
in his younger days. The other was to strengthen
economic ties with the view of promoting closer and
more friendly relations between the two countries. In
other words he wanted to build up the To-A Kogyo
Kaisha on a firmer basis. Unfortunately he became ill
in the midst of his tour and was obliged to give up
many important plans because of his unexpectedly early
return to Japan.

Viscount Shibusawa kept up his active interest in
the above two companies, even after he withdrew from
the business world in the year 1909.

He did this because he felt that they were important instruments to promote international good-will

between the two countries. In the year 1920, there came into existence another organization which was called Nikka Jitsugyo Kyokai (Japan-China Industry Association).

Stimulated by the intense economical competition all over the world since the cessation of the great European War, the business men of Japan came to realize the importance of entering into negotiation with those of China. In this movement, all the leading business men of the large cities of the country were to join. The question of leadership was regarded of the utmost importance, as both the scale and scope of the project were vastly comprehensive, and as we Japanese say, " the white feathered arrow stood for " the Viscount. The choice fell upon him. The Viscount was then eighty one years old.

Through this Association several important contacts between the Viscount and his colleagues on the one hand, and influential visitors from China on the other, were made. Among them, the visit of Mr. Yu Chia Hsing and his party is worth mentioning.

The party arrived in Japan on the second of June, 1926. They were kept busy with entertainments and conferences during their tour of a few days. Under the auspices of the Japan China Industry Association, the Viscount opened his Asukayama villa for their entertainment at a sumptuous luncheon party.

In this visit of Yu Chia Hsing an important understanding was reached between the visiting party and some of the Japanese leaders in the business world. The understanding was the formation of two Committees in Tokyo and Shanghai after the fashion of the Japanese American Relations Committees in Tokyo and San Francisco, the object being to foster trade, joint-investments, and commercial arbitration. No concrete result was obtained owing to unexpected changes which occurred later.

The Viscount expressed his views concerning the promotion of Japan China friendship in the following words :

" The difference between man and animals exists in the fact that man makes progress, while animals remain stationary. In order to promote his progress he must learn many things through education. His primary aim should be to receive political and military training. But the age in which we are living attaches special importance to economic development. But here again it is highly necessary for us to know what will be the ultimate goal of the economic development, for though advancement might be made to a certain extent, yet the obscurity of the objective makes the economic foundation weak. It is like a child's play of piling up blocks which tumble down almost at the point of completion.

" The great European War of 1914–1918 is a very good example. This war was an economic one which ended in the self-destruction of economic life. To-day Great Britain and Russia, who are turning their attention toward the East, seem to be chiefly aiming at economic interests. They want to foster it even if they have to resort to armed forces. They fight for the promotion of economic interests and for the time being, they seem to have succeeded, but in reality the war destroyed the very thing to be constructed. The very hand which has erected a huge structure a moment ago smashes it in the next minute. What a foolish and wasteful act! We must protect ourselves from such a nonsensical deed. And how? Not by merely giving to man intellectual training only, but moral training also.

" The summary of what I have been trying to express is

this—that civilization must depend upon the advancement of economic power ; that economic progress cannot be achieved by simply aiming for personal gain and the prosperity of commerce and industry *per se*, unless it is based on the strong foundation of morality ; and that there is no other way but to fall back on the practice of the principle of the union of economics and morality, if we desire human progress. When this principle is thoroughly understood and faithfully followed, good will and friendliness between our two countries will be perfectly maintained. Much more so since we have a racial and cultural affinity."

The last friendly gesture the Viscount made toward China was at the time of the great calamity of the nation wide flood in the summer of 1931. The continued heavy rains produced a vast inundation in the regions along the river Yung Tsu Kiang and in the districts of North and South China. Especially the flood which invaded five Shengs of Hu Pei, Hu Nan, Kiang Hsi, An Hui, and Kiang Su along the banks of the river Chang Kiang was the most frightful disaster seen in the whole of China in the last eighty years. The area of flooded land extended to fifty nine thousand square miles, which corresponds nearly to the area of Japan proper. The lives lost were estimated as thirty four million. The property lost amounted to two billion Yuan, in addition to the losses caused by the rottening of stored grains and by the impossibility of sowing autumnal seed. Nearly one hundred and twenty thousand acres of cultivated land were inundated. This meant that seventeen per cent of the entire area of cultivated land was devastated.

Under this terrible calamity, the Government of China

made a huge effort to devise various emergency measures. Other nations manifested their sympathy in concrete ways.

In Japan, Premier Wakatsuki called together the representatives of the organizations closely related to China on the 25th of August, 1931. The result was that an organization called Chyu Ka Minkoku Suisai Dojo Kai (the Relief Society for Flood Sufferers of the Chinese Republic) was formed. The Viscount who had been somewhat indisposed and confined at home was chosen as the President of the society. Baron Goh was made the Chairman of the committee. Mr. K. Kodama and Mr. F. Abe were made the vice-Chairmen. On the 25th the organization was completed. The gift of one hundred thousand yen from the Imperial Household was sent to Mr. Soong, the Chairman of the Flood Relief Committee through Mr. Shigemitsu, the Chargé d'Affaires.

In the Relief Society for Flood Sufferers of the Chinese Republic, the Viscount and Mr. Kodama occupied important positions as the President of the society and a vice-Chairman of the committee respectively. This fact goes to show what an important position the Japan-China Industry Association was occupying in business circles as the Viscount was its President and Mr. Kodama the vice-President. The official members of this Association met twice, on the 21st and 24th, and formed a concrete plan to raise two million yen for relief purposes. This was done previous to the meeting called by Premier Wakatsuki.

One of the methods of raising subscriptions was the radio speech of the Viscount, the first attempt of the Japanese Radio Company to introduce a microphone into

a private home.   This arrangement was necessary as the
Viscount was still in the state of convalescence.   The
Viscount made a powerful appeal to the entire nation
on behalf of the suffering neighbors.   Up to the 15th
of September the amount of more than four hundred
and ninety thousand yen was raised.   As the first dispatch for relief work, a large quantity of polished rice,
wheat, flour, woolen blankets, condensed milk, and drugs
were sent by a special steamship to Hankow.   Baron
Fukao, the Chairman and Mr. Funatsu, the vice-Chairman of the visiting Committee, started for Shanghai on
board the Nagasaki Maru, ahead of the cargo steamer.
The Baron carried with him the sum of one hundred
thousand yen as a present to the Chinese Government
and twenty thousand yen to be distributed among the
Japanese residents in the suffering districts.   The good-
will messengers reached Shanghai on the 17th and called on Mr. Soong, the Chairman of the Flood Relief
Society in the office of the society.   Mr. Soong deeply
appreciated what the Japanese public did for the allevia-
tion of the sufferers.

A complete understanding between the Japanese messengers and Mr. Soong was reached as to the disposition
of the goods.   The arrangement was that when the cargo
boat shoud arrive at Shanghai on the 22nd, Mr. Soong
and his committee would visit the steamer for inspection
and receive the lists of the articles from Baron Fukao
and Mr. Funatsu, then letting the boat continue on to
Hankow where the distribution of the articles should be
made.   But Mr. Soong having received the news of the
Manchurian incident suddenly left Shanghai for Nanking on the 20th and wrote to Baron Fukao asking him

to postpone the date of the transference of the goods.
On the 23rd another letter of Mr. Soong reached the
Baron. It reads :

" We the Relief Committee deeply appreciate the compassion
manifested by His Imperial Majesty the Emperor of Japan and
also the sympathy shown by her general public, but we beg of
you to understand that it is impossible for us to accept the gift
with equanimity when we think of the Manchurian incident."

This was a plain announcement of a refusal to
accept the consolatory articles sent from Japan by the
specially equipped steamer. Baron Fukao earnestly
strived to prevail on the Chinese Relief Committee to
change their mind, on the ground that the present mission was totally different from the Manchurian event,
in that the mission had come with the genuine
sympathy of the Japanese people to their close neighbors.
This solicitation of Baron Fukao was backed with a
strong appeal made in the name of Viscount Shibusawa
to the effect :

" A friendly call on the flood stricken neighbors transcends
all political questions. Even at the time of war the Red Cross
activity is acknowledged by the enemy. If so, the sympathy of
the general public of Japan should not be denied on account of
the Manchurian incident."

But all the effort ended in vain. With deep regret
the cargo boat sailed back to Moji leaving Shanghai on
the 26th. Thus the last international goodwill effort of
Viscount Shibusawa ended in a peculiar anomaly.
Nevertheless this effort of the Viscount will remain as
one of the memories of what he did for China almost
to the very last of his earthly career, which was for-

ever closed three months later.

In this connection it is interesting and significant to note a recent incident which transpired in Nanking with reference to the Economic Mission of Japan to China headed by Mr. K. Kodama, ex-President of Yokohama Specie Bank. On the 16th of March Chiang Kai Shek, the Generalissimo gave a reception in honor of Mr. Kodama and his party. Toward the close of the function the Generalissimo proposed to pause for a moment to do honor to the memory of the late Viscount Shibusawa, to whom he had just paid a high tribute. Thus the good the Viscount did for China in the days gone by was finally vindicated in this beautiful act of her supreme ruler. A seed sown hardly fails to bring forth the fruits of its kind.

We will now turn our attention to the international activity of the Viscount with regard to the United States of America.

It goes without saying that a major part of the international activities of the Viscount consisted of his efforts for the promotion of better understanding and more friendly relations between Japan and America. Facts and data in this field of the Viscount's activity are so abundant and complicated that the author is simply overwhelmed by the task of reducing them to a readable form in a few pages. The question in this case is not so much what should be written as what should be left unwritten. He is like a young woman bewildered as to which piece she should choose in the midst of an endless variety of goods displayed in a large department store.

The Japanese Association of the League of Nations, now the Japanese International Association, has been issuing a magazine known as "Kokusai Chishiki" (International Knowledge), and its memorial number of the late Viscount Shibusawa was issued on the first day of February, 1932, the year following his death. Close friends of the Viscount paid high and beautiful tributes to him. The author was asked to write an article in his capacity of Secretary of the Japanese American Relations Committee, of which the Viscount was the virtual Chairman from the time of its organization in 1916. His subject was "Japanese American Friendship and the late Viscount Shibusawa." The following is an excerpt from it :

"During eight years from 1923, in which the great earthquake and fire took place, to 1931 nearly three hundred foreigners (a great majority being Americans) called on the Viscount. Of the three hundred, two hundred and thirty-six were men and sixty-four women. Classified according to their professions, there were fifty-six business men; fifty-four religious leaders; thirty-two newspaper and magazine writers ; eighteen diplomats; sixteen scholars ; sixteen bankers ; six educators ; six government officers ; three persons interested in international work ; one lawyer ; one social worker ; one militarist; one physician ; and two boys. Most of the sixty-four women were married women, and among them were writers, social workers, and artists.

"The visitors were all of them picked persons, who at home occupy positions of influence and confidence. Therefore when they returned home from their long journey, they were invited by colleges and universities, churches and clubs, to lecture on their experiences. Some of them contributed fresh articles to magazines and newspapers. They spoke or wrote about curious and strange manners and customs; the superb beauty of sceneries; and exquisite fine arts. And on the top of it all, they would talk or write about Viscount Shibusawa, the grand old man of Japan.

"The motives of the visitors were deeply significant, and two or three typical ones might here be cited.

"Mr. A. said: 'Your Excellency Viscount Shibusawa, I came with a letter of introduction of a friend of mine who admires you. He told me that it is delightful to see Nikko, Hakone, and Mount Fuji, but that I cannot say I have seen real Japan unless I have met Viscount Shibusawa and so be sure to pay your respects to him.'

"Mr. B. said: 'Your Excellency's good name is widely known to us, and as I have long been desiring to have the privilege of meeting you even for a few minutes during my tour of Japan, I feel now that my object of visiting Japan is completed.'

"Mr. C. said: 'I am greatly pleased to see you again. You look younger than the time when I met you a few years ago. You are growing younger instead of getting older. I heartily congratulate you. Viscount, really I am ashamed to stand in your presence to-day on account of the immigration law of 1924. The law disgraced us Americans more than it did you Japanese. Nearly all thoughtful Americans are thinking so too. The public opinion of America supports its revision. This change of the national sentiment against the law is largely due to the broad-minded and patient attitude manifested by the leaders like your good self here in Japan. I earnestly hope that your own eyes will see the law amended.'

"Mr. D. said: 'I am a regular contributor to a magazine of large circulation and anxious by your permission to publish in it my interview with the grand old man of Japan.'

"Mrs. E., mother with her son said: 'As my son has just reached adolescent age, I felt it helpful for him to get a practical education in seeing what is going on in countries other than his own. This is the sole object of our overseas tour at this time. A mere hand shake with you will be to him a rare privilege. I am very happy to be able to pay my respects to you to-day. I bring to you best wishes from my husband.''

Viscount Shibusawa welcomed every visitor with

sincerity and frankness, and spoke to each somewhat as follows:

"I am very grateful to you for calling on me to-day. I don't deserve such words of commendation. Is this your first visit to Japan? Have you seen much of Japan? If I am to tell you why I came to take a deep interest in the promotion of Japanese American friendship, I must go into the story of my own life, but that will be impossible in a brief interview. I shall therefore summarize the story so that you may understand how I was led to become a pro-American Japanese.

"I was fourteen years old when Commodore Perry with his squadron entered into Uraga Bay. I was a farmer boy living in a village abont fifty miles north of Tokyo then called Edo. From my childhood days I had been fond of reading books—Chinese classics. I studied nothing but Chinese. I don't know your language, and am not able to talk to you directly except through an interpreter.

"The mood of those who studied Chinese classics in those days was antagonistic to the Government and they hated foreigners. I was unconsciously affected by the atmosphere, and identified myself with the movement of the 'Away with barbarians and down with the Tokugawa regime.' Although our plot did not materialize yet we, the village young fellows, planned a scheme to burn down a neighboring castle and then to march to Yokohama to drive out foreigners. Judging from the knowledge I have now, it was a most absurd attempt.

"Later it so happened that I was to be a retainer to Prince Yoshinobu Tokugawa, a powerful Daimyo of the day. I entertained my anti-foreign spirit just as strongly as ever. Here I must tell you more particularly why I got into this spirit of hatred against foreigners. Among the books I read there was a book entitled the "Shin Ei Kinsei Dan" (Modern Story about China and England), in which what was known as the battle of Tau kuang (道光) was discussed. The story told in the book was briefly this that the Chinese authorities burned the cargo of opium which England imported into Hongkong; and that thereupon England declared war against China in which China was defeated and forced to cede Hongkong to England. From the book I obtained impressions that England was unreasonable; that foreign countries were aggressive; that while they boasted of their civilazation they practiced the barbarous principle of 'the strong preys upon the weak'; that Japan must never keep intercourse with foreign countries; and that it was better for Japan to drive out every foreigner from the country at the earliest possible date, as otherwise Japan might meet irreparable disaster. Still later my Lord Prince Tokugawa was promoted to the Shogunate, and in 1867 I was dispatched to France as one of the attendants to Prince Mimbu, the younger brother to the Shogun. The Government of France extended an invitation to the Shogun's Government to send a national representative to the International Exposition of Paris. Prince Mimbu was appointed as the official delegate of Japan to the Exposition.

" Another objective of the Prince was to remain for five years in Paris for study. The time for the departure came. All of us were taken to the steamer in which we soon began to feel monotony and loneliness. In order to scatter this atmosphere we discussed politics and talked about current topics. I was an avowed anti-foreigner whose zeal never abated even after he had entered the foreign steamship. There was a fellow passenger, one of the attendants to Prince Mimbu. He was an expert in diplomatic affairs. His name was T. Tanabe. One day Mr. Tanabe told me about the history of the modern diplomacy of Japan touching the Japanese-American Treaties of 1851.

" Here for the first time I was indelibly impressed with the superb personality of Townsend Harris, the first American Minister to Japan. I felt that our Bushido, which so far I had believed to be the indigenous product of Japan, was most admirably demonstrated by Minister Harris a foreigner.

" While Minister Harris was conducting his diplomatic affairs in the Legation established in the temple called Zenpukuji in

the Azabu ward, his interpreter Mr. Heusken was assassinated
at night. The attitude the Minister assumed on this occasion
greatly moved me. If there was a man to be indignant in this
case, it was Minister Harris. But instead, the Ministers of
England and France were highly excited, and withdrew from
Tokyo to Yokohama as a demonstration of their displeasure and
dissatisfaction.

" Not only did they remove their legations to Yokohama, but
they also strongly urged Minister Harris to follow suit. He
refused to listen to such a proposition stating that such an action
would humiliate the Japanese Government.

" If the rowdies should attack me because of my stay here in
the Legation, let it be so. We should be prepared to encounter
such an emergency as this if we are to lead a junior nation to
a better and more advanced civilization. Although criticism is
due the Government upon its inadequacy of protecting foreign
residents, yet Heusken was also to be blamed about his care-
lessness in going out at night, in spite of the fact that the
authorities had publicly issued a warning for foreigners not to
go out at night on account of a wide spread disturbance then
going on.

" Such was the stand the American Minister took in the face
of the bloody event closely related to him, and he was calmly
attending to his daily routine as though nothing exciting in and
about his legation took place.

" My anti-foreign notion was completely blown away then, and
from that time I began to study America and Americans. The
more I studied, the higher and firmer my confidence in and
respect for America grew.

" Superficially speaking, there seems to exist a vast difference between Japan and America, so much so that complete
understanding and neighborly sentiment between them can
never be realized. For instance : Japan is a monarchy and
America a republic ; Japan is small and America big ; Japan
is poor and America rich ; and Japan is old and America

young. But when we study the characteristics of the two nations from spiritual and moral standpoints, we can find many
traits in common, such as justice, humanity, fair play, the
square deal, self-sacrifice, loyalty, philanthropy, chivalry,
cooperation, unity, patriotism, public spiritedness, orderliness, and
respect for law. Hence it is perfectly practicable for us two
peoples to enter into friendly relations if we thoroughly understand each other. The way of Chung Shu (忠恕) which regulates the intercourse between one individual and another, so
that they may live in peace and harmony, can be equally
applicable to that between one nation and another.

"As to the immigration law you referred to, leaders in your
country seem to recognize the necessity of its revision and it may
not be very far off till we see the law changed. I wish you
to see to it that any obstacle which hinders the smooth relations
between our two countries should be removed at the earliest
possible date.

"I must beg your pardon for this so inadequate reception.
Please endeavor to promote peace between our two countries and
among mankind."

Such were the spirit and the method in which he
used to welcome casual visitors from distant countries.
Besides, he frequently entertained foreign visitors at
luncheons and dinners to exchange more fully ideas
for strengthening mutual confidence and trust.

The first experience Viscount Shibusawa had in
entertaining a foreign visitor to Japan on a large scale
and in an elaborate manner was the one when he acted
as the chairman of the committee for welcoming General
Grant, ex-President of the United States of America,
in the summer of 1879. His visit to Japan was heralded several weeks in advance. He was to land at
Nagasaki first. In Tokyo a reception committee was

organized, and the Viscount, who twelve years before had enjoyed gala days in Paris the center of the world's culture and social intercourse, could not be left off the committee.   He was chosen as the chairman of the committee.   An illustrious representative of the nation which gave birth to Townsend Harris, whom the Viscount idolized almost as an incarnation of Bushido, was about to enter Tokyo.   What a splendid opportunity it was for the Viscount, the chairman of the committee, to demonstrate his ability as the host to a most distinguished guest.

A grand banquest, a theatrical entertainment, and the display of the ancient military arts such as shooting the target by the archer from the saddle of a running horse, dogs chasing by riders on horseback, and the horse race of jockeys bearing on their backs flowing hoods in the shape of large pipes.

These entertainments were given in Uyeno Park, and His Imperial Majesty the Emperor Meiji was present in honor of President and Mrs. Grant.   Everything went off nicely to the great entertament of the distinguished visitors.   To commemorate this great occassion and historic event, two trees were planted by President and Mrs. Grant.   They are called the Grant hinoki (cypressus lawsoniana) and Grant gyokuran (magnolia grandiflora).   The former was planted by the President and the latter by Mrs. Grant.   Both of them are still flourishing having fought the rains and winds for nearly sixty years.

Viscount Shibusawa's American and European trip in the year 1902 was his first to America and his second to Europe.   In this trip the Viscount left his footprints

President Grant.

on the soil of America extensively, and his name as
Baron Shibusawa was printed on the memory of many
leaders of the country. He told us that this journey
of his was literally a pleasure tour, in which, however,
one definite mission entrusted to him by the Federated
Chambers of Commerce of Japan was included—the mission
to promote mutual understanding and good-will
between the people of the West and the people of
Japan by informing the former of the commercial and
industrial condition of Japan. He landed at San Francisco
on the 30th of May, 1902, and spent one whole
month in America in general observation. By coming
into direct contact with things that were going on in
America, he was astonished at seeing such an intense
business life and such rapid progress. He felt that what
he had read in newspapers and had heard from friends
who had visited the country did not tell him even half
the truth he witnessed himself.

He proceeded to Chicago, taking the northern route.
Along the railway he saw the vast prairies and could
judge the kind of soil by observing the thick growth
of vegetation. In Chicago he was struck with wonder
because of the marvelous prosperity so evident in the
city. He ascribed this incomparable thrift of the city
to the fact that it was the distributing center of agricultural products. He was profoundly impressed by the
prosperity of Chicago because he took it as the result
of national wealth caused by agricultural products.

Again commercial and industrial activities in large
cities struck him with amazement—the hydroelectricity
of Niagara; the steel factories of Pittsburgh; the
railway car manufacturing company of Philadelphia;

the passenger and freight car manufacturing company of Chicago ; the cotton goods factory of Boston ; the silk goods factory of Patterson ; and the tobacco factory of New York. These concerns he visited, but he regretfully stated that he could not inspect the silk goods factory on account of the strike. Although the Viscount did not take down the names of the presidents, vice-presidents, and other leading officers of the above mentioned institutions, yet one can safely imagine that he must have met with some of them at least in each of the institutions.

The Viscount's interview with President Theodore Roosevelt in this trip was a memorable one. The Viscount and his small party, consisting of one interpreter and two business men, were taken by Minister Takahira to the White House. They were led to the library on the second floor. The President entered the room at 12:08 and beginning with Minister Takahira, he shook hands with the visitors.

The Viscount expressed his deep appreciation of the honor of the audience accorded him and his party by the President. The President, instead of making a direct answer to the greeting of the Viscount, asked him what route he took. Then the following conversation took place between President Roosevelt and the Viscount.

Viscount : We landed in San Francisco last month. We passed through Chicago, Pittsburgh, and Philadelphia, arriving at New York City three days ago. We reached this city last evening.... Japan has reached her present stage of civilization through the influence of your great country, and the entire nation remembers it with a profound gratitude.

President :   I have been informed about the progress Japan has
recently made. Her fine arts and military discipline
are the objects of the world's admiration. Especially the latter was praised by the army officers of
the different nations represented at the time of the
Chinese Boxer trouble. Our officers told us that
the military experts of Russia, Germany, and England were unanimous as to the strict orderliness of
the Japanese army, and even went so far as to say
that it could be taken as our model.

Viscount :   I deeply appreciate the high estimate you placed
upon our fine arts and military system, and cannot
be too grateful for it, but as I am a business man,
it rather pains me to know that our commercial and
industrial development has not reached the point to
draw your attention to it as that of the fine arts
and military training has done. I shall make a
special effort henceforth to develop commerce and
industry, so that I may receive your favorable comment upon them the next time when I shall be privileged to enjoy an audience with Your Excellency.

This gentle sarcasm, of which the Viscount not infrequently made good use, seems to have conveyed to
the President the sentiment of the Viscount, because
the Viscount used to tell us whenever he referred to
this incident in the interview between himself and the
President that the President smilingly acknowledged his
slip in not having referred to the business features of
Japan while welcoming a business visitor from that far
off country, and that he promised the Viscount to
comment on the business activity of Japan the first
thing whenever the next interview between them might
take place.

President : I understand that your mission on this trip is to promote a better understanding and good-will between the people of the West and your people through commercial and industrial relations. The mission is a highly commendable one and I shall do whatever lies within my power to assist this noble cause. Have you already met the President of the Chamber of Commerce of New York?

Viscount : Not yet, Sir. But as I am expecting to go back to the city, and also brought with me a letter of introduction from Minister Buck to the President of the New York Chamber of Commerce, I anticipate the pleasure of meeting him.

President : I shall confer with the Secretary of State and try to facilitate your journey. Please let me know the schedule of your itinerary in this country.

Viscount : I most deeply appreciate your consideration. I shall submit it to Your Excellency.

President : Please convey to His Imperial Majesty the Emperor, and also to your Government, that Minister and Mrs. Takahira are fully discharging their high functions as the accredited representatives of the Japanese Empire, gathering around them a host of friends in our official and diplomatic circle. I prize my association with him and have confidence in him.

Viscount : Most assuredly I shall do so.

The President graciously prepared a letter of introduction to Mr. Morris K. Jessup, the President of the Chamber of Commerce of New York, in which he commended Baron Shibusawa to Mr. Jessup as a man who has the most vital relations with the welfare of Japan's commerce and industry......a gentleman who occupies a very high position in social and industrial circles.

There was a business man in New York whose name should not be omitted in connection with this trip of the Viscount. He was Mr. Frank A. Vanderlip, the vice-President of the National City Bank. A few days after the Viscount paid his respects to the chief executive of the great Republic—namely on the 25th of June, 1902, Mr. Vanderlip called on the Viscount in one of the hotels in New York. In those days Mr. Vanderlip was making himself famous as the author of the book entitled " The American Commercial Invasion of Europe." This was translated into Japanese and the Viscount wrote an introduction to it. It so happened that the Viscount was reading the manuscript when Mr. Vanderlip called on him in the said hotel. The two men could have hardly dreamed then that this interview would form the occasion which caused Mr. Vanderlip to organize a Vanderlip party, eighteen years later in 1920, for visiting Japan to hold a conference with the Viscount and his colleagues—a conference which greatly contributed to the promotion of neighborly feelings between the two countries. If such a book as might be called The History of Peoples' Diplomacy between Japan and America is to be written, this conference should certainly receive due recognition in that book.

In speaking of the Viscount's visit to America in the year 1902, we mentioned only two names of prominent men, President Roosevelt and Mr. Frank A. Vanderlip. But he must have met many more leaders on this trip as he visited so many large factories and business institutions, thus the name of Baron Shibusawa becoming quite widely known in America.

But compared with his second visit to America this first one was only a prelude. We shall now try to describe this second trip. It took place in the year 1909 seven years after his first one. The first trip was made largely for pleasure in order to take his mind off from arduous duties crowding and pressing upon him. The second one was undertaken for the specific purpose of promoting better understanding and closer relation between the people of Japan and America. At this time the Viscount had already withdrawn from the major part of his numerous business relations, and was ready fully to devote his time and energy to public and international activity.

The international relationship between Japan and America since the visits of Commodore Perry to Japan in the years 1853–4, down to the day of the conclusion of the Russo-Japanese war in 1905 through the arbitration of President Theodore Roosevelt, had been smooth and cordial. But the war and its conclusion produced undesirable sentiments among the Japanese people both at home and in America. The home people were strongly conscious of the fact that they were victorious over Russia and entitled to more favorable terms than those concluded at Portsmouth. This belief led them to blame President Roosevelt the arbitrator, and Marquis Komura the chief delegate of Japan.

And this created resentment among the Americans. Then the haughty behavior of the Japanese immigrants in California, being elated by the consciousness of their kinship with the victorious race, made them obnoxious

to the citizens of California. Thus the anti-Japanese
sentiments in California were becoming stronger and
more bitter so that their influence poisoned the minds
of the American people.

The movement to segregate the Japanese school
children in the American primary schools in California, and the denunciation of the method of picture
marriage, were the concrete challenge of the California
exclusionists.   However these movements were somewhat mitigated by the conclusion of the "Gentlemen's
Agreement" in 1907.   Marquis Komura was the
Minister of the Foreign Department at that time.   He
saw that the Japanese-American relationship should be
placed on a securer basis than it was.   His idea was
that, as America is a country controlled by public
opinion, it is necessary to directly appeal to the people,
in addition to the regular and official method of diplomacy.   In other words, the Marquis would have Japanese leaders organize what might be called the peoples'
diplomacy and make a friendly gesture toward the
American people.   Viscount Shibusawa, who was up
to the previous year the President of the Tokyo Chamber of Commerce, and others were approached by
Marquis Komura on this question.   The Viscount was
in hearty sympathy with the proposition and took up
the question with B. Nakano, the President of the
Chamber.

Then a concrete plan was formed and submitted to a
conference of the representatives of the Chambers of
Commerce throughout the country.   It was to extend
an invitation to the American Chambers of Commerce
of the Pacific coast to send their representatives to visit

Japan. The motion was unanimously adopted and a formal invitation was extended. This resulted in the visit to Japan of a party consisting of more than fifty persons in 1908. Their days were crowded with inspections of social, educational, and industrial institutions; entertainments; garden parties; and sight-seeing. The program went off satisfactorily and every member of the party seemed to have enjoyed his or her trip.

As a return courtesy, an invitation from the Chambers of Commerce of the Pacific Coast was extended to Japanese business men to visit their country in 1909. The invitation was accepted, and Viscount Shibusawa was chosen as the President of the visiting party, which consisted of a similar number of persons as the American party, including a few ladies. The name of the party was Nihon Tobei Jitsugyo Dan (The Commercial Commissioners of Japan).

This being an unprecedented and significant undertaking, the Imperial Household, the Government, and the business circles placed high hopes in it, and gave the party a most enthusiastic send off by treating them with parting luncheons and banquets.

The party landed at the port city of Seattle in the early part of September, where it is needless to tell that it was most loyally and cordially welcomed by the reception committee.

The arrangement for the Commercial Commissioners of Japan to travel through the great country of America was to make the special train their sleeping quarters from the beginning of their journey to its end. This meant for them to spend about ninety-six nights before they concluded their tour in San Francisco on the thirtieth of November. The party visited fifty-three cities during its three months journey. How strenuous and crowded their contacts with the hosts of those cities were is discernible from the report the Viscount made on his return.

" From the day we entered the train in Seattle on the fifth of September until the thirtieth of November when we alighted from it at San Francisco, we travelled the continent in the same train specially provided for our use. We were to spend our nights in the sleepers of the train. When the train reached a stopping place automobiles numbering from forty to fifty might be waiting for us. The train generally reached the station at seven o'clock in the morning to meet the engagements of nine o'clock. We took breakfast in the train, and then we were severally grouped to ride in the cars sent for us. Often we were taken to the City Halls, where one hundred and more might be waiting to welcome us. The leader of the hosts addressed us words of welcome to which I as the chairman had to respond. After that, we were taken to schools and public parks for inspection. Soon the luncheon time came. We were taken into Club houses where large numbers of men might be waiting to greet us. After the luncheon, two or three persons spoke to welcome us. Responses were made by an equal number of the visitors. Thus the luncheon gathering continued till three or four o'clock. Then again we were taken in the cars for inspection trips, after which we were rushed to our home in the train. Change of dress for the evening function had to be hastily attended to. With full dress and wearing our decorations, off we started for the banquet hall, which was usually in some hotel. There were more speakers at the banquet. Consequently the meeting dragged on to one o'clock or still later. We returned to the train and prepared ourselves for sleep. Then the train began to roll on to the next destination. The next day's program in the next city would be similar to what took place in the preceding one. Thus day in and day out, we were welcomed and entertained."

Mr. M. Zumoto, who joined the party in America at the request of the Viscount to do the interpreting work for him, commented on the tireless effort the Viscount made during the journey, saying that it was nothing short of a miracle to see a man of seventy years of age meet such assiduous and incessant demands pouring upon him as the leader of the party. The majority of the members of the party who were much younger than theViscount seemed to have fallen far behind the Viscount in this endurance test.

The preparation of each city for the reception was quite elaborate. Each city struck a medal and designed a badge to memorialize the occasion. None appreciated these manifestations of cordiality and hospitality of the hosts of each city more deeply than the Viscount. The friendships he formed with leaders in political, social, economical, educational, and religious spheres throughout America, and the impressions he obtained in this trip made him more than ever a most staunch friend of Americans.

We shall cite here an instance which will throw light on the dignity and importance of the Commercial Commissioners of Japan on the one hand, and on the other, the great significance which the American public attached to this party. The instance was the reception given by President Taft to the party at the Lafayette Club by Lake Minnetonka, on Sunday the nineteenth of September. After the exchange of greetings, the party was taken into the dining hall for luncheon.

Toward the close of the function speeches were exchanged between the President and the Viscount.

The Viscount said:

"...We are plain business men holding no office in the Government. Our mission is to promote peace and good-will between our two peoples. But on the verge of our departure, His Majesty the Emperor was gracious enough to grant unto us an unprecedented favor by ordering the preparation of a farewell function for us. He despatched the Minister of the Imperial Household to the gathering to convey to us his farewell advice to the end that the enterprise pleased His Majesty, the Emperor, and therefore he earnestly hoped for its success. The public also gave such an enthusiastic ovation at the farewell as could be accorded only the departure of an expeditionary army. From this you can readily see how wholeheartedly the entire nation endorsed our visit to you. You can also construe the above mentioned demonstrations as the sure expression of the friendly sentiment our people hold toward your great Republic."

To this President Taft responded:

"It gives us a rare joy to meet here with the gentlemen of Japan who occupy among their countrymen positions of influence and intelligence. We shall all be pleased to show you whatever you desire to see as a token of our appreciation of the courtesy and hospitality some of us received from your people when we visited them. If we can offer to you anything that will benefit your country, we shall only be too glad to do so.

"Some of our people are worrying about the anti-Japanese agitation created among certain classes of people in the past, but to-day we hear less about it. It will never disturb our historic good relations. Those of us who are informed of the real conditions existing between America and Japan will not be carried away by any sensational statements mentioned in irresponsible newspapers. Now I have the honor of proposing a toast to the

health of the august Sovereign of the most advanced and powerful nation in the far east—His Majesty the Emperor of Japan."

Thus three Banzais were heartily shouted by the
hosts and the guests. The sentiment expressed by President Taft was the keynote to which all the rest during the trip was attuned. The party certainly fulfilled
the mission of the peoples' diplomacy and the name of
Baron Shibusawa was widely known to the American
people from that day.

The correspondence between American friends and
Viscount Shibusawa and their visits to him began to
increase from that day and continued until the day
he breathed his last. How profoundly the experience
in this mission impressed the Viscount could be seen
from the fact that he made it an annual event for
many years, till the number of the party was greatly
depleted, to hold a memorial banquet for their reunion
in the evening of the 19th of December, which was
the date they safely reached home, and to send greetings from them to those who helped to make the trip
memorable as well as successful.

There can be no doubt that the mission of the peoples'
diplomacy contributed to a large extent to promote
better understanding and friendly feeling between the
two nations. But it would be expecting too much of
the mission to believe that it swept away all trace of
anti-Japanese sentiment existing in some sections of
America. Hence disturbing news reached Japan in the
year 1913 that the Legislature of the State of California
was going to pass a prohibitory law for ineligible
aliens to own real estate for agricultural purposes in
California. The news also alarmed the leaders at home.

Then they organized the Nichi-Bei Doshi Kai (the Japanese-American Emergency Society). Viscount Shibusawa was elected its President and B. Nakano the vice-President.

To deal with the emergency the Viscount sent to America Dr. J. Soyeda, one of the Viscount's lieutenants for several years, and Mr. T. Kamiya who was educated in America. Their purpose was to express sympathy with the sufferers; to investigate the real situation; and to try to check the passage of the intended alien land law.

The two messengers learned in their steamer that the law was passed, but they proceeded on their voyage. On their arrival in San Francisco they conferred with the Japanese leaders and American friends who were not in sympathy with the Legislature. Their presence consoled and steadied the panic-stricken minds of the immigrants. Dr. Soyeda and Mr. Kamiya proceeded to Washington and had an interview with President Wilson and Mr. Bryan the Secretary of State, both of whom deeply regretted the action taken in the California legislature.

The third trip to the States of the Viscount took place in 1915. This was the year when the Memorial Exposition of the Opening of the Panama Canal was held in San Francisco. Therefore the apparent objective of the Viscount's trip was to inspect the Exposition, although the real and more serious objective which prompted him was the promotion of good-will between the two peoples.

Two things militated against the creation of enthusiasm among the Japanese people for the San Francisco Exposition. The one was the anti-Japanese attitude the

people of California assumed in 1913 and the subsequent
estrangement; and the other was the European war
which absorbed the attention of the entire nation of
Japan, especially of her business men. The authorities
of the Exposition were placed in a very embarrassing
position, because they could not get the expected support from the nations of Europe. This emergency drove
them to look for assistance from the Orient.

The Viscount, who achieved a grand success in the
peoples' diplomacy of 1909 by forming genuine friendships with prominent men of the leading cities in
America, would not let slip any opportunity to renew
and strengthen the neighborly feeling between the two
countries, and to him this Panama Memorial Exposition
of San Francisco loomed up as another epoch making
occasion to deepen the international friendship between
the two nations. So off he started for America on
board the Shinyo Maru on the 23rd of October 1915.

In July of this year, Judge Gary of the United
States Steel Corporation had visited Japan and was
grandly feted both by high officials and business leaders.

The Viscount also entertained him at his Asukayama
home. The Viscount took much pride in his friendship with the Judge.

This trip of the Viscount was fraught with many
important events of permanent value to the cause of
Japanese American relationships. He was loyally welcomed by the officers of the Exposition, and his presence
there added to it brightness and enthusiasm. He received a stimulus on this trip to organize a Japanese
American Relations Committee, which will fully be discussed later. He renewed his acquaintance with Mr.

Frank A. Vanderlip and President Roosevelt, which he formed on his first trip to the States in 1902. In Boston, he called on President Eliot of Harvard University. In Washington, an audience with President Wilson was granted to the Viscount, and the President's intercession on behalf of Dr. Teusler, of St. Luke's International Medical Center whose cousin was Mrs. Wilson, was to the Viscount a sacred trust which he felt must be fulfilled at any cost. Dr. Teusler was in America at this time busily engaged in raising subscriptions for the building fund of the institution and knew that in the previous year the Viscount, the chairman of the Japanese Advisory Council of St. Luke's International Medical Center, had received in behalf of the institution the gift of fifty thousand yen from the Imperial Household. President Wilson was no doubt informed of these intimate relations between Dr. Teusler and the Viscount.

In conversation with Dr. Eliot and Mr. Vanderlip, the Viscount touched on the far reaching question of the relationship of Japan with America regarding China. The view of the Viscount was that, as the result of the European War, America will be obliged to find markets in China where there is no telling but that a trade competition between America and Japan might not take place. He thought that the best way would be to cooperate in carrying on business there, because the practicability of cooperation between America and Japan was a proven matter as could be seen in the joint enterprises of the Shibaura factory and the Tokyo Electric company.

Now coming back to the Japanese American Relations Committee, it should be stated at the outset that the organization of the body by the Viscount was one of his most far reaching contributions for the promotion of the friendly relations of the two countries. It was organized in Tokyo in February of 1916, pursuant to the promise he made to Mr. Wallace M. Alexander, the then President of the Chamber of Commerce of San Francisco.

The aim of this organization is expressed in its first Article :

" The aim of the organization shall be to bring about a better understanding between the people of Japan and the people of the United States of America in order that friendly relations between them may permanently be maintained ; and also to take such measures as necessary to solve any difficulty which may rise between them at any time."

Article V reads as follows :

" The membership of the Organization shall not exceed thirty in number."

This limitation in the number of members was due to the agreement made between the Viscount and Mr. Alexander.

The charter members of the Organization are representative men in political, social, educational, religious, and business circles. Their names and offices are as follows :

Anesaki, Dr. Masaharu, Professor in Tokyo Imperial University.

Asano, Mr. Soichiro, President of Asano Cement Co., Ltd.

Furukawa, Baron Toranosuke, President of Furukawa

President Theodore Roosevelt.

President Taft.

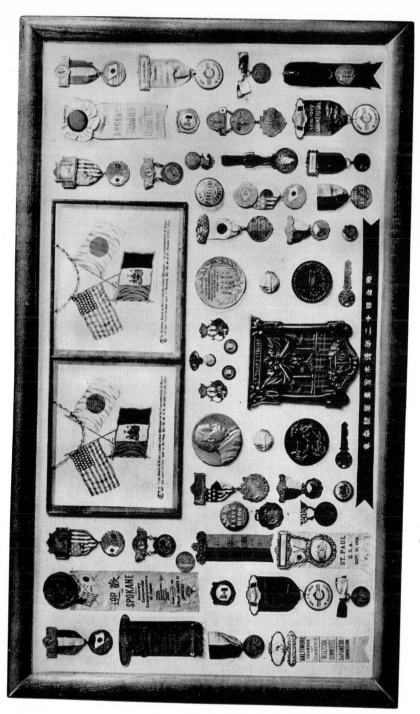

Collection of the Medals Commemorating the Tour to U.S.A.

Mining Co.

Hayakawa, Mr. Senkichiro, Managing Director of Mitsui Bank.

Horikoshi, Mr. Zenjyuro, Proprietor of Z. Horikoshi & Co.

Inouye, Mr. Junnosuke, President of Yokohama Specie Bank.

Kaneko, Viscount Kentaro, Member of Privy Council.

Kondo, Baron Rempei, President of N. Y. K.

Kushida, Mr. Manzo, Chairman of the Board of Directors of Mitsubishi Bank.

Mishima, Viscount Yataro, Governor of Bank of Japan.

Morimura, Baron Ichizaemon, President of Morimura Gumi Co.

Nakano, Mr. Buei, President of Tokyo Chamber of Commerce.

Nitobe, Dr. Inazo, Professor in Tokyo Imperial University.

Okura, Mr. Kihachiro, President of Okura Gumi Co.

Sakatani, Baron Yoshiro, Member of the House of Peers.

Shibusawa, Baron Eiichi, President of Dai Ichi Ginko.

Shidachi, Mr. Tetsujiro, Governor of Industrial Bank of Japan.

Shimura, Mr. Gentaro, Governor of Hypothec Bank of Japan.

Shimada, Mr. Saburo, President of the House of Representatives.

Soyeda, Dr. Juichi, Governor of the Imperial Railway Bureau.

Takada, Mr. Shinzo, President of the Takada Trading Co.

Uriu, Baron Sotokichi, Admiral.

Zumoto, Mr. Motosada, Editor and Publisher of the Herald of Asia.

Of these members, Viscount Shibusawa and Mr. Nakano constituted the Executive Council. Mr. Horikoshi and Mr. Zumoto were Secretaries. There was neither president nor chairman in the organization although the Viscount was its virtual president in the sense that he assumed the responsibility for the welfare of the organization instead of " Lording it over."

Twenty years have elapsed since in 1916 the Japanese American Relations Committee was organized by the members just mentioned, and it is quite natural that we find considerable changes in the membership. We would introduce to the reader the present members of the Committee who are ever ready to rally round the banner of the organization in time of need. They are :

Akashi, Mr. Teruo, President of Dai Ichi Ginko.

Anesaki, Dr. Masaharu, Professor-Emeritus of Tokyo Imperial University.

Asano, Mr. Soichiro (II), President of Asano Cement Co.

Eguchi, Mr. Sadaye, Member of the House of Peers.

Fujiyama, Mr. Raita, Member of the House of Peers.

Fukai, Mr. Eigo, Ex-Governor of Bank of Japan.

Furukawa, Baron Toranosuke, President of Furukawa Mining Co.

Hara, Mr. Kunizo, President of Japan Aircraft Co.

Hara, Mr. Tomitara, President of Hara Co.

Harada, Dr. Tasuku, Formerly Professor of University of Hawaii.

Horai, Mr. Ichimatsu, Governor of Japan Industrial Bank.

Ichinomiya, Mr. Reitaro, Director of Yokohama Specie Bank.

Ikeda, Mr. Seihin, Governor of Bank of Japan.

Isaka, Mr. Takashi, President of Tokyo Gas Co.

Ishii, Viscount Kikujiro, Member of the Privy Council.

Kagami, Mr. Kenkichi, Ex-President of N. Y. K.

Kaneko, Count Kentaro, Member of Privy Council.

Kushida, Mr. Manzo, Director-in-Chief of the Mitsubishi Firm.

Morimura, Baron Ichizaemon (II), President of Morimura Gumi Co.

Okura, Baron Kishichiro, President of Okura Gumi Co.

Otani, Mr. Noboru, President of N. Y. K.

Sakatani, Baron Yoshiro, Member of the House of Peers.

Shimizu, Mr. Teikichi, President of the Shimizu Gumi Co.

Takaki, Mr. Yasaka, Professor in Tokyo Imperial University.

Togo, Baron Yasushi, President of Japan Wireless Telegraph Company, Ltd.,

Uriu, Baron Sotokichi, Admiral.

Yamada, Dr. Saburo, President of University of Seoul.

Yuki, Mr. Toyotaro, ex-Governor of Japan Industrial Bank.

Zumoto, Mr. Motosada, Editor and Proprietor of the Herald of Asia.

The members of the Executive Council are Viscount Ishii, Baron Sakatani, and Mr. Fujiyama.

The Secretaries are Dr. Bunshiro Hattori, Professor in Waseda University, Mr. Kitaro Shiraishi, Director of the Shibusawa Holdings Co., and Dr. Kyugoro Obata.

There are twenty-seven members in the Committee, and of that number seven persons bear the honor of being the surviving charter members. They are Dr. Anesaki, Baron Furukawa, Count Kaneko, Mr. Kushida, Baron Sakatani, Admiral Uriu, and Mr. Zumoto. But this fact does not mean that institutions like the Bank of Japan, Industrial Bank of Japan, the Mitsui, Dai Ichi Ginko, Yokohama Specie Bank, Nippon Yusen Kaisha, Morimura Gumi Co., and Okura Gumi Co., etc. ceased to be represented in the organization. These institutions are just as faithful in charter membership as the seven veterans. The only difference is that their representatives have changed.

Backed by this powerful organization and through it, the Viscount carried on his international activity between Japan and America. It has been a quiet and steady work. The most conspicuous work in the history of this organization was the two conferences held under its auspices in Tokyo in the spring of the year 1920.

The motive of these two conferences was to consider the grave question affecting the Japanese farmers in California. Early in 1920 it was known that the anti-Japanese group in California was going to submit the enactment of the alien land law to a referendum in the fall of that year. This was the revival of the anti-Japanese movement of 1913 in California in the worst form, and the immigrants were alarmed by what might take place.

In order to cope with the situation, the Japansse American Relations Committee planned conferences with two groups of American leaders. One was a group of California leaders who would face the referendum movement, and the other was a group representing Eastern leaders.

Mr. Wallace M. Alexander headed the California group. Mr. Alexander is a veteran business man who was elected president of San Francisco Chamber of Commerce several times, and who proposed to Viscount Shibusawa the organization of the Japanese American Relations Committee in Tokyo to match up with the Japanese Relations Committee of San Francisco Chamber of Commerce. The group was composed of Dr. Benjamin Ide Wheeler, president-emeritus of the University of California; Mr. Walton N. Moore, a former president of San Francisco Chamber of Commerce; Mr. William T. Sesnon, another former president of San Francisco Chamber of Commerce; Mr. Loyal A. Osborne, vice-president of the Westinghouse Electric Company; Mr. Walter E. Clark, vice-president of the Atlantic Ocean Ship Building Company; and Mr. Frederick H. Randall, a California lawyer. In addition there were a few ladies, numbering seventeen altogether. The party arrived in Tokyo on the sixteenth of March, 1920.

From the seventeenth to the twenty-fourth, the visiting group of men attended sessions of the conference with some of the members of the Japanese American

Relations Committee, devoting to it their forenoon hours from 9.30 a.m. to 12.30 p.m. The conference seat was the assembly hall of the Bankers' Club. The organization of the conference was effected in the following form:

Viscount Shibusawa, the convener; Count Kaneko, the chairman; Baron Sakatani and Mr. Alexander, the vice-chairmen; and Dr. Hattori and Mr. Randall, the secretaries. The other Japanese members were Dr. Anesaki, Professor in Tokyo Imperial University; Dr. Dan, Director-in-Chief of the Mitsui Firm; Mr. Kushida, Chairman of the Board of Directors of the Mitsubishi Bank; Mr. Inouye, Governor of Bank of Japan; Dr. Soyeda, Director of Bank of Taiwan; and Mr. Zumoto, Editor of the Herald of Asia. The name of the conference was the Japanese American Unofficial Conference. Its aim was to discuss questions of better information and understanding, instead of forming resolutions about them. The agenda for the conference were the questions of immigration, land ownership, joint investment, cable rates, exchange professors, and publicity. On each question opinions were expressed from both sides and the conference ended in a most happy condition.

Immediately after the conclusion of the first conference, the second one followed, deliberating on the same questions and in the same place. The American group of the second conference consisted of Mr. Frank A. Vanderlip, the Chairman of the Board of Directors of the American International Corporation, and the leader of the party; Mr. Lyman Gage, a former Secretary of Treasury; Mr. Lewis L. Clarke, President of the American Exchange National Bank; Dr. Jacob Schur-

man, President of Cornell University; Mr. George East-
man, President of the Eastman Kodak Company; Mr.
D. P. Kingsley, President of the New York Life
Insurance Company; Mr. Seymour Cromwell, vice-
President of the New York Stock Exchange; Henry
W. Taft, New York's foremost lawyer and brother of
President Taft; Mr. Lionberger Davis, a financier of
St. Louis; and Mr. Julian Street, a well-known author.
Including their wives, daughters, and private secretaries,
the party consisted of twenty-four members.

They travelled on board the Kashima Maru and arrived at Yokohama early in the afternoon of the twenty-
fourth of March. Mr. Z. Horikoshi, who was commissioned by the Viscount to help organize the Vanderlip
party, accompanied the party from New York all the
way through the long journey. His full knowledge of
American life and tactful chaperonage were said to have
given a sense of security and comfort to every member
of the party.

Important and enlightening as the conference was for
its American members, yet the attending circumstances
during their visit to Japan at this time were no less
significant. To begin with, the Vanderlip party was
welcomed by a special organization called the "Welcome
Society of the American Guests." Prince Yoshihisa
Tokugawa, the son and heir of Yoshinobu Tokugawa
the last Shogun of the Tokugawa regime, was the
Honorary President of the Society and the Viscount
the President.

In the evening of their arrival at Tokyo an elaborate
welcome meeting was held at the Peers' Club. Formal
greetings were exchanged between the Viscount and Mr.

Vanderlip. As an entertainment a Noh drama was put on. Luncheon, garden and dinner parties were held almost every day and night under the auspices of the Premier, the President of the Tokyo Chamber of Commerce, and Baron Mitsui, and others.

Toward the close of the conference, Mr. Vanderlip and his colleagues prepared their farewell party at the Imperial Hotel. They and their ladies dressed in *kimono*. Many notables and their wives were invited to this function. It was a grand success in creating a cordial spirit between the hosts and guests. Mr. Clarke also gave a farewell entertainment one evening at the Imperial Hotel to quite a large select group of ladies and gentlemen. These functions as the by-products of the conference contributed as much towards understanding and amity of feeling as the conference itself.

What effect did these two conferences have upon the Referendum movement in California in the fall? The measure to prohibit Japanese immigrants owning land in California went through with a large number of votes. But it was stated that there might have been a still larger majority for the Referendum, if the publicity work which was originated in the Japanese American Unofficial Conferences had not been carried on against the movement.

The fourth visit to the States of Viscount Shibusawa was made in the fall of 1921 at the time of the Washington Conference. Ever since the close of the above two conferences, the Viscount's mind had been filled with the desire of solving Japanese American questions in a fundamental manner. He felt the Washington

Conference might offer an opportunity to solve them. He wanted to be in America at that time so as to prevail on the conference to take up Japanese American questions as a part of its deliberations. But he scrupulously avoided any occasion to be misconstrued by the American public as though he was a part of the official delegation. He came to America as the representative of the Japanese American Relations Committee which is a private institution. He was accompanied by Dr. Soyeda, Mr. Zumoto, and Mr. Horikoshi members of the Committee. He settled down in New York making his headquarters at the Hotel Plaza. Dr. Soyeda went on to Washington and served as a medium between the Viscount and the conference. The Viscount kept busy every day calling on old friends and receiving visitors in the Hotel. While in New York he paid his visit to Mrs. Theodore Roosevelt at Oyster Bay and offerred flowers at the tomb of her late husband. He called on President Butler and Mrs. Andrew Carnegie. He was twice invited by Judge and Mrs. Gary, once to a luncheon at their country home and once to a dinner at the city residence, at which time the table furniture from the plates to the coffee cups were pure gold. Later he made the comment that the gold utensils had been too much for his appetite! He was also invited to a dinner party under the auspices of Mr. and Mrs. L. L. Clarke, which was composed of Marquises, Viscounts, Barons, and their ladies, and business magnates, representing Italy, France, England and America. Mr. and Mrs. Frank A. Vanderlip entertained the Viscount and his party at luncheon and the theatre. Mr. A. Barton Hepburn, Mr. Charles Mitchell, and Mr. Thomas W. Lamont were other

friends who assured the Viscount their hearty cooperation
in bringing about closer relations between the two countries. He travelled to Rochester, N. Y. to make his
courtesy call on Mr. George Eastman and was royally
entertained by him and his friends, the leading citizens.
He went to Pittsburgh to offer a wreath at the tomb
of Mr. Henry J. Heinz and was very graciously received
by Mr. and Mrs. Howard Heinz as their house guest
for a night. Then the Viscount came to Philadelphia
to renew his acquaintance with ex-Ambassador Morris
and Mr. John Wanamaker. The latter received him
at his office in the department store. The Viscount
was to be his guest over the night. A big banquet was
held in honor of the Viscount. The evening was passed
very pleasantly. After all the guests had left, the
two old gentlemen fell into an endless conversation
until Mr. Rodman Wanamaker the son interposed to
have them go to bed. The next day was Sunday and
Mr. Wanamaker, superintendent of the Sunday School
of his church, the Bethany Presbyterian, took the Viscount into the church, and showed him the different
classes. Then the closing exercises came and the superintendent introduced the Viscount to the gathering.
The Viscount made a brief address which was followed
with the ceremony of the presentation of a Japanese
Bible from the school to the Viscount. Mr. Wanamaker had bought a Japanese Bible and had put on
it the Viscount's name in gold. On Monday the Viscount was to make his last call on Mr. Wanamaker and
went to the department store again. He was taken into
the art gallery where famous original paintings of Europe were displayed. In the midst of these art collec-

tions, Mr. Wanamaker was to present a souvenir to the
Viscount but on account of illness, he could not be
present. Mr. Frank A. Brown, the general secretary of
the National Sunday School organization and a very
close friend of Mr. Wanamaker, presented it to the Viscount on behalf of Mr. Wanamaker. The souvenir was
a Waltham gold watch of a special make. Anticipating
the visit of the Viscount long before, Mr. Wanamaker
had planned to demonstrate his genuine friendship in
this manner. On the back of the watch Eiichi Shibusawa in Japanese, a photograph of his autograph, was
engraved. The Viscount carried this gold watch until
his last day.

The names of Messrs. John Wanamaker, Henry
Heinz, and Frank A. Brown naturally call to our
memory the eighth World Sunday School Convention
held in Tokyo in October 1920. The Convention meets
every four years. The Seventh Convention was held
in Zurich in 1913, and Rev. Dr. Kozaki and Rev. Dr.
Ibuka attended it. Early in that year Mr. Heinz stopped
in Japan on his way to this Convention. Mr. Heinz,
Marquis Okuma, and Viscount Shibusawa met for a
social function, and the Viscount suggested that the
eighth World Sunday School Convention should be held
in Tokyo. Marquis Okuma seconded the suggestion.
This moved Mr. Heinz to the degree that he too endorsed
the plan to hold the next Convention in Japan.
Doctors Kozaki and Ibuka were authorized to extend
to the Zurich Convention a formal invitation to hold
its eighth Convention in Tokyo in 1916. The invitation was extended and accepted, and so Tokyo was to
be the seat of this great Convention in 1916.

On the return of Drs. Kozaki and Ibuka, the report of the meeting was held at the residence of the Marquis in October 1913. This meeting resulted in the creation of the Patrons' Association of the Eighth World Sunday School Convention in Tokyo, and during the next month the Association formed regulations to guide and govern the work of the preparation for the coming Convention. But in 1914 the European War broke out and it at once cast a gloom over the prospective gathering.

In the year 1915 the Viscount was commissioned by the Federated Chambers of Commerce of Japan to attend the Panama Memorial Exposition held in San Francisco. Also he was requested to confer with the authorities of the World Sunday School Association.

The Viscount met with such leaders as Messrs. Wanamaker, Heinz, Brown, and Kinnear in Philadelphia. It was decided in this group council that the Convention should be held in Tokyo as soon as the War in Europe ceased. The Viscount returned home at the close of the year. The armistice was declared in 1918 and the activity of the Patrons' Association was begun afresh. The officers of the Association were Marquis Okuma, President; Viscount Shibusawa, Baron Sakatani, Mayor Tajiri, and Mr. Fujiyama, President of Tokyo Chamber of Commerce, vice-Presidents.

Two thousand delegates representing thirty three countries were to meet in Tokyo, with additional home delegates numbering one thousand, making the total three thousand. Hence the vital question was how to secure a meeting hall large enough to hold this number. The authorities decided to build a new hall to accommodate the Convention on a vacant lot near the Tokyo Station. A large wooden building of three stories was prepared stuccoed in white, attractive both inside and out. It was completed toward the close of September. Inspection was made and everything found satisfactory. But alas, in the afternoon of the 5th of October at 3 : 50 it took fire and was reduced to ashes. The worst of it was that the Convention was to be opened that very evening. Two questions called for a speedy decision. One was where to hold the opening meeting, and the other was where the sessions of the Convention for the coming ten days or so should be held. The first question was solved by making quick arrangements to use the assembly halls of the Y. M. C. A. and the Salvation Army Headquarters. The second which taxed the brain of the leaders was happily solved by renting the Imperial Theatre for the sessions of the Convention. It was an exceedingly delicate matter to stop the performances going on every night in the theatre, but the Directors of the theatre headed by Baron Okura unanimously decided to suspend the plays during the Convention, undergoing heavy financial risk as well as the complaints of the patrons. But no murmur was raised on the part of the spectators. They were sympathetic with the leaders. Thus the announcement of the use of the Imperial Theatre during the Convention was made while the opening exercises were going on. An unspeakable sense of gratitude and relief came to the entire Convention, and that feeling formed the keynote of the daily sessions. And the eighth Convention of the World Sunday School Association went into history with a fine record.

From Philadelphia the Viscount proceeded to Washington, D. C., where the Disarmament Conference was going on. He went to Mount Vernon to pay his respects to the memory of George Washington and offered a wreath at the hero's tomb. Once more he returned to New York and after spending a few days there left the city for good. He came to Washington for a second time and attended the final session of the conference, in which the Anglo-Japanese Alliance was forever buried. The Japanese Delegation thought it improper to bring into the conference Japanese American questions as the conference included several European Powers.

Thus the proposition of the Viscount was unaccepted. He was now ready to start on the return journey. He wanted to take in New Orleans and thence to proceed toward Los Angeles. Just on the verge of his departure a telegram reached the Viscount. It was a message sent by Dr. R. B. Teusler of New York, requesting the Viscount to be present at the gathering of the American Advisory Council of St. Luke's International Medical Center. His attendants, including the physician in charge, agreed that it was not wise for the Viscount to go back to New York. But he set his mind to go and took the train for New York to be on time.

Needless to say that Dr. Teusler was exceedingly pleased to have the Viscount present on this occasion.

It was in December that the Viscount and his small party reached Los Angeles. It was the rainy season in that section of California. A big reception was given under the auspices of the Los Angeles Chamber of Commerce in honor of the Viscount. The Japanese community also gave a brilliant banquet. One afternoon he drove to San Diego to visit Mr. Lyman Gage who had been a member of the Vanderlip party. The road was badly wrecked by the rain, but he safely arrived and spent the night at the Hotel Coronardo. The next morning Mr. Gage, eighty seven years of age, drove his own car to the hotel and chatted with the Viscount for about an hour.

On this return trip the Viscount visited Fresno, Sacramento, and Livingston, where he met both Japanese and Americans. On the North Pacific Coast he visited Portland and Seattle where he was warmly welcomed by his old friends such as Mr. O. M. Clark of Portland and Mr. J. D. Lowman of Seattle. The leaders of the Japanese Communities in the two cities gave the Viscount a most cordial welcome.

He returned to San Francisco at the close of the year 1921. He spent his New Year's Eve and New Year's Day in Fairmont Hotel, waiting for the steamer to take him to Honolulu.

On the day before he left San Francisco, the Japanese Relations Committee of the San Francisco Chamber of Commerce, headed by Mr. Wallace M. Alexander, gave a farewell luncheon to the Viscount. Table speeches were made, and Mr. Alexander presented to the Viscount on behalf of the Japanese Relations Committee of San Francisco Chamber of Commerce, a souvenir of a gold tablet on which a statement of appreciation was engraved. It reads :

Presented to
Viscount Eiichi Shibusawa
by his friends
the Japanese Relations Committee
of the
San Francisco Chamber of Commerce
in grateful recognition of his untiring
and unselfish devotion and zeal
in the interest of closer and more
friendly relations between the peoples
of
Japan and the United States.
January
1922

The next day the city papers mentioned both speeches. A lady who was staying at the Fairmont, occupying a suite of rooms, telephoned the Viscount and requested him to send to her his secretary. The Viscount acquiesced and the secretary was sent to her. She told him how deeply she was impressed by reading the newspaper account of the speech the Viscount made the day before, especially the expression of " carrying with him his coffin." She told him that, though a woman, she would do her utmost in the same work, and that as a pledge, she would present to the Viscount a special keepsake which she desired to be fastened to his watch-chain. Struck by her zeal and eloquence, the secretary received the charm on behalf of the Viscount taking it for granted that he would accept such a high compliment. The Viscount received it in good humor and pursuant to her request he ever after wore it fastened to his watch-chain. As a return compliment, the Viscount presented to her a book containing a collection

President Wilson.

Charter Members of the Japan

Organized

Mr. S. Asano.

Dr. M. Anesaki.

Viscount E. Shibusawa.

Mr. Z. Horikoshi.

Baron R. Kondo.

Count K. Kaneko.

Mr. M. Kushida.

Baron K. Okura.

Baron Y. Sakatani.

Mr. S. Shimada.

Mr. G. Shimur

Dr. J. Soyeda.

Mr. B. Nakano.

Baron T. Furukawa.

Mr. S Hayakawa.

Mr. J. Inouye.

Viscount Y. Mishima.

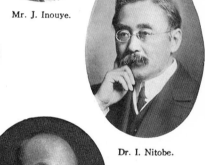

Baron I. Morimura.

Dr. I. Nitobe.

Mr. T. Shidachi.

Mr. S. Takada.

Baron S. Uryu.

Mr. M. Zumoto.

Present Members of the Japanese

Mr. T. Akashi.

Dr. M. Anesaki.

Mr. S. Asano.

Mr. S. Eguchi.

Mr. E. Fukai.

Mr. K. Fukui.

Baron T. Furukawa.

Mr. K. Hara.

Mr. T. Hara.

Dr. T. Harada.

Mr. I. Horai.

Mr. R. Ichinomiya.

Mr. T. Isaka.

American Relations Committee

Mr. K. Kagami.

Count K. Kaneko.

Mr. M. Kushida.

Baron I. Morimura.

Baron K. Okura.

Mr. N. Otani.

Mr. T. Shimizu.

Mr. Y. Takaki.

Baron Y. Togo.

Baron S. Uryu.

Dr. S. Yamada.

Mr. T. Yuki.

Mr. M. Zumoto.

Members of Executive Council

Viscount K. Ishii.

Baron Y. Sakatani.

Mr. R. Fujiyama.

Secretaries

Dr. B. Hattori.

Mr. K. Shiraishi.

Dr. K. Obata.

of the fifty-three scenic pictures along the Tokaido the highway the ancient Daimyo used to travel between Kyoto and Yedo.

The Viscount later found that the lady occupied an important post in the municipal government of San Francisco during the World War, and that she was a cousin of one of the San Francisco friends of the Viscount.

The final task in the voluntary goodwill mission of the Viscount on his way back home was to visit Honolulu where he had many influential friends both American and Japanese. The special concern of the Viscount's visit to Hawaii at this time was to soothe the ruffled feelings of the capitalists who were sorely tried by the persistent strikes of the Japanese employees in the sugar cane plantations. The strikes were well planned. They were widespread, and doggedly persistent, so much so that some of the employers came to harbor a strong suspicion that the Japanese Government might have been operating behind the scene. These strikes took place in January 1920, and were finally settled in June. But their evil effect upon the employers continued for a long time. The Viscount wanted to quench the fire of smouldering discontent in the hearts of the employers, assuring them that he would strongly advise the Japanese leaders not to repeat such unfortunate social and racial discord in the future. In the midst of luncheons, banquets, and teas put up in his honor, the Viscount accomplished this particular mission.

Thus far we have devoted our discussions of the international activity of the Viscount to China and America as typical cases. However his international interest extended to nearly all the countries of the world. He entertained the idea that the world's peace and order could be maintained if America, England, and Japan could be united in friendly relationship.

So he paved the way for creating and sending a party of Japanese business men to England. The economic mission to England of Baron Dan and his party in 1921 was the result of the Viscount's effort.

We can also see his international services in the following capacities: chairman of the Armenian Sufferers Relief Committee; president of the Siberian Captives Relief Society; president of the Association of Consolation for the Sick and Wounded Soldiers of the Allied Nations; chief-director of the Franco-Japanese Society; chairman of the Japanese Roumanian Commercial Relations Committees; president of the Japan-India Society; and president of the League of Nations Association of Japan.

The reputation of the trustworthiness and dependability of Viscount Shibusawa as an international figure could be seen from the following two facts: the establishment in the Tokyo Imperial University through the Viscount of the Hepburn chair of the constitution, history, and diplomacy of the United States of America, in December, 1917; and the invitation of the American Government to the Viscount to act as arbitrator in case a difficulty might arise concerning the exchange of steel and steamships between America and Japan.

It is very interesting to know that Mr. A. Barton Hepburn's early interest in Japan was created by his distant cousin, Rev. J. C. Hepburn, a Presbyterian missionary early in the Meiji Era, and the author of Hepburn's Japanese-English Dictionary. Mr. Hepburn was the chairman of the Board of Directors of the Chase National Bank at the time he conceived this beneficent enterprise of contributing one hundred and twenty thousand yen to the University. By this time he was known as one of New York's prominent financiers. He was a business man, but his mind was philosophically inclined. He had been watching the turn which the great European War was taking and the way his country was affected. He felt very keenly the madness and cruelty of the war which was apparently bringing no good to any land. But quietly philosophising and scrutinizing some of the causes of the world war, he came to the conclusion that the lack of true understanding and the existence of misunderstanding among nations were the main causes of the war. In this mood of of contemplation he turned his thought to the relation of America and Japan and saw that they had so far been good neighbors historically and geographically.

He further saw that it should be the duty of leaders in both countries to keep intact this beautiful international relationship and never allow it to be disturbed by such a terrible occurence as was transpiring in Europe. He was convinced that the fundamental and permanent measure or precaution to be resorted to is the constant effort to promote and spread mutual understanding through higher education. Thus Mr. Hepburn sent a long letter to the Viscount through Mr. R. Ichinomiya the manager of the New York Branch of Yokohama Specie Bank.

The Viscount was pleasantly surprised by such a far-reaching letter from his American fellow-banker.

He took up the matter with President Yamakawa who was much pleased with the spirit and gift of Mr. Hepburn. The President took the proper steps and the chair was speedily created. Having heard the news of the matter from the Viscount, Mr. Hepburn was highly pleased with the outcome. The Viscount reported to Mr. Hepburn that the fund would be handled most carefully and profitably by its trustees, who were Ambassador Morris, Viscount Ishii, Baron Megata, Mr. Junnosuke Inouye, and the Viscount himself. Later on Viscount Ishii was appointed an ambassador, Baron Megata passed on, and Mr. J. Inouye was busy. All this made the Viscount's responsibility as a trustee heavier, but he bore the burden until his death.

Mr. Shiraishi makes a cogent statement in his book about the Viscount under the heading of " The Japanese-American Ship-Steel Exchange Arbitrator," He says :

"...One may be inclined to believe that, as the matter of the Japanese-American Ship-Steel Exchange was a temporary measure for which there was no occasion for the Viscount to act as an arbitrator, it is unnecessary to pay special attention to it. But he would sadly fail to catch the meaning of the invitation extended by the American Government to the Viscount to take up that post—the invitation which is a clear evidence of how universally he was trusted by the Americans and of how strong a bond of friendship he established between America and Japan."

Its meaning becomes deeper when the magnitude of the subject-matter for the arbitration is seen from what it involved—namely the matter of constructing thirty ships on the part of Japan and of selling to Japan 122,921 tons of steel on the American side, and of paying to the Japanese ship-builders the price for the ships built about $ 43,023,750. No wonder that Ambassador Morris in his official letter addressed to the Viscount in regard to this important matter has this brief but significant sentence :

" I highly congratulate Your Excellency for your personality and prestige, which command the deep confidence not only of your own people, but also of the American people."

There are three events which should receive due recognition before this chapter is closed. They are the erection of the huge monument of Townsend Harris in the premises of Gyokusen-ji of Kakisaki, Shimoda, Izu, on the first day of October, 1927; the observance in Uyeno Park in 1928 of the fiftieth anniversary of the visit to Tokyo of General and Mrs. Grant, by erecting a monument; and the reception meeting held in Seinen Kan in 1929, under the auspices of Japan International Children's Friendship Society to welcome more than thirteen thousand American dolls sent from American friends sponsored by Dr. Sidney L. Gulick.

These three events brought together representative men and women of the two countries to fraternize with each other, deeply impressed by the significance of each event. This is specially true with the unveiling ceremony of the Harris monument in Kakisaki, because no such gathering of high dignitaries of the two countries under such happy auspices could have taken place in the past or could occur in the future in so remote and secluded a place as Kakisaki. In this connection, it should be stated to the credit of the generosity of the America-Japan Society that the renovation of the temple was made possible by the contribution of a large amount of money from the Society in response to the appeal made by the Viscount to Prince Tokugawa, the President of the Society, in behalf of the temple. The entire responsibility of erecting the monument rested upon Ambassador Bancroft, his friend, Mr. Henry M. Wolf of Chicago, and Viscount Shibusawa. The reader will find historical interest in the past by reading the inscriptions on the monument on its two faces. The major part of the inscription on the back was given in Chapter IV, but as one-third of it was not quoted there, the entire inscription is given here:

INSCRIPTION ON THE FRONT FACE OF THE MONUMENT

" In Memory of
TOWNSEND HARRIS
American Consul-General

who by the Treaty of Yedo July 29, 1858 opened Japan to the world and on this spot September 4, 1856 raised the first consular flag in this empire and here resided until November 23, 1857.*

Erected by
Viscount E. Shibusawa
Edgar A. Bancroft
(Late American Ambassador to Japan)
and
Henry M. Wolf, of Chicago.
September 4, 1927
Paragraph from the Consul's Diary:

---

*He left Shimoda finally on June 30, 1859.

" Thursday September 4, 1856. Slept very little from excitement and mosquitoes; the latter are enormous in size. Men on shore to put up my flag staff. Heavy lot. Slow work. Spar falls, breaks cross-trees, fortunately no one hurt. At last get a reinforcement from the ship, flag staff erected. Men form a ring round it, and half past two p. m. of this day I hoist the first consular flag ever seen in this empire. Grave reflections. Ominous of change. Undoubted beginning of the end. Query,—if for real good of Japan? "

TRANSLATION OF THE INSCRIPTION IN JAPANESE ON THE BACK OF THE MONUMENT

" Townsend Harris, the first Consul-General of the United States of America to reside in Japan, arrived at Shimoda, Idzu, in August 1856. In those days, our people of all classes were poorly informed about the world's affairs, and most of them took it for granted that all foreign Powers were insatiably greedy and aggressive. Nothing daunted by this unfavorable atmosphere, he spared no pains to point out to our authorities the advantage of starting commercial connection with foreign nations, and explained to them the established usages and conventions of international intercourse. His painstaking efforts at enlightening the minds of the officials of the Shogunate were finally crowned with success in concluding a commercial treaty between Japan and America. This formed a model for the treaties which the Shogunate subsequently negotiated with other Powers. As a matter of fact, however, there were not wanting among our countrymen people who entertained toward Mr. Harris a deep feeling of indignation, because they thought that the treaty which he had succeeded in arranging was won by intrigue and chicanery on his part.

" In the meantime, Mr. Harris was promoted to the post of Minister Plenipotentiary and his official residence was moved to Edo. The Shogunate was then increasingly involved in difficulties, domestic as well as foreign. To add to its troubles, the Representatives of the Powers, generally lacking proper understading of Japan and of things Japanese, not infrequently acted in an arbitray and arrogant manner, thereby aggravating the public agitation against the Government. But so far as Mr. Harris was concerned, he always conducted himself fairly and squarely, constantly showing his sympathy to Japan. His honorable attitude was most strikingly demonstrated in connection with the death of Mr. Henry C. J. Heusken, his official interpreter, who was assassinated in January 1861 by rowdies on the bank of the Furukawa in Azabu. All the foreign Ministers, with one exception, were highly wrought up by the incident, and blaming the Shogunate for its incompetency to protect them, they closed their legations at Edo and withdrew to Kanagawa. But the American Minister who happened to be the one most intimately concerned, did not approve the step taken by his colleagues of the other Powers. He refused to stir from his official quarters at the Zempukuji Temple, but calmly attended to his duties as usual as if wholly unconcerned about his own safety. The courageous and magnanimous attitude taken by Mr. Harris on this critical occasion made a strong appeal to the imagination of our people, who were now convinced of the genuineness of his sentiment toward them, and who from that moment began to put trust in America as a true friend of Japan. Japan and America owe a heavy debt of gratitude to Mr. Harris whose noble personality thus initiated the relationship of mutual friendship which has happily united the two nations during these seventy years.

"For this reason I had a conference sometime ago with the late Mr. Edgar A. Bancroft, the then American Ambassador to Japan, and his friend Mr. Henry M. Wolf of Chicago, who was staying with him, in connection with a plan for perpetuating the memory of America's first envoy to Japan. The plan we agreed upon was the erection of a monument at the Gyokusenji Temple, Shimoda, Idzu, where Mr. Harris set up the first consular flag of the United States on Japanese soil. But to my great sorrow, Ambassador Bancroft died during his incumbency, and Mr. Wolf returned to his homeland. Thus the responsibility of carrying out the plan we had agreed upon devolved upon me alone.

"While in my youth I was exerting myself in the affairs of my country, I heard much of the achievements of Mr. Harris, and have always held him in high admiration for his lofty character. Hence, when I journeyed through the United States in 1909 as the Chairman of the Honorary Commercial Commission of Japan, I made special efforts to visit his grave in an old cemetery in the city of Brooklyn, and reverently laid a wreath at his tomb. The time of my visit there was well nigh toward the close of autumn, and the maple leaves overshadowing the grave were almost turned to scarlet, as if testifying to the genuineness of the great heart lying underneath. Buried in a deep reverie I found it not easy to tear myself away from the sacred spot. I then composed two poems, one in the Japanese and the other in the Chinese style and dedicated them to the memory of the admired hero.

"Now in erecting this monument in honor of Mr. Harris, a paragraph from his diary is inscribed on the front face, as it affords us an insight into the conscientious catholicity of mind with which he grappled with his difficult task. On the back, I have thus far tried to outline the circumstances which led me to take part in this undertaking. To complete the sketch, I wish to quote my two poems above referred to—all this by way of a humble tribute to his precious memory :

"*Late in autumn in the moss grown grave yard,*
A traveller from afar mournfully stands at the tomb,
Lo the sunset glow transfuses the overshadowing maple into scarlet,
An apt symbol of the genuine heart of the ancient hero."

"*The visitor at the tomb*
A glimpse of the hero's heart caught
In the maple aglow with the sinking sun."

Viscount Eiichi Shibusawa,
Grand Cordon of the Order of the Rising Sun,
Senior Grade of Third Class Court Rank."

The Japanese American friendship dolls sent from America were distributed to every primary school throughout Japan, the occasion having had its own welcome ceremony. Then later, the Japan International Children's Friendship Society through the school authorities appealed to every pupil of the primary schools in Japan to contribute a penny per capita, so that some kind of a return courtesy could be shown to the American friends who sent so many lovely dolls. The society invited the best known doll makers and ordered them to make Japanese dolls corresponding in number to the States of America—48.

They were made and the public were invited to inspect them for a few days in one of the department stores.

Mr. R. Sekiya, a high official in the Department of Education served as the vice-president of the society from the beginning and it fell to him to carry these forty-eight Japanese dolls to the United States.

Mr. Sekiya and the dolls received an enthusiastic welcome in large cities.

Thus what looked at a time to be a trivial enterprise receiving cold criticisms grew into an affair of international significance of an enormous proportion hardly anticipated in the beginning.

In these days of exclusive and extreme nationalism all over the world, minimizing internationalism, it is highly refreshing and strongly heartening to recall the

memory of one, in whose life nationalism and internationalism were most effectively developed and blended
in a perfect harmony—Viscount E. Shibusawa.

CHAPTER XI

STUDENT OF LITERATURE:
PROSE AND POETRY
(Chinese and Japanese)

IN the closing period of the feudalism of the Tokugawa regime, the cultural interest of the samurai
and the well-to-do farmers was confined mostly to
the gekken and jyujitsu or jyudo as military arts, and
penmanship, reading, composition, calculation (soroban),
and poetry as literary arts. Viscount Shibusawa as the
only son of one of the leading farmers in the village
received both military and literary trainings in his early
youth.

He had native capacity for achievement in any of
the arts. He could have been a first rate writer if he
had devoted his time and energy to literature. He
could have made himself a poet both of the Japanese
and Chinese styles, if he had made up his mind to
cultivate this particular line of literary taste. But his
supreme interest rested in the promotion of the general
welfare of mankind.

To him the military and literary arts, however fas-
cinating and tempting it was to indulge in them, were
nothing more than means to an end. His interest in
humanity was supreme, and everything else was subor-
dinate to that interest. Consequently, anything that would
subserve human interests appealed to the mind of the
Viscount in proportion to the degree of the intensity
of that appeal.

The exquisite taste of the Viscount in literature must

have been created in this way. Of course we should
never ignore the fact that his early habit of reading
classical books had so fashioned his mind as to find
delight in the reading itself. The style of his expression in his ordinary conversation was naturally influenced
by his reading. His incessant and extensive reading
supported by his extraordinary power of memory made
him both a choice conversationalist and a good writer.
In public address, he was at his best when he spoke
extemporaneously. His speech was invariably systematic,
graceful, coherent, and well-balanced.

Except on strictly formal occasions, he always spoke
without a manuscript. His literary habits may best be
seen in his correspondence with his foreign friends.

When a letter came addressed to the Viscount from
one of his American friends, it was first translated by
his English secretary into Japanese. Then it was submitted to the regular secretary who made quite careful corrections to make it plainer and smoother. Then
it was typed.

This typed letter clipped together with the original
was presented to him. He read it, and as he read it
corrected the sentences in the letter—here and there.
When he got through with it he signed his full name
to it, giving the date of his inspection. If a reply to
it was needed, he wrote down " to be answered." Often
he gave oral instructions to his English secretary for
the answer. Then the secretary prepared the answer
according to the instruction. He took it to the regular
secretary who corrected and polished the whole composition. It was typed.

Now it was ready for the final inspection in which

several changes or additions were made. This was translated into English and was sent to the friend. Therefore in the files of the letters for translation the pencil corrections are conspicuously seen. The process was a tedious and circuitous one, but the Viscount never gave up this method for years.

Often the manuscripts of his public addresses taken by stenographers were submitted to him, and he took pains to go over them and correct them. He read the proof sheets and made other corrections to suit his taste.

When he prepared a pamphlet or a booklet, he not only corrected the manuscript before it went to the printer's office, but read the proof. This was not all. He often sent it to a recognized scholar for further correction and approval.

Another indication of his exquisite taste for literary style could be seen from his habit of committing to memory beautiful and inspiring sentences in famous essays and discourses. Needless to say that he knew by heart Lun yu (論語), which is to us a choice book both for its sound ethical teaching and literary beauty.

He frequently recited a famous verse composed by one of the immortal poets of China. The verse is known as Chih Pi Fu (赤壁賦), and the poet's name is Su Tung Po (蘇東坡). The poet lived in the latter part of the eleventh century A.D. under the Sung Dynasty. The poet Su made several visits to Chih Pi Fu a scenic spot in Huang Cheu (黄州), when he was exiled to that province, evidently to take his mind off from the world's troubles. He composed two odes on the same subject Chih Pi Fu and it is on the first one that universal praise as a fine literary product is lavished. This is the one the Viscount used to indulge in reciting.

It will be impossible to translate this wonderful verse into a foreign language in the poetical form, but its general meaning may be brought out in a prose form. How great an esteem this verse had from Chinese scholars can be seen from the comment a famous scholar, Hsich Fang Te (謝枋得) the author of a book entitled Wen Chang Kuei Fan (文章軌範) who lived in the thirteenth century, made on it. He says:

" No one short of superhuman talent and superb knowledge could compose this verse. Supremely pure and free of human taint, it expresses the sublime sentiment of one who by riding on the chariot of clouds or taking the wings of the wind, reached the highest heaven whence he looks down upon the whole universe."

We Japanese read Chinese poems in a different way from what the Chinese do, placing our emphasis on their meaning, rather than on the rhythm or music.

In the following pages, the author will quote the Chih Pi Fu, and poems composed by the Viscount, giving to them free translation in English.

He may also bring in a few Japanese poems composed by the Viscount.

前赤壁賦　　蘇東坡

壬戌之秋七月既望蘇子與客泛舟遊於赤壁之下。
清風徐來水波不興舉酒屬客誦明月之詩歌窈窕
之章少焉月出於東山之上徘徊於斗牛之間白露
橫江水光接天縱一葦之所如凌萬頃之茫然浩浩
乎如馮虛御風而不知其所止飄飄乎如遺世獨立。
羽化而登仙於是飲酒樂甚扣舷而歌之歌曰桂棹
兮蘭槳擊空明兮泝流光渺渺兮予懷望美人兮天
一方客有吹洞簫者倚歌而和之其聲嗚嗚然如怨
如慕如泣如訴餘音嫋嫋不絕如縷舞幽壑之潛蛟。
泣孤舟之嫠婦蘇子愀然正襟危坐而問客曰何爲
其然也客曰月明星稀烏鵲南飛此非曹孟德之詩
乎西望夏口東望武昌山川相繆鬱乎蒼蒼此非孟
德之困於周郎者乎方其破荊州下江陵順流而東
也舳艫千里旌旗蔽空釃酒臨江橫槊賦詩固一世

之雄也而今安在哉況吾與子漁樵于江渚之上侶
魚鰕而友麋鹿駕一葉之扁舟舉匏樽以相屬寄蜉
蝣於天地渺滄海之一粟哀吾生之須臾羨長江之
無窮挾飛仙以遨遊抱明月而長終知不可乎驟得
託遺響于悲風蘇子曰客亦知夫水與月乎逝者如
斯而未嘗往也盈虛者如彼而卒莫消長也蓋將自
其變者而觀之則天地曾不能以一瞬自其不變者
而觀之則物與我皆無盡也而又何羨乎且夫天地
之間物各有主苟非吾之所有雖一毫而莫取惟江
上之清風與山間之明月耳得之而爲聲目遇之而
成色取之無禁用之不竭是造物者之無盡藏也而
吾與子之所共適客喜而笑洗盞更酌肴核既盡杯
盤狼藉相與枕藉乎舟中不知東方既白。

Souvenir Watch.

Memorial Tablet.

Harris Monument and Memorial Photograph at Gyokusen Ji.

Harris Monument at Gyokusen Ji.

Prose Translation of the Ode on Chih Pi Fu
by Su Tung Po

" One autumn evening next to the full moonnight I
with my guest indulged in a boat ride on the river
along the Chih Pi Fu. A gentle breath sweeps over
the stream but not a ripple stirs. I opened a flask of
nectar and exchanged cups with the guest. I sang the
" Poem of Bright Moon," and a " Verse of Beauty."
Meanwhile the moon rose above the eastern mountain
and gracefully moved between the Great Bear and Aquila.
A white mist thinly veiled the river. Yonder heaven
kisses the water. Embarking in a small boat, we sailed
on and on over the ocean-like river. It looks as if we
were being carried on through an endless expanse riding
on the wind and were entering into a mystic region far
above the world, being transformed into winged creatures.
Then again we drank the wine and highly enjoyed our
pleasure. Beating the side of the boat, I sang the song :

> Let the oar speed the boat,
> Let the helm steer it against
>   the shining water ;
> Away runs my thought to the Court,
> Where once I mingled with high
>   minded courtiers.

" The guest began to play his flute tuning it to my
song. The music sounded as though it were expressing
sentiments of reproach, yearning, weeping, and appealing.
Its whispering cadence like a silken thread lingers long.

" If a dragon, living deep in the mountains, heard the music, it might be stirred to rise and dance. Were a widow in a lonely boat to listen to it, she might sob over it. Saddened in my heart, I braced myself and asked the guest why this was so. He said to me :

' The moon shines bright. The light of most of the stars is drowned in her brilliancy. The night-heron flies off towards the south.'

" Is this not a poem composed by Tsao Meng Te, a mighty warrior, hinting at his own valour. Towards the West there lies Hsia Kou and towards the East, Wu Chang. Between them mountains and waters intermingle. The entire stretch is covered with green groves. But is this not an old battle field where even this mighty hero was defeated by Cheu Lang? When Cheu Lang conquered Chin Cheu and was coming down to Chiang Ling towards the East speeded by the swift current, his boats one following after another stretched to a great distance and the banners of the boats covered the sky. Cheu Lang taking the wine with him into the boat sailed down the river. With a long sword on his left side, he composed a poem. Was he not a rare hero? But where is he now? He is forgotten. The guest further speaks and says :

' You and I are no heroes. We are none but fishermen and hunters. We are friends of fish and deer. We live like a May-fly which is born in the morning and dies in the evening. We are like a tiny grain floating on an ocean. It is beyond our present reach to indulge in luxurious pleasure, flying like birds and to enjoy the endless brightness of the moon. This is why the faint cadence mixed with the autumnal wind creates

in our hearts an unspeakable sadness.   To this I
answered thus :

' Do you know too the nature of the water and the
moon ?   The drops of water may pass on, but there is
no end to the water itself.   The moon may wax and
wane, but the moon as such remains forever.   If you
look into a thing from the viewpoint of change, heaven
and earth do not pause even for a second, but from the
standpoint of permanence, things and I are endless.
Why, then, do we envy anything?   Moreover, most
things in the universe belong to their masters.   What
does not belong to us, should not be exploited by us.
But the cool wind that sweeps over the river can be
felt, and the moon which shines over mountains can be
seen.   None can prevent us from enjoying them, and
there is no wearing out in their use.   These are inexhaustible sources the Creator has bestowed upon us.
You and I enjoy them to our fill.'

" At this, the guest was merry and smiled.   He washed
the cup and again began to drink.   We drank and ate
till the fish and fruits were all gone.   We grew so stupid
that the cups and plates were left scattered, and we fell
asleep in the boat, only to wake up when the eastern
sky became bright with the sunrise."

The next poem is of the same type with the one we
have just finished.   This was composed by the Viscount
when he was nineteen years old and busy with his farm
life.   The reader will be reminded by reading this poem
of the strong moral stamina which characterized the life
of the Viscount.

內山峽

澁澤青淵

襄山蜿蜒如波浪。西接信山相送迎。奇險就中內山峽。
天然崔嵬如刱成。刀陰耕夫青淵子。販鬻向信取路程。
小春初八好風景。蒼松紅楓草鞋輕。三尺腰刀涉棧道。
一卷肩書攀峥嵘。涉攀益深險彌酷。奇巖怪石磊磊横。
勢衝青天攘臂躋。遠近細辨濃與淡。幾青幾紅更渺茫。
四望風色十分晴。探盡眞趣游子行。恍惚此時覺有得。
始知壯觀存奇險。君不見遁世淸心士。吐氣吞露求蓬
慨然拍掌歎一聲。汲汲名利客朝奔暮走。趁浮榮不識中間存
瀛又不見將一隅誤終生。大道由來隨處在天下萬事成
大道徒將一隅誤終生。
於誠父子惟親君臣義。友敬相待弟與兄彼輩著眼不
到此。可憐自甘拂人情篇成長吟澗谷應風捲落葉滿
山鳴。

UCHIYAMA GORGE

SEI-EN SHIBUSAWA

"The long stretch of the mountain ranges of Jōshyū presents the appearance of mighty waves. Their western crest overlaps with the mountain of Shinshyū. The entire scene looks sublime, and the most sablime is the Uchiyama Gorge. The cliffs on both sides stand steep like high walls. Sei-en, from a village on the bank of the river Tone, journeys on toward Shinshyū for a business deal. It was the season when the scenery in the mountains was at its best. Green pines and red maples made his steps brisk. Carrying a sword by his side, he climbs up a ladderlike road, and bearing a book on his back, he treads a perilous path. The higher he mounts, the more fearful grows the climb. Rocks and stones of weird forms lie around. His enthusiasm burns in him like a prairie fire, and he climbs up brushing away every obstacle in the path. He rises high till he vies with the clouds above. At about two o'clock in the afternoon he reached the summit. Clouds were dispersed and all around was clear and bright. Far and near the colours of the mountains became distinct, some light and others dark. In the four directions as far as eye can see, greens and reds intermingle. There for the first time he realizes that the sublimest of all views are to be enjoyed on high mountains. Thus he reached the height of indulgence in true pleasure, and for a moment fell into a trance during which he was inspired. Coming back to his senses he was greatly stirred and spoke thus :

'Have you not seen a hermit of high thinking? He takes pride in a solitary life, talking sharply and living plainly. Then again, have you not seen a seeker of gain and fame? He is busy from morn till eve to attain an ephemeral glory. They know not that a true way lies between the two extremes, and spoil their whole life by falling into the rut of a narrow view of life. A true way has existed everywhere from time immemorial. It is sincerity. Everything under heaven is controlled by it. Affection between parent and child; fairness between master and servant; and mutual respect between elder and younger brothers, are nothing but the application of sincerity to different relations and circumstances. Their eyes fail to see this truth. They naively run counter to humanity.'

"When he loudly sang this poem the entire valley re-echoed the song and the whole mountain rang with the mournful rustle which scattered the leaves of the trees."

We will mention a few shorter poems which have international significance. He composed two poems on George Washington; one each on Commodore Perry, Townsend Harris, and Theodore Roosevelt, when he paid his respects to the tombs of these immortal heroes.

The poem on Townsend Harris has already been mentioned in this book in connection with the monument dedicated to his memory.

ON GEORGE WASHINGTON

一。
國初大憲燦明章。
錢石心兼錦繡腸。
民衆到今懷舊德。
古墳無樹不甘棠。

二。
聯邦到處足觀光。
來弔英魂感更長。
靈域不關都市熱。
茅茨風冷鎖針陽。

I

Kokusho taiken meishō san tari,
　　Tesseki no kokoro kinshyū no harawata wo kanu,
Minshyū imani itarumade kyūtoku wo omō,
　　Kofun ki to shite kanshō narazaru nashi.

II

Rempō itarutokoro kankō taru
　　Kitarite eikon wo chosureba kan sarani nagashi,
Rei-iki kansezu toshi no netsu
　　Bōji kaze hiyayaka ni shite shayō ni sasu.

I

The Father of the nation laid its foundation firm,
  He blended unbending will with a tender heart,
The people till this day sustains to him profound gratitude,
  Every tree surrounding his tomb praises his virtue.

II

Every place in the States is worthy of visit,
  But here, pondering over the memory of the great
    soul, my feeling deepens;
This sacred spot transcends the fever of the city,
  The sinking sun marshals the cool wind to sweep
    over the greensward.

ON COMMODORE PERRY.

併將暗淚濺墳塋
日暮蕭々風送雨
來與幽魂訂舊盟
異洲早已記英名

Ishyū hayaku sudeni eimei wo kisu;
  Kitarite yūkon to tomoni kyūmei wo tadasu;
Nichibo shōshō kaze ame wo okuru;
  Anrui wo awase motte fun-ei ni sosogu.

This warrior sailor distinguished himself abroad long ago:
  Here to the great soul my homage I do pay;
The sun-set clouds send showers down;
  Tears mingling with the rain fall on the tomb.

ON PRESIDENT THEODORE ROOSEVELT

欽　憶　利　迭
將　起　器　裁
英　當　誰　兵
略　年　能　備
拜　婁　試　事
靈　氏　錯　還
壇　業　盤　難

Tagai ni heibi wo saisu koto mata katashi
　　Riki tare ka yoku sakuban wo kokoromin,
Omoi okosu tōnen ro shi no gyō,
　　Eiryaku wo kinshi motte reidan wo haisu.

Disarmament is a difficult task,
　　Who can cut this Gordian knot?
What if he were still alive at this time?
　　Recalling his superior statecraft I bow before his tomb.

ON A NEW YEAR MORN IN SAN FRANCISCO

金　米　客　不
門　壽　裏　嫌
迎　算　韶　無
得　來　光　酒
太　猶　亦　答
平　缺　覺　佳
春　五　新　辰

Kirawazu sake no Kashin ni kotōru naki wo.
　　Kakuri shōkō mata shin wo oboyu,
Beiju samshi kitareba nao go wo kaku,
　　Kinmon mukae etari taihei no haru.

Never mind if there is no nectar to felicitate the New
Year morn ;
There is something refreshing in spending a
happy day abroad ;
The eighty third milestone in life's journey being passed,
The traveller welcomes the early spring of
the Pacific at the Golden Gate.

ODE ON MOUNT FUJI

自是扶桑第一尤
崑崙不許說朋儔
玲瓏高聳青空裏
屹爾臨他五大洲

Onozukara kore fusō dai ichi no yū ;
　　Konron yurusazu hōchyū wo toku wo ;
Reirō takaku sobiyu seikū ri,
　　Kitsuji to shite nozomu tano godaishyūni.

Fuji is indeed a peerless mountain in all Japan ;
　　Mount Konron stands pale before it ;
In shining grandeur it towers above the clouds ;
　　It challenges the five great continents to furnish
　　its rival.

The following Japanese poems are selected from nearly
three hundred. The Viscount was a student of the
Chinese classics from his early days ; but there is hardly
any sign that he had devoted time and attention to the

study of Japanese classics. Out of his own sheer taste, and exploiting his only leisure hours during convalescence from illness at different times, he expressed his thoughts, impressions, and feelings in Japanese verse. His creative and imaginative power as well as his fine sensibility re-acted upon various kinds of external stimuli—political, social, moral, economic, and scenic. In other words, the Viscount passessed a genuine poetical temperament, which, if couched in verse, could produce poetry. To be sure he was an amateur in this line, because he deliberately limited himself to remain such. He faced larger issues which demanded his services and he was constantly conscious of the fact. He was more of an amateur in composing Japanese poems than Chinese for the reason that he had given less attention to the former than to the latter.

On Matsushima, one of the three famous sceneries in Japan:

一、
大方のものは聞きゝしに
劣れるを
みるにましたる
松か浦島

二、
すみわたるみつに
千島の影みねて
夕日ほのめく
浦の松か枝

I

Ōkata no mono wa
　　Kikishi ni otoreru wo
Miruni mashi taru
　　Matsu ga ura shima.

II

Sumi wataru mizu ni
　　Chishima no kage miete
Yūhi honomeku
　　Ura no matsu ga ye.

I

Usually what is learned by hearsay
　　Betrays its reputation when seen;
But half of the truth is not told,
　　In the case of the charm of Matsushima.

II

Thousands of islets are reflected
On the face of the clear water,
Pine trees on them are adorned
With the glory of the sinking sun.

*Two poems sent by the Viscount to Mr. Y. Sasaki,
President of Dai Ichi Ginko, as a token of his deep
appreciation of the gift of an old potted dwarf plum tree.*

ゆきしもにうちくたかれし
ふる枝にも
つほむは梅の
ちからなりけれ

二、
つほみつゝ冬こもりして
もろともに
春まちてさけ
鉢のむめか枝

I

Yuki shimo ni uchikudakareshi
furu ye ni mo,
Tsubomu wa ume no
chikara nari kere.

II

Tsubomi tsutsu fuyugomori shite
morotomo ni
Haru machite sake
hachi no ume ga ye.

I

It is the strength of the plum
To bud on the old branches
Beaten for many winters
By snow and frost.

II

Oh, thou plum tree of the pot
Thou hast bravely weathered winter storms,
And patiently waited for spring
To blaze again in full bloom.

ON BUTTERFLIES

一、

おとろきてたちつゝ花に
ねる蝶は
子等に追はれし
夢や見るらん

二、

うちつけにちりくる花と
汝もひしは
このまに飛へる
小蝶なりけり

I

Odorokite tachi tsutsu hana ni
Neru chō wa
Kora ni owareshi
Yume ya miru ran.

II

Uchitsuke ni chiri kuru hana to
　　Omoishi wa
Kono ma ni toberu
　　Kocho nari keri.

I

That frightened butterfly,
　　Now sleeping on the flower
May be dreaming of
　　A dragon that chased her around.

II

What seemed to be leaves,
　　Promiscuously falling,
Were small butterflies flying
　　Among the trees in the woods.

ON THE CLOSING DAY OF THE YEAR

迎るも送るもおなじ
歳ながら
暮れ行く今日の
惜くもあるかな

Mukōru mo okuru mo
　　Onaji toshi nagara

Kure yuku kyō no
Oshiku mo aru kana.

The cycle of the year goes on unimpeded
    But facing the closing day of the year,
One can not help wishing
    To have it linger longer.

WELCOMING A NEW YEAR ON A SICK BED

祝ふけふかな
ひとりこゝろに
くるとしを
みことは人にまかせて
ほ

Homigoto wa hito ni makasete,
    Kuru toshi wo
Hitori kokoro ni
    Iwō kyo kana.

Leave the greetings of the New Year to friends,
    One who is lying on a sick bed
Will welcome the New Day,
    Alone in his own heart.

SUFFERING FROM TROUBLE
OF THE INNER EAR

耳なきをなにかこつへき
世のなかの
うきこときかぬ
よすかと思へば

Mimi naki wo nani kakotsu beki
Yono naka no
Ukikoto kikanu
Yosuga to omoe ba

Why should one bemoan deafness,
If he take it as a means
To keep him shut away from the noise
Of this fleeting world?

MISCELLANEOUS POEMS

一、

いかてかくよきにはうとき人心
あしきにさとくたちめくるらん

二、

世をわすれよにわすらるゝ老か身に
病はなとかつきまとふらん

三、打ふしなから鏡を見て

おもやせてうつる鏡のおもかけは
われたにわれを見まかへにけり

四、憎きもの

ひかことゝさすかにわれを知るらんを
鷺を烏といひくろめたる

五、女學生に示す

開けゆく世の色と香を身にしめて
むかしのさまに咲けをみなへし

六、卒業生に送る

とく飛びて高く雲井に羽うたなん
ふみのはやしに巣たつひな鳥

I

Ikade kaku yoki ni wa utoki
Hito gokoro
Ashiki ni satoku
Tachi meguru ran.

II

Yo wo wasure yo ni wasuraruru
Oi ga mi ni
Yamai wa nado ka
Tsuki matō ran.

III

*UCHI FUSHI NAGARA
KAGAMI WO MITE*

Omo yasete utsuru kagami no
Omokage wa
Ware dani ware wo
Mimagae ni keri.

IV

NIKUKI MONO

Higagototo sasuga ni ware wo
Shiruran wo
Sagi wo karasu to
Ii kurome taru.

V

JOGAKU SEI NI SHIMESU

Hirake yuku yo no iro to ka wo
Mi ni shime te
Mukashi no samani
Sake ominaeshi.

VI

SOTSUGYO SEI NI OKURU

Toku tobi te takaku kumoi ni
Ha uta nan
Fumi no hayashi ni
Sudatsu hina dori.

I

What a puzzle it is
That the human heart is so slow for good
While it moves quick and clever
In seeking to do evil?

II

Why does sickness haunt
The one who has long ago
Forsaken the world
And been forgotten by it?

III

LOOKING IN A MIRROR
WHILE LYING ON A SICK-BED

So haggard became my face that,
When I looked into the mirror,
I failed to notice whether the reflection
Was mine or that of some one else.

IV

A HATEFUL THING

Covering one's own faults
Of which he is clearly conscious,
He would cajole others
To take a crow for a swan.

V
TO A SCHOOL GIRL

Oh, thou graceful flower Ominaeshi,
Take in all the colours and ordours of modern culture
And bloom out into the beauty
Of the full stature of classic womanhood.

VI
TO A GRADUATE

Swifty fly high up in the heavens
Thou newly fledged songster
Now leaving the dear little nest
Back in the woods of learning.

Thus far, we have scanned the literary side of the life of Viscount Shibusawa through the classic poem which he loved to recite and the poems of his own composition both in Chinese and Japanese styles.

We shall conclude this chapter by quoting a piece of prose in the Japanese style with its translation into the English. The title is the "Uya Tan Jo."

雨 夜 譚 序

みしかしと悟れは一瞬にもたらす、なかしと觀すれは千秋にもあまるはけに人の一生にそありける。されとそのみしかしといひ、なかしと思ふも、必すしもきえゆく年月の數によるにはあらす。その身に遭遇する事草の多少によりて、この觀念に長短の差別を來するものそかし。そもゝゝおのか生涯をいはむに。むかし故郷にありし頃は、犖とり簀になひて、霖雨には小麥の蝶に化せむを懼れ、旱りには又苗代水の足らさるをかこちけるか、世のみたれゆくさまをなけきて、負氣なくも、國家の憂をおのか憂とせしより、住みなれし草の庵を立出、西の都に赴きしに。ゆくりなくも一橋の公にめされて、三とせの春秋を過しぬ。此の公大樹の職を繼給いし後、其實弟なる德川民部公子の

泰西留學に扈從せよとの命蒙り、慶應の三とせといふ年の正月、御國
を首途せり。かくて英佛蘭伊白なとの國々を歷遊し、その年の冬より
佛國にて留學し給ひしか、折しも御國の政變により、其志も遂け得す、
空しく歸國せしは、明治元年の冬なりき。飛鳥川淵瀨かはれる世とな
りければ、おのつからむかししのはれて、公の幽居し給ふ駿河の國な
る靜岡の里に移り、餘所なからもその傍にて殘生を途らむとほりせし
も、あくる二年の冬はかりに、やむことなき仰をうけ給はりて、あつ
まのみやこにまゐ登り、四年か程職事にあつかりぬ。さるに官邊の勤
仕は素よりおのか本意にあらされは、同し六年の夏、せちに請ひ奉り
て、其職をいなみ、今の身となりぬ。かくて後二十年あまりの年月を
經れとも、維新前後の五七年こそ、いとなかゝりし心地せられしか、
おのか境界は世の變遷につれて推しうつれるさま、故郷にて、飼ひた
りし蠶の卵種より孵化して、四たひ眠食をかさね、また變化してもと
の卵種になれるか如し。これ偶然のことゝはいへ、おのか志のある所
をみるに足れり。おのれ別に人にすくれし才藝あるにあらねと、たゝ
此の年月一つの眞こゝろをもて、萬つの事にあたりつれは、かの一信
敵萬軍の古諺の如く何事につけても、さのみ難きを覺えす、何わさを
とりても、さはかり破れはとらさりき。そのなし得たる跡につきても
めてたきふしこそなけれ、心に恥ち身に疾ましき事とては秋毫の末も
あらす。今はた三十年あまりの、種々の事共を想ひめくらせは、ゆめ
うつゝわきためなけれと、身に實歷せしものはまのあたりの如くおも
はれて、忘れんとするも忘れかてなれは、さいつころより、うからや
からの請のまにゝゝ、すきこしむかしかたりを、雨夜の徒然にうちい
てしを、傍にて筆記せしものありて、その水莖の跡いつしか數かさな
れるをみれは、われなから千秋を經し觀あり。終にこれを雨夜譚と名
つけて、ひとつの冊子とはなしぬ。されとこは只々半生の經歷を略述
せしまてにして、もとより世のため人のためにとてなしゝわさにはあ
らす。おのかなからむ後、うからやからの人々これを讀みて、我佛た
ふとしと思ひなは、かねての望みは足りぬへくなむ。

　　　　　ゆつりおくこのまこゝろのひとつをは
　　　　なからんのちのかゝみともみよ

　　　　　　　　　　　　　青淵老人しるす

An Introduction to the Rainy Night Talks.

Such is our life that it is shorter than the tick of a clock when we emphasize its briefness, or it is longer than thousand autumns when we take the opposite view. Whether we think it short or think it long does not necessarily depend upon the actual number of months and years we have spent. Rather we believe that the idea of the distinction between shortness and permanency of time is governed more or less by the nature of the experiences we enjoy.

Now I shall narrate what I have undergone in my past life. While I was living with the folks at home decades ago I handled a plough and shovelled earth.

In a rainy season, I worried over the ruin of the wheat crops, and in a drought I feared there would be a scarcity of the water for the beds of rice plants. In the meantime ominous clouds gathered upon the political horizon of the country. Though it was presumptuous yet I identified myself with the cause of the nation. I left my humble but dear home for the western capital, then the political center. Upon reaching it I was most unexpectedly invited hy the Prince of Hitotsubashi to serve him and three years were spent in his service.

Not long afterward the Prince was made the 15th Shogun of the Tokugawa Regime and he ordered his young brother Prince Mimbu to go to France for study. I too was appointed to accompany the young Prince. Thus it was in January, 1867 that we started on a long journey.

On our arrival in Europe, the Prince and his suite visited England, France, Holland, Italy and Belgium. Towards the close of the year the Prince settled down for study in France. No sooner had he begun his academic life than he received the news of political change at home. Being prevented from carrying on his original plan, the Prince was obliged reluctantly to return home in the winter of the first year of the Meiji Era, 1868.

As the bed of the river Asuka changes from the shallow to the deep, and from the deep to the shallow, so does the nation. In the midst of the change the memory of the past revived afresh, urging me to betake myself to spend the rest of my life in the city of Shizuoka in Suruga, where the Prince was spending his quiet life, and where I might serve him by living close to him. But in the winter of the second year of Meiji, 1869, a call came from a source which was almost irresistible to come up to the eastern capital, where I had to spend my life as a government officer for four years. As this kind of service was not one for which my lot was cast, I resigned the office in the summer of the sixth year of Meiji, and entered into the present status of my life.

Two decades have passed since then. But years which I felt to be the longest were some six years, centering in the Meiji Reformation. Thinking of the vicissitudes through which I came, I am reminded of the experience I had in my country home while feeding the silk worms. The worm is hatched from the egg. It passes through four stages of development, ending its life again in the form of an egg. This illustration looks like a mere accident, but it sufficiently explains the trend which my mind took.

I am far from claiming that I am endowed with talent excelling others, but I have through all these years clung to one thing, which is sincerity, and conducted all my affairs according to it. An old adage has it that one grain of sincerity corresponds to an army of ten thousand soldiers. Hence I never encountered any hardship in all my dealings which could not be overcomed, nor was I ever defeated by them. Looking back over the deeds done I can find nothing of which I may boast, but with a good conscience I can say that there is nothing in heart and in conduct of which I am ashamed.

Indulging in reminiscent phantasmagoria connected with various phases of my life covering the last thirty years, there are matters which can hardly be distinguished as realities or dreams. But those which belong to the realm of my personal experiences remain to me as if they were but the events of yesterday, and they are unforgettable if I try to forget them. Lately at the request of my kinsfolks, I began to give my reminiscent talks. These were taken down by a copyist and the papers accumulated to a considerable pile. Merely looking at them gives me the impression that, after all, my life has covered many years.

At last, I caused it to be published under the title "Uya Tan" (Rainy Night Talks). Of course, this is no more than a cursory review of half of my life's career and not intended to be published for the benefit of the public.

It was solely intended for my kinsfolks who might read it after I have passed on, and find in it sources of gratitude as well as pride towards the one promoted into the ranks of " Hotoke " (ideal life.)

Let this crystal of a sincere heart
Be a bequest from the one
Who would have it be set up
As a guidepost in life's journey.

Written by Sei-en, the Aged.

CHAPTER XII

MORAL INTENSITY

ONE of the most praiseworthy and admirable qualities in the life of Viscount Shibusawa was his unwavering adherence to his moral convictions. He was preeminently a man of moral intensity. His keen intellect and indomitable will were permeated and controlled by this ethical note. He was widely known among his countrymen as a possessor of full orbed common sense, who could disentangle the most perplexing problem quickly and fairly as if by instinct. When necessary, he gladly compromised and yielded to the appeal or solicitation of the party involved in the difficulty. He was a harmonizer and peace-maker. But he was that only within the limits of his moral ideals. Contrary to those ideals not an inch would he budge. Conscience to him was an absolute authority. Its voice was as sacred and irrefutable as that of his sovereign.

The Viscount often used the words " do-ri " (reason), "do-ri-tadashii" (reasonable), and it is significant as well as interesting to note that he always put before the words " reason " or " reasonable " 神聖なる = shinsei naru (sacred), and 眞正なる = shinsei naru (truly right). From this the reader will easily see that the Viscount meant by " reason " moral truth, and not syllogistic truth—cold mathematical exactness. It is always refreshing for the author to recall that, whenever he brought a problem or a question for counsel, the reaction was invariably whether it was morally reasonable or not, instead of whether was it expedient or not. This should not be taken as though the author is intimating that the Viscount despised the principle of expediency. Unlike the cynical and conservative type of moralist, the Viscount placed a high premium on expediency. In fact it was the Viscount's burning passion and untiring effort to destroy on the one hand the traditional notion that morality and economy are incompatible, and on the other to instill into the popular mind that they are complementary and harmonious in the life of a man as the two blades of a pair of shears. The point he wanted to emphasize was that the correct relationship between morality and economy came from the harmonizing of economy with morality, and not morality with economy. For him, to reverse this relative position of the two principles would have meant to put the cart before the horse. He published his sentiments on this question in a record under the title of the " Dōtoku Keizai Gōitsu Setsu," (An Argument on the Harmony of Morality and Economy). Its translation reads as follows :

" Morality and economy primarily were meant to walk hand in hand. But as humanity has been prone to seek gain, often forgetting righteousness, the ancient sage anxious to remedy this abuse zealously advocated morality on the one hand, and on the other warned people of profit unlawfully obtained. The later scholars misunderstood the true idea of their predecessor and made the hasty conclusion that righteousness and gain are incompatible that ' if one be virtuous he cannot be rich ; if rich cannot be virtuous'; and that one looses righteousness if he obtains profit ; and he loses profit if he approaches righteousness. They forgot that productiveness is a way of practicing virtue. They little thought that all sorts of industrial work and the existence of cooperative systems are conducted according

to certain regulations based on moral reason and mutual
confidence. The result is that they came to believe that
proverty is clean and wealth unclean. This misunderstanding
tended to separate learning from practical living. Moreover, as
learning was regarded from olden times a matter which belongs
to the higher class, it was taken for granted by the Samurai in
the feudal period that learning was a monopoly of the non-
productive class of people above the Samurai. The productive
classes, representing agriculture, industry, and commerce were
illiterate, knew nothing about classical learning, and regarded
morality as useless and even harmful.

"The teaching of Confucius, in which I believe, is far different. In "Lun Yu" (論語) we find this sentence: 'With
coarse rice we eat, with water we drink, and my bended arm
for a pillow—I have still joy in the midst of these things.'
Careless reading of the statement is apt to lead the mind of
the reader into the belief that Confucius utterly disregarded
riches and honors, but this is a mistake caused by a wrong explanation of the statement. If an emphasis is placed upon the
clause, 'I have still joy in the midst of these things,' a totally
different meaning of the whole expression can be brought out.
The true meaning of the word will then be that a sage who is
deeply interested in ethical life still finds joy even in plain living, although it is not an ideal one. The word 'still' makes
the meaning clearer than ever.

"That Confucius warned against profit unrighteously obtained,
and believed that gain righteously earned to be in harmony with
morality, can be construed from the fact that he sharply criticised riches and honors whenever they were obtained through
unrighteous methods. He says: 'Riches and honors acquired
by unrighteousness are to me as a floating cloud.' 'Riches and
honors are what men desire. If they cannot be obtained in the
proper way, they should not be held.' From these sayings, we
can see that he did not despise riches and honors as such, but
that he warned men against unrighteous methods in acquiring

them. When Tsze-lu (子路) asked his master who is a complete man, the master said, 'The man who in the view of gain thinks of righteousness.' Again in the chapter on 'Nine Subjects of Thought to the Superior Man' this expression is used—namely " When he (the superior man) sees gain to be got, he thinks of righteousness.' In characterising the qualifications of a scholar, Tsze-chang (子張) used the same expression as that used by Confucius, the Master, as 'The man who in the view of gain, thinks of righteousness.' From these it is clear that gain righteously obtained is not a thing of which the superior man should be ashamed.

" Adam Smith, an English scholar and the nestor of the science of political economy, was professor of ethics and philosophy in the University of Glasgow and founded a school of ethics based on the principle of sympathy. Later he founded the modern science of political economy through the publication of his book entitled 'National Wealth.' Here we can see that wise men both ancient and modern agree in their thinking.

" Therefore I believe that harmony between profit and righteousness is an immortal principle common to the Orient as well as to the Occident. Tsze-kung (子貢) puts this question to his master : 'Suppose the case of a man extensively conferring benefits on the people, and able to assist all, what would you say of him ? Might he be called perfectly virtuous ?' To this the master replied, 'Why speak only of virtue in connection with him ? Must he not have the qualities of a sage ? Even Yao (堯) and Shun (舜) were still solicitous about this.' If moral life is limited to 'eating coarse rise and drinking water', the 'extensively conferring benefits on the people, and able to assist all' will be altogether out of question. But Confucius the master replied : 'Why speak only of virtue in connection with him ? Must he not have the qualities of a sage ? Even Yao and Shun were still solicitous about this.' By this he meant that such philanthropic action is more than virtue and is one of the qualities a sage possesses, in which Yao and Shun were afraid to be deficient. In summing the matter up, this can be said that the ' extensively conferring benefits on the people, and able to assist all,' is the sacred duty of His Imperial Majesty, the Emperor of Japan. At least such is the conduct of a sovereign who rules a country according to Wang Tau (王道). Consequently one who rules the people should not neglect the work of productiveness. This is my firm conviction.

"My learning and ability are limited, and deeds done insignificant, but I have firmly adhered to the conviction that morality and economy can be perfectly harmonized. I go further and believe that this harmony can be demonstrated by facts. I am not speaking of this conviction of mine as the latest development in my mind. It has remained in me for many decades. First of all, my great desire has been that if we hope for the genuine prosperity of the country, we must endeavor to enrich it ; that if we want to make the country wealthy, we must depend upon the activity of industry and commerce conducted according to modern scientific methods ; that the promotion of industry and commerce calls for the organization of the cooperative system, which in turn must be controlled by sound and solid moral reason ; and that there is but one standard for moral reason, which is Lun Yu 論語, the teaching of Confucius the sage. Though unworthy, yet I have steadily tried to conduct my business affairs according to Lun Yu making up my mind that heretofore scholars of Lun Yu made a sad mistake by treating morality and economy as incompatible principles, while they are really harmonious.

"With this determination, I have carried on my business for several decades, and believe that fortunately I have not made any grave mistake in my career. But to-day, progress is made on all sides and human affairs are being improved. Here in the midst of this intense progress, a question whether morality is making progress apace with other matters comes up, and regrettable as it is, the answer to it is No. In some cases it appears as though it has greatly retrogressed. Is this contributory to the welfare of the country ? Is there any one who will dare to say that it is well for the country if it becomes wealthy, even though its morality is low and the practice of love and righteousness neglected ? If such a tendency is allowed to reach its extreme, it is sun-clear that we shall meet many disasters, examples of which are too common both in the Orient and the Occident to enumerate. Thus indulging in my thoughts, I have a fond dream that my view on the harmony between morality and economy based upon the principle of Lun Yu may spread among men, so that some day they will fall in line with this view."

The moral intensity of the Viscount is also seen in his insistence that the moral training of a man is just as necessary as the intellectual training. In Japan of the Meiji Era, many scholars and educators either consciously or unconsciously had imbibed the notion that if a person were intellectually enlightened, he will naturally become a moral person, thus giving a superior position of importance to intellect over morality. There existed a strong tendency among the intellectual leaders that the moral life of a man is dependent upon his intellectual life. A great scholar like Dr. Nobushige Hozumi held this view, and there is an interesting record handed down to us concerning the conversation between the Viscount and Dr. Hozumi on the question of morality. Dr. Hozumi was a famous scholar of civil law, being for a long time a professor in the Law College of the Tokyo Imperial University and its Dean. He was the author of several books on law, and later was honored as a member of the Privy Council and still later as its President. He was early united in marriage with the oldest daughter of the Viscount.

He was a profound scholar and a gentleman. So his words carry weight. Dr. Hozumi said:

" Mere formality does no good. When a person becomes intellectual, he naturally acquires the ability of distinguishing good from bad and of preferring good to bad. To coerce a man to believe a creed or faith is to make him its blind follower. The effect upon him will ruin his after life."

The reaction of the Viscount was expressed in the following words:

" When I first heard this, I felt it to be true; but on second thought, I reached the conclusion that the ability of discriminating good from evil, does not necessarily make a man to prefer good to evil. On the contrary, he may be led to deny morality. As an old adage says ' Intellect is apt to heighten evil.' Thus I reached the conclusion that one should have a principle of some form to guide and direct his own life."

The Viscount told some of us that he had a similar talk with Dr. David Starr Jordan, then the President of Stanford University, Dr. Jordan taking the same view as Dr. Hozumi. Dr. Jordan was no less a great scholar than Dr. Hozumi, though along different lines of scholarly pursuits. Morally, Dr. Jordan was a recognized man of high character, being a genuine lover of peace among men. As the Viscount's argument with Dr. Jordan was advanced at the time of the European War, although the United States had not yet been drawn into it, he could array many such facts as poison gas, submarine torpedoes, and bombing airplanes, used in the great war, to enforce his view that intellectual and scientific civilization without the stabilizing force of morality is a most dangerous thing. The Viscount sharply criticized the attitude of the Germany of that time as an ambitious nation set for world conquest because of her enormous material power, accumulated at the expense and sacrifice of a finer quality of human life—morality.

Japan, now emerging from the depths of her heart-searching experience of the 1936 February 26th incident, is scrutinizing the causes which led her into this unpremeditated trouble and is trying to find a measure that will forever prevent the recurrence of such a national disaster.

Minister Hirao strongly advocated, as perhaps none of his predecessors did, the imminent need of character education among students, which had long been neglected.

Count Kaneko, a veteran member of the Privy Council, referring to the recent incident in his council address, attributed it to a defect of the educational system of Japan as adopted by the authorities of the early part of the Meiji Era. On this point, the views of Minister Hirao and Count Kaneko are the same.

In other words, the high officials deplore the long existing tendency in our educational system of minimizing the cultural side of character building, allured by intellectual culture. The day the Viscount looked forward as surely coming seems to be dawning now.

The difference between the view held by Dr. Hozumi and that by the Viscount on the question of intellectual and moral education seems to be quite fundamental. As we have already seen Dr. Hozumi, and Dr. Jordan too, believed that the intellectual awakening of the human mind would lead it to a moral awakening, making the latter dependent upon the former. But the Viscount dissented from this view going even so far as to say that the mere intellect of a man may ruin his morality. The Viscount refused to give priority to the intellectual side of a man over his moral side. He insisted that an equal emphasis should be placed on both simultaneously, and that they should receive parallel care and training. But in a deeper examination of the views propounded by the two solons, we can see that the difference of view is a matter of emphasis, and the change of the emphasis is caused by the atmosphere of the environments in which they had lived and moved. As a great scholar and a professor in one of the world's greatest Universities, it was quite natural for Dr. Hozumi to be an exemplary personality. His colleagues and the large number of students expected him to be a moral man, and he too assumed that responsibility as one of the prerequisites of his position. And for him to stand before a large group of intellectuals day by day as a leader of thought and character was his delight and pride. The nature of the institution was perfectly conducive to moral living, and it was just as natural for him to be ethical as for water to seek its level. But as a professor and a scholar, he was expected to give the best and most up-to-date knowledge to satisfy the thirsty minds of ambitious youths. For this, most thorough preparation and strenuous effort should be given. Hence the emphasis was placed on the intellectual side, but minimizing in no sense the value of the moral side.

With the Viscount, life was totally different. The atmosphere which surrounded him was antagonistic to

and destructive of his moral life. He was constantly
tempted or allured to compromise and reshuffle his
moral notions in the face of economic invasions.

Every morning he had to sharpen his moral weap-
ons to fight blind forces of gain and expediency. Not
for a moment could he relax his moral vigilance. Thus
it behooved the Viscount constantly to fight the subtle
power of lucrativeness, summoning all the moral elements both actual and potential in him. Is it any
wonder then that the Viscount placed a tremendous
emphasis on the moral side of his life?

As the Viscount was an intellectual giant in the sense
that he could see a matter through and scrutinize a
situation quickly and decisively, it was no burden to
him to deliberate and dispose of any business question.
But from every direction he received strong pressure
on his sense of righteousness, and he had to hold himself ready to fight and overcome it. He fought through
his long business career and maintained his moral integrity intact and unsullied as no other business man of
Japan did. Again and again he gladly sacrificied profit
when it did not tally with his sense of moral reason.
Materially he was poorer because of it, but morally he
was richer by far. He lost many opportunities of ac-
cumulating wealth, or rather passed them by unconcerned,
for the sake of a moral choice. This unselfish spirit
and steady insistence on righteousness were widely
known by the people, and he became a very center of
confidence among them. In this sense, he was the
richest man in all Japan, and Japan owes a permanent
debt to the Viscount. He is indeed a national treasure,
increasingly shedding his influence upon the business

world as the years advance.

We shall cite a couple of examples in which he clearly demonstrated his rigid insistence on moral reason.

There is a concern known as the Ishikawa Jima Ship Building Co., Ltd. which was organized in January, 1893.

"It was about the time the Ishikawa Jima Ship Building Company was formed, that the company received an order of a boiler. The materials for it were imported from a foreign country. On the arrival of the goods, it was found that there was a slight difference in the measurement between the imported goods and the ordered ones, when assembled. The difference was indeed very slight, so slight that there could be no difference in the construction and efficiency between the ordered boiler and the newly manufactured one. But the customer would not accept it. Then only one way was open. It was to send for new material, but that would take a long time, for which arrears would have to be paid. This would in the end mean that the boiler would be delivered to the customer free of charge. The order from such a stubborn customer should be rejected, and the boiler should be disposed of to some one else, was the opinion of the company. At the same time, the value of such a boiler became higher. Therefore the management thought the above the most feasible way out and the matter was brought to the attention of the Board of Directors. The Viscount, the Chairman of the Board, who generally left matters like this to other Directors, happened to be present in this meeting. He was dissatisfied at the attitude taken and said : ' Does the Ishikawa Jima Company break the contract in order to make profit thereby ?' To this, no one dared reply. Finally, the demand of the customer was accepted and a boiler in conformity to the order was delivered to him. This act of the company was deeply appreciated by the customer who straightened out the account in such a way that it caused no loss to the company.

"That warning of the Viscount became the guiding principle

of the Ishikawa Jima Company, and the credit of the company was thus forever established." (Fifty Years History of the Ishikawa Jima Ship Building Co., Ltd.)

Another instance was in connection with gas works under the control of the Tokyo Prefecture. In spite of the wise management and desperate effort of the Viscount, as the head of the Bureau of Gas Enterprise, the losses exceeded the profits. This fact together with the further fact that electric lights were being successfully used in Europe aud America cast a gloom over the future prospect of this gas enterprise, and it was in the assembly of the Tokyo Prefecture that the following resolution was passed in July, 1881.

" It is unreasonable to place the Gas Bureau which is a profit making enterprise under the direct control of the Tokyo Prefecture. Moreover, it is against the purpose of the " Common Fund," which is a reserve for an emergency, to apply it to the ordinary business necessities in the use and supply of gas."

The resolution meant the disposition of the enterprise by sale. Mr. Soichiro Asano, who was selling coal to the Bureau, heard of this. He went round among the influential Assembly men and urged them to sell it. Mr. Asano's intention was to buy it cheap and to make a huge profit out of it. He had sized up the situation, and found it in his favor. So he called on the Viscount, with whom he was on intimate terms, and solicited the Viscount to join him in requesting the authorities to offer the sale to them.

To this proposal, the Viscount made the following reply :

" The Bureau has thus far spent an enormous sum of money. How can I, as a responsible party, dispose of it as for nothing.

The members of the Prefectural Assembly are pessimistic over the prospect of the demand of gas because of the possible use of electric lights. But this is an over-strained worry. I am firmly convinced that this work of supplying gas should not be abandoned as it has a bright future. When the question of its management is raised as to whether it should remain in the hands of the Prefecture or be transferred to a private company, proper consideration should be given to it. As I am not insisting on leaving the Bureau as it is, I shall have no objection to sell it to a private concern, when an opportunity to do so presents itself. But I am decidedly opposed to sell it just at this time. Much more is it out of the question that I should take a leading part in the movement of buying the common property of the citizens for the purpose of profiteering. I shall oppose your own private attempt to buy it, as it is detrimental to the public welfare."

Mr. Asano, listening to the argument advanced by the Viscount, clearly saw its reasonableness and also the firm determination of the Viscount. Then and there he dropped the question, being convinced more than ever of the irresistible power of the moral sense of the Viscount. The Viscount not only turned down Mr. Asano's proposition, but argued the case with the Governor of Tokyo Prefecture and a few leading members of the Prefectural Assembly in favor of retaining the management of the gas works for some years to come, on the ground that the consumption of gas by the citizens will surely increase and profit be made. His prophecy came true a few years afterward, and the works were transferred to a private party with comparatively little loss to the Prefecture.

In the preceding chapter we discussed the Viscount's interest in the Oriental classics. He was a great reader;

composed poems both in Japanese and Chinese styles; and loved beauty expressed in literature; but his intense concern was for truth—moral truth. He identified himself with several literary organizations whose membership consisted of well-known scholars of Chinese classics of high moral standing. He formed what was known as Rongo Kai (論語會) and also Yomei Kai (陽明會). The former was a family affair in which he gathered together his sons, grandsons, and the young folks of his close relatives at his home twice in a month, to listen to the dissertations on Lun Yu (論語) by eminent scholars. The Viscount often participated in the discussions. Sometimes he invited a Christian teacher to lecture on the New Testament.

In later years, he used to hold the Yomei Kai in one of the rooms of his office. The name Yomei Kai was taken after the name Wang Yang Ming (王陽明), a famous Chinese scholar who insisted on the harmony of knowledge and conduct.

In all this the Viscount's primary interest was a moral one, aiming at the character building of men in an intensely practical fashion. He wanted to be a good and useful man, and believed that not only he alone but others can and should attain to that status.

The Viscount was 76 years old when he was about to visit America for the third time, and a well-known scholar of the Chinese classics, Chyushyu Mishima, then 86 years old, sent two Chinese poems to the Viscount for felicitation. The Viscount sent a letter of acknowledgement, in which this significant statement was made:

" It is a great pity that the mad chase after fame and gain is not limited to the life of tradesmen, but that all humanity seems to be addicted to it. I cannot say that my life has been as pure as the moon light. But I shall endeavor not to cheat my own conscience nor to lead others astray."

The older he grew, the more intensely he came to yearn after a high and blameless life. Being profoundly practical, he placed a tremendous stress upon conduct; but at the same time he emphasized the uprightness of the inward life. In other words, the Viscount had the conviction that a man must first *be* good in order truly to *do* good.

The moral intensity of the Viscount reminds the author of the life and career of a powerful leader in the business world of America—Judge Elbert H. Gary, who was a staunch friend of the Viscount and of Japan. He became President of the Federal Steel Company in October, 1898, "then the biggest steel concern, but one, in the United States," and later the Chairman of the executive committee of the United States Steel Corporation.

Miss Ida M. Tarbell, the author of the "Life of Judge Gary," has many statements in her book which speak of the Judge's moral qualities. She says:

" He (Judge Gary) had a passion for square dealing. You had to show him that the thing you were trying to put over was fair before you could get his approval."

Judge Gary was practicing law in Chicago at the time when the invitation to take the position of the presidency of the Federal Steel Company was offered to him by John P. Morgan. The Judge declined to accept the position on the ground that he could not afford to give up professional work which was yielding him an annual income of $75,000, but Morgan assured the Judge he need not worry about that. These incidents show us what kind of stuff the Judge was made of and what kind of credit he was commanding. Indeed, it was said of him that the expression ' Gary is fair ' had long been current in the legal circles of Chicago.

In a letter addressed to President Roosevelt with the date of March 15th, 1907, the Judge has this statement :

" If any company in which I am interested is wrong, it must get right. All of us must be measured by the standard of right. The application of this principle, from which as President, I think you have never deviated, is building for you a monument which will be permanent and will be the last pride of all your friends. It is embodied in the sentiment expressed by you : A square deal for all."

Mr. Charles Schwab was one of the lieutenants of Andrew Carnegie in the latter's steel works. How deeply Carnegie trusted Mr. Schwab could be seen from the promise the former made to the latter to offer him $5,000,000 for five years. From this, it was said that Mr. Schwab was a million dollar salary man. Mr. Schwab went into the United States Steel Corporation when Carnegie sold to it his big concern. Morgan liked Mr. Schwab, and there was a time when Judge Gary felt that Morgan's confidence and affection for him were being transferred to Mr. Schwab.

In a big banquet given in honor of Judge Gary, Mr. Schwab was the speaker and the speech made by him that evening reveals not only the high esteem in which the Judge was held by his colleagues, but more

important than that, the triumph of the moral principles to which the Judge had constantly resorted in
all his business dealings. The full quotation is worthy
of transcription here :

"Several times during the past week, I have endeavored to
write something that I might say to you on this occasion that
would be appropriate, Judge Gary, and that would express the
sentiment of your friends here assembled, but each time I tore
it up as unsatisfactory, and I made up my mind that I would
say to you exactly what I personally felt, feeling assured that
in the saying of it I would express what was in the hearts and
minds of every gentleman here.

"I am thankful for this opportunity of saying one thing,
Judge. You and I have been associated in business, or we were
for some years ; we have had many differences, and I am glad
of this opportunity to say publicly that with my bounding
enthusiasm and optimism I was wrong in most instances—indeed
in all instances—and you were right. The broad principles that
you brought into this business were new to all of us who had
been trained in a somewhat different school. Their effect was
marvelous, their success unquestioned. It was a renaissance and
a newness of things in this business that was necessary and
invigorating. Judge, we feel that your position in the steel
industry is unique. I have been present at many gatherings
where men have been honored for scientific attainments in steel.
I have been present at gatherings where men have been honored
by reason of their operative ability in the manufacture in steel,
but, sir, this is the first time in the history of the industry when
the great heads of all the big concerns in the United States and
Canada have gathered to do honor to a man who has introduced
a new and successful principle in our great industry."

What was this "new and successful principle in
our great industry"? Nothing more or less than the
moralization of business!

What a boundless confidence Morgan placed in Judge Gary and his ability can be seen from the following incident narrated also in Miss Tarbell's book.

" In the fall of the preceding year (1909), Judge Gary had commissioned an executive in a western mine to look up certain information. When this came to the ears of the president of the subsidiary company, he promptly dismissed the man. The man complained to Judge Gary, who ordered him to be reinstated. President Carey resented the action, contending—and in this he was backed by the presidents of many of the subsidiaries—that the chairman had no right to go over the head of the president in reinstating an officer, that if he did so it would ruin discipline.

" Considerable excitement developed, and one member of the finance committee, who sided with the president, went to Mr. Morgan with it. If the finance committee pronounced in favor of Gary in this matter, he reported, the presidents of the subsidiaries threatened to resign in a body."

" Tell them," announced Mr. Morgan, "that their resignations will be accepted."

" The matter was thoroughly threshed out before the committee and the chairman unanimously sustained."

The Government sued the United States Steel Corporation and lost. The chief counsel of the Corporation, Lindabury, was quoted to have stated :

" It was the conduct of the corporation which saved it, and that conduct was due to Judge Gary's foresightedness and his conviction that sound ethics are the basis of all sound business."

Judge Gary said :

" The highest and best rewards come from honest and proper practice. Bad results in the long run come from selfish, unfair, and dishonest conduct."

" You cannot separate them (business and morality). The

moral principles are at the base of all permanent business success—they go together. In the long run, every business question
every public question, must be settled by what is right and
what is wrong."

Mr. Leet, the Secretary of Judge Gary said :

" He has a passion for exact justice. He wants justice more
than anything in the world."

Miss Tarbell joins Mr. Leet in the same strain. She
says about the Judge :

" A note that runs through all of Judge Gary's speeches and
letters and through the comments of his contemporaries is his
desire that things be fair. As a matter of fact, Judge Gary
does not think that anything but justice works in the long run
in handling human affairs. He is a profound believer in the
essential moral quality of the universe. To him the effort to
do business without considering the moral law is foolish and
stupid."

There is danger for a man of exact justice to fall
into a habit of life of stiffness, narrow-mindedness, and
intolerance. But Judge Gary was a broad-minded, toler-
ant, and sympathetic man. He was a man of " infinite
patience," " likable and approachable." " He, (Judge
Gary) has put the Golden Rule in the Steel Corporation's business."

Judge Gary used to send his printed addresses to
the Viscount—the addresses he delivered before the
Board as its Chairman. The author was always delighted and inspired in reading them because of the ethical
note which permeated them.

Judge Gary's Golden Rule here spoken of must be the
Christian rule which reads " Whatsoever ye would that

men should do to you, do ye even so to them," while
Viscount Shibusawa's was the Oriental form which
reads: "What you do not want done to yourself, do
not do to others."

The Viscount used to comment on the Christian
Golden Rule as too positive and aggressive and on the
Oriental rule which he scrupulously followed as gentler
and more liberal.

Miss Tarbell in the last sentence of the last chapter
of her book on the life of Judge Gary has this statement:

"No man in contemporary affairs has more honestly earned
the high title of Industrial Statesman."

If she were to write a biography of Viscount Shibusawa, she might have concluded her book with the same
beautiful peroration, for no two other men could have
been found in business life who so signally left footprints
of moral insistence in the field of industry in their
respective countries.

As we have already seen, the Viscount had entertained a high hope and an unshakable optimism that
the future generations would gladly fall in line with
his view of the harmonization of morality and economy.
From this conviction of his, we may safely conclude
that the Viscount "is a profound believer of the essential moral quality" of humanity, if not "of the
Universe" as Miss Tarbell speaks of Judge Gary.   In
other words, he must have tacitly admitted the existence
of a moral government deep in the nature of human
life.   Otherwise, the Viscount could not have looked
forward so confidently as he did to the Golden Age of

man's moral triumph.

On this point, Judge Gary was in perfect agreement with the Viscount, but the Judge did not stop there. He went further and as Miss Tarbell characterized him, " he is a profound believer in the essential moral quality of the Universe," of which humanity is but a small fraction.

Here Judge Gary parts company with Viscount Shibusawa, and here again the difference of belief of the two great men was caused by the difference of their early training or environment. The Viscount had grown up in an atmosphere where man is the supreme center of interest. How did this earth on which we are living come to exist? Who supplies the vast amount of air which we constantly breathe, and without which we cannot live? What is the first cause which brought about the vast variety of results, such as the starry heavens, which Emmanuel Kant said were one of the two wonders for us, the other being the existence of conscience in man? These questions were too remote and impractical for the realistic mind of the Viscount.

With Judge Gary, the situation was different. He was from his very childhood trained according to the Christian religion. With Emerson, the Judge believed in the existence of one great Over-Soul—creator of man and the universe, whom the Christian calls God ; the great and only Being who is omnipotent, omnipresent, omniscient, and supremely righteous ; and upon whom the entire universe including mankind depends. He is immanent in, and transcendent of, all things. Every man " lives, moves, and has his being in Him." He is fundamentally and broadly ethical, because He is " righteous " ; and " merciful and gracious, long-suffering, and abundant in goodness and truth."

Judge Gary believed in the Creator as his supreme sovereign to whom he was responsible both for his inward and outward life—motives as well as conduct. The Judge had constantly held himself accountable to Him in all his deliberations, and it was this great living background which not only sustained him during a quarter of a century in his vital relations with America's greatest industry, but also made him the peerless " Industrial Statesman."

Dr. Nitobe once told the author that the Viscount would have been a Christian if he could have read English books. Dr. Nitobe's idea might have been that the plain and dignified style of the King James Version of the English Bible would certainly appeal to the exquisite literary taste of the Viscount, while the Japanese translation of it is too coloquial and prosaic to rouse his interest. But whether the Viscount would have been a Christian or not, he would not have passed by the Creator and Upholder of the moral order of the Universe as a total stranger, or his high moral quality would surely have revealed to him the reason why he had been so zealous in upholding the moral cause through all his life, if his soul could have caught a glimpse of the holy mien of that Being.

It would be no mere idle speculation then to say that Viscount Shibusawa might have been Judge Gary and vice versa, if their environments were exchanged. At any rate, it is no small event in human annals that such men as Viscount Shibusawa of Japan and Judge Gary of the United States were born on earth, bearing witness consciously or unconsciously to the existence of an unimpeachable moral law, whose Author will finally judge every man by that law; and giving a mighty stimulus to many ambitious youths of future generations to emulate them in a fair and righteous life.

In "The Doctrine of the Mean," there is this expression which Viscount Shibusawa loved to repeat, and to write down on sheets of silk in his inimitable handwriting :

"Sincerity is the way of heaven. The attainment of sincerity is the way of men."

Who can attain to it? The answer is,

"He who attains to sincerity is he who chooses what is good, and firmly holds it fast."

CHAPTER XIII

IMPRESSIONS OF FOREIGN FRIENDS

BELIEVING that it would interest the reader if a chapter is devoted to a collection of the impressions of foreign friends of Viscount E. Shibusawa, the author addressed the following letter to about thirty foreigners who were close friends and admirers of the Viscount:

Under the patronage of the Viscount Eiichi Shibusawa Memorial Foundation, Inc., (Zaidan Hōjin Shibusawa Sei-en Ō Kinen Kai), I am preparing a brief biography of the Viscount in English entitled "An Interpretation of the Life of Viscount E. Shibusawa." The intended book will consist of fifteen chapters covering about 300–350 pages. One chapter will be devoted to a collection of the impressions of the Viscount's foreign friends about him.

Although I am aware of the fact that you are constantly occupied and your time is too valuable to be disturbed, yet knowing that you were one of the Viscount's close friends, I am taking the liberty of requesting you to send me a brief statement of a few hundred words, say (200–300) along the line just suggested, with your autographed signature. The book will be made public on the sixth anniversary of the Viscount's death, November 11th, 1937, the Armistice Day of the Great World War, but I am anxious to collect full data about his life as early as possible. Hence this my request!

Anticipating your warm support and kind cooperation in this humble project, and trusting that this will find you in the best of health, I beg to remain,

Yours most cordially,

Kyugoro Obata

Judge Gary.

The Viscount and Judge Gary.

Responses came together with words of encouragement and commendation, some in separate letters and others incorporated in the statement of impressions.

By way of acknowledgment and appreciation the author would mention excerpts from letters which will not be reproduced in full in this chapter:

Mr. Frank C. Atherton: "I am sure that such a book would be very well worth while, for I consider the Viscount one of the outstanding world leaders of his generations."

Dr. Sidney L. Gulick: "With all good wishes for the success of your undertaking and early awaiting the results......"

Dr. Herbert S. Houston: "I was delighted to have your letter and to know you are preparing a documented life of our illustrious friend, the late Viscount Shibusawa."

Mr. Thomas W. Lamont: "I wish you all success in this work which I know is a labor of love for you."

Dr. John R. Mott: "I commend with all my heart the undertaking to which you have set your hand. There could be no one who could render the service as well as you can."

Colonel Robert Sandall: "General Evangeline Booth has directed me to send you the enclosed reference to Viscount Shibusawa, which it has been the General's great pleasure to prepare in response to your request for such, in connection with your life of the Viscount."

Mr. Frank A. Venderlip: "I am glad to know that you are preparing a biography of the late Viscount Shibusawa. Biographies compiled on order are difficult to write and do not always result in the best sort of biography. The author naturally feels under compulsion to put the subject in the most favorable light, and the interpretation is apt to be somewhat one-sided. I would venture to suggest caution in that direction."

Dr. John Wood : " It is a great joy to learn from your letter of December 5 that you are going to write a Life of Viscount Shibusawa. Few men of our generation I think are deserving of such commemoration as he."

For the sake of convenience, the author has arranged the " Impressions " according to the alphabetical order of the names of the contributors :

FRANK C. ATHERTON

My first acquaintance with Viscount Shibusawa was in December of the year 1915, when he was returning to Japan from a trip to the United States. The day he was in Honolulu, a group of Americans entertained him at a luncheon, at which time I had the honor of introducing him to many leading Americans and Japanese who were assembled in his honor. During the course of his address, he made the following significant statement :

There has been talk from time to time of a possible war between Japan and the United States, growing out of immigration laws, the question of land ownership by Japanese in California, and certain discriminations against their attending the public schools. I do not believe that there will ever be a war between these two great countries on account of these differences. If a war should ever come, it will be for the trade of China. One of the reasons for my visit to the United States was to talk over the situation with leading business and financial men in that country so that we might come to a better understanding in regard to the development of trade by both Japanese and American business men.

This statement made a deep impression upon me and I have often quoted it.

As I look back upon this meeting with the Viscount, I feel that the force of his personality, his deep desire to improve the relationships existing between Japan and the United States, and his hope to accomplish it by personal conference were among the influences which led later to the formation of the Institute of Pacific Relations. The Viscount, in his talk, was emphasizing some of the foundation stones upon which the Institute has since been built. It aroused in us a desire to help further his splendid ideas.

At this time Mr. Lloyd Killam, one of the secretaries of our Young Men's Christian Association, was working particularly among the young Orientals of this community and was urging upon us the need for securing land and erecting a building, and the employment of secretaries to further such work. We had just secured a desirable piece of property and told the Viscount of our general plan. He immediately expressed a deep interest and offered to try to interest some of his friends and associates in Japan in this undertaking.

By the summer of 1917 we had the plans for the building completed and were starting to raise funds. In October of that year, I left for the Phillipines on a business trip, stopping in Japan for a few days on my way westward. The Reverend T. Okumura, a Japanese minister who had been at work in Hawaii for many years, was in Japan at that time on a furlough and advised the Viscount of my contemplated arrival in Tokyo. Hardly had I reached the city when the Viscount extended to me a cordial invitation to attend a dinner at the Banker's Club in Tokyo, while my steamer was in port. He also asked that I tell those present of our plan to develop a large inter-racial work for the young men of Hawaii. Upon my arrival at the club that evening, I found assembled about thirty leading business and professional men of the city. At the close of the dinner the Viscount told of his visit to Honolulu lalte in 1915 and his becoming acquainted with our work and plans for the young men here. He then called upon me to speak at some length of the progress we were making. I had brought with me a set of the plans for the new building, and after describing its general lay out and how it was to be used, passed the pictures and plans around the table. Much interest was shown in the enterprise. At the close of the dinner the Viscount said he hoped those present would be sufficiently interested to assist.

On my return to Honolulu in January, 1918, I was unable to leave the steamer at Yokohama due to illness, but the Viscount caused to be delivered to me a draft for $10,000 in United States gold, as a gift to the proposed building from himself and many of the leading business men and firms in Japan. This he had raised by his personal efforts. Such a generous interest in an enterprise for young men of various races several thousand miles from Japan touched me deeply and showed the Viscount to be a broadminded and splendid type of world statesman.

In 1921 the Viscount again passed thru Honolulu on a trip to the mainland United States. He spent several days here and many of us had an opportunity for extended conferences with him. The building to which he and his friends had so generously contributed was completed and in use. In spite of his age, he went all over the plant and showed keen interest in the program being carried out—this following a luncheon in his honor. He spoke on that occasion in appreciation of the work and the pleasure that he felt in being able to assist in such an enterprise.

When a few years later a small group here in Honolulu were laying plans for the gathering of representatives of various nations around the Pacific to meet here to discuss problems affecting international relationships, we naturally looked to the Viscount for advice and assistance in securing the interest and support of leaders in Japan. His response was prompt and most helpful. Not only did he manifest a personal concern in the undertaking but cooperated whole-heartedly, and as a result a fine group from Japan attended the first conference. He maintained a deep interest in the Institute during the remainder of his lifetime, giving generously of his time and means to the furthering of its work.

When the Institute held its third conference in Kyoto, in 1929, the Viscount took a real interest in the subjects to be discussed and the work and policies of the organization. He gave a luncheon for the delegates in Tokyo and set aside a time for many of us to have personal interviews with him. He also entertained several of us in small luncheon groups.

Naturally, he was greatly distressed at the legislation passed by the Congress of the United States in 1924, which practically closed the doors to all immigrants from Japan. He felt that this raised a serious obstacle in the way of building up more friendly relations between the people of Japan and the United States, to which he had been devoting so many years of his life. He hoped to live to see the day when this Act would be amended.

Nevertheless, he still maintained his faith in the people of the United States and worked unceasingly towards building up good will and understanding between the peoples of these two races. One could not meet the Viscount without being deeply impressed with his ability, fine personality, sincerity and broad and sympathetic outreach. During our many years of friendship, I exchanged letters with him at frequent intervals and had these several opportunities of meeting him personally. Association with him was stimulating, for his vision, courage and kindliness and idealism impressed me deeply. He was a world's statesman of the highest order— one who made a great contribution to his own country and to furthering international understanding and good will. He was an inspiration to all who had the privilege of knowing him and calling him Friend!

Honolulu, Hawaii
August 24, 1936

GENERAL EVANGELINE BOOTH

In the quietude of a quaint old Japanese garden, resplendent with magnificent chrysanthemum blossoms, I met the venerable Sage of Japan, Viscount Shibusawa. I recognized at once that he linked the Old and New. Alive to all ages, in him reverence for tradition blended with appreciation of worth-while innovation; national love was coupled with an international outlook; the chivalry of a samurai was linked with the shrewd manner of an up-to-date business man. Indeed, it might be said, he clothed Japan's remarkable development of the Present with the Grandeur of the Past.

He greeted me with the charming ingenuous simplicity of a child, yet conducted me around the gardens of his home with the stately dignity of the Philospher he was.

With delightful naivete he displayed two relics which he accounted precious; one the photograph of of William Booth, my father and himself taken together in 1907, the other, which he considered sacred, a faded pillow-cover upon which the Founder had laid his head. In William Booth he met a kindred spirit; both possessed the genius of passion for the people; both possessed the indomitable force of the unbendable will; both were blessed with the vision of the prophet.

As we talked, it was easy to learn that the Viscount had great love for The Salvation Army and deep appreciation of all it was achieving for Japan.

The influence of this great man has remained with me and will do.

Evangeline Booth

General

SIDNEY L. GULICK

January 2, 1936
Ashland, Oregon

Dear Mr. Obata:

Gladly do I respond to your request of December 5th for a statement of impressions of the late Viscount Eiichi Shibusawa.

My first contact with the Viscount came about through the little group of forward-looking, idealistic patriots, of which he was a member, who were deeply concerned over the materialistic trend of the times. President Naruse of the Woman's University called upon me in Kyoto to describe a plan for the formation of an association of like-minded persons and to invite me as a missionary to become a member of the organizing group. He told me quite fully about Baron Shibusawa as he then was and his anxiety on account of the rampant materialism and blatant atheism that were undermining the higher life of Japan. The Baron felt that although he was a Confucianist he would like to join with men of other faiths who would unite in seeking to promote a spiritual and idealistic interpretation of life.

I was deeply interested in the plan and shortly thereafter was happy to receive and accept an invitation from the Baron to attend an organizing meeting. It was held in his villa in the suburbs of Tokyo in the Fall of 1911. At that first gathering there were perhaps a dozen persons present. I vividly remember the Baron acting as chairman as well as host. After a delicious though simple banquet in Japanese style—all seated on zabuton on the soft tatami, the Baron started the discussion by stating his own views of the situation. That statement confirmed what President Naruse had already told me. Each one of us then stated in turn his views.

Among those present I now recall President Naruse, Professor M. Anesaki, Tetsujiro Inouye, and Wamin Ukita. Several broad-minded Buddhist and Shinto priests were also present whose names I no longer recall. upshot of that evening's conference was the decision to form the Kiitsu Kyokai (Association Concordia). The Association met once in two or three months, always at the Baron's villa, he himself the genial and gracious host.

I first learned of the Baron's special interest in American-Japanese relations when Dr. Shailer Mathews and I visited Japan in February 1915. Our errand was to convey to Japanese Christians the Message of the Federal Council of the Churches of Christ in America and to tell them that the leaders of the Churches had started a program of education on the problem of American-Japanese Relations. The Baron welcomed our visit most heartily. A special and large meeting of the Kiitsu Kyokai was held, the Baron being the generous host, the particular interest of that meeting being the address by Foreign Minister Kato.

But I especially recall the Baron's cooperation in securing the permission of the Government for a visit to the United States of Mr. Bunji Suzuki to represent Japanese labor at the meeting that autumn of the American Federation of Labor. But for the Baron's influential support I am confident that my plan to bring Japanese and American labor leaders together would have failed. As it turned out, the Baron himself came to the United States that fall in order to promote better understanding between America and Japan. While he was in San Francisco that October a banquet was given by George Shima, "the Potato King," at which the Baron and Mr. Samuel Gompers were the two guests of honor. Consul-General Numano and Mr. Paul Scharrenburg, Secretary-Treasurer of the California State Federation of Labor, were other distinguished guests.

Throughout the years, until his lamented death, the Viscount was ever among the most earnest advocates and promoters of understanding and goodwill between Japan and the United States. I realized this afresh when I made my second visit to Japan (1922–1923) on behalf of the Federal Council of the Churches, of whose Department of International Justice and Goodwill I was then the Secretary. Again I was the recipient of the Viscount's gracious hospitality and valuable assistance, as I sought to deliver the Message of the American Churches to the Christians of Japan and to assure the people generally that the Federal Council of the Churches was pushing forward its program of education on American-Japanese Relations.

Probably nothing in his long life more deeply grieved and disappointed the Viscount than the ruthless Asiatic Exclusion Law adopted by the United States Congress in 1924. Yet notwithstanding that grievous disappointment, he never gave up hope that in due time the people of the United States would see the light and would practice the Golden rule. It was his influence, I doubt not, that had much to do with the adoption by the Japanese Government of the sane and dignified policy of protest without threats of any kind and of declaring its belief that America's sense of justice and fair dealing on which it relied would in the end lead it to remove the humiliating stigma which the United States Congress had placed upon Japan by that exclusion law.

Among my most delightful memories of the Viscount was his charming cooperation in connection with the adventure of the 13,000 Doll messengers of Friendship that went to Japan in 1926 from the children of America to those of Japan. He also had much to do with the coming to America from the children of Japan of the three score handsome, or I should rather say superb Doll Ambassadors of Goodwill, a couple of years later. The Viscount graciously consented to serve as Chairman of the Japanese Committee on World Friendship Among Children, entering into the spirit of that highly idealistic and somewhat humorous adventure with the enthusiasm of youth. He presided at several great public gatherings when the American Dolls were welcomed, and on their memorable journey to and through the United States. I love to look at the photograph of the Viscount holding in his arms one of those blue-eyed American Dolls and smiling as he listened to its gentle voice saying, "mama."

When the sad news of the Viscount's death reached the United States I felt that I had lost a warm personal friend and that a mighty force in the promosion of the cause which had been central in my own life for the past quarter of a century had suddenly vanished. In the Viscount's death not only Japan but also the United States lost a great leader in all good deeds that make for friendly and mutually advantageous international relations. I am wondering who in Japan will rise up to become a worthy successor.

Ever cordially yours,

Sidney L. Gulick

HERBERT S. HOUSTON

(Dr. Houston believing that the article he prepared at the time of Viscount Shibusawa's death would meet the author's request better than anything he can now do, sent it to him with the advice to acknowledge the fact that it was first published in the New York Times and later in the official periodical of the Japan Society of New York. Hence the author attaches this explanatory note.)

A tragic touch is given to Viscount Shibusawa's passing to join his ancestors at the moment his country seemed to be on the verge of war with China. Japan's greatest peace advocate was likewise the most famous Japanese disciple of Confucius. In his truly noble soul there seemed to be no place for envy, uncharitableness, or any form of intolerance. He was not only a supporter but the mainstay of every good cause in Japan. The Shinto Shrines at Nikko, the Buddhist temples at Kyoto, and the Christian schools and churches in Tokyo found his generous purse always open and ready to aid. For two of the three generations through which he lived he was the first citizen of Japan.

As long ago as 1879, when General Grant made his historic visit, it was Shibusawa who was his host. Even before that, at the beginning of the Meiji Era in 1867, he was a man of light and leading. And earlier still, when Perry sailed into the harbor of Yedo in 1854, he was a stout lad of 14. His long span of life covered the whole history of modern Japan. In fact, he embodied the tradition and spirit and vision of his country, in her rise to power, as did no one else. It would be hard to find a man of any country who typified its best qualities so fully as Shibusawa typified the best qualities of Japan. In America we would have to compare him with Washington and Lincoln; in England with Gladstone, before the home-rule bill; in Italy with Garibaldi. Such comparisons might, at first glance, seem to be extravagant; but in fact they are needed to throw into proper relief the truly representative character of Shibusawa's great career. He was neither soldier nor statesman, in any official way, but as a business man and public leader he was Japan— eager, tireless, aspiring, full of vision and courage.

One day last summer, in his beautiful library in Tokyo—given to him as a token of affection by the Japanese people—I heard the story of his life from his own lips. In a small group of friends—the scholarly Nitobe, the accomplished journalist, Zumoto, who acted as interpreter, the impressive Uchida, member of the House of Peers, and the efficient secretary, Obata—the aged Viscount began with his boyhood, as the son of a farmer; his first intense dislike of the foreigner and of foreign influence; his fighting spirit of nationalism, so strong that it could see no merit in anything or anybody that was not Japanese; his earliest contacts with the career and work of our first American Minister, Townsend Harris; his amazement in finding that his anti-foreign preconceptions were not supported by facts; his gradual, but reluctant, admissions—first to himself and finally to others—that his preconceptions were really prejudices; and then, at last, his complete conversion to a world philosophy of mankind's true greatness when freed from the bias of race and standing on the broad foundation of a common humanity.

In all this moving narrative of emancipation, as he described it, Viscount Shibusawa freely acknowledged America and Americans as his teachers. He recalled his visits to this country and all that he had learned, the visits of scores of Americans to Japan and all that they had brought and left, to the upbuilding of his country. With a feeling of pride he told how his admiration of America had become so great that he was often described as being more American than Japanese.

And then the autobiographical drama came to a sudden and unexpected climax. As the little group sat in rapt interest—Greeks could have listened to Homer with no closer attention—the old man's face clouded and he spoke, first in apologetic reserve and then with a burst of Samurai fire, of the passage of the Japanese exclusion law; of his utter incredulity when the matter was first broached; of his dazed acceptance of the fact of the law's enactment; of his pride wounded in the house of America, his guide and exemplar and friend. It was too much. Like a great Cryptomeria tree on the road to Nikko, he bowed before the storm of his feelings and tears streamed down his face. We all bowed our heads. At length I ventured to say that America was still the friend of Japan; that she continued to show it, in many ways—in the rising walls of the new St. Luke's Hospital; in prompt succor during the earthquake; in building a beautiful embassy in Tokyo, the finest in any capital in the world; and then, taking my courage in both hands, I boldly declared it as my own personal belief that a growing body of American opinion considered the exclusion act a mistake and I was sure that, in due course, it would be repealed.

When my words were translated the Viscount said, simply, "Yes, I hope it will be repealed"—and then added, "but I am a very old man." I knew, of course, that he meant he would not live to see the repeal. And he hasn't—but the forces of good-will he inspired will continue to promote better understanding and hasten the time when his great heart's desire will be fulfilled.

In his own country he was universally looked upon as the Foreign Minister of the Japanese people. He knew and loved the Chinese. Their great philosopher, Confucius, had in him the most devoted disciple in this generation. In this time of war and rumors of war, Shibusawa stood stoutly for peace. Militarists might be too quick on the trigger in Manchuria but he, even in his old age, could aid mightily in Japan in keeping the hearts of the people set on peace. It was his powerful influence that had much to do in changing the policy of Japan in Korea, twenty-five years ago, from military ruthlessness to the constructive ways of peace. His own grandson for many years has been an important factor in that work of reconciliation and progress.

Japan, in the spirit of her greatest friend of peace,

Shibusawa, will somehow find a way to carry on with China. And thus the soul of this great man will go marching on.

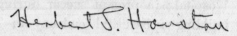

THOMAS W. LAMONT

From the time of my first visit to Japan in 1920, I cherished sincere admiration for and vivid memory of a warm friendship with one of that country's Grand Old Men. Viscount Eiichi Shibusawa was a leader of finance and industry and devoted for years to the promotion of warm and friendly understanding between his country and mine. He was a tireless worker for peace. Himself a person of mental training and discrimination, he was supporter of Japanese culture.

Upon the occasion of my 1920 visit to Japan the Viscount received my wife, myself and my immediate staff at his own home and entertained us with extraordinary grace and courtesy. Afterwards, I had the privilege of a long and constructive discussion with him, conducted through the medium of our good friend, Mr. Obata. Thus it was a particular privilege for me to be able to assist in the welcome accorded Viscount Shibusawa on the occasion of his visit to America in the Fall of 1921.

He and I corresponded regularly, and his letters brought to me a freshness of viewpoints which seemed only to grow keener with the advancing years. No one of us can forget the zeal and effectiveness of his efforts to assist his country in that trying period fol-

The Viscount and Friendship Dolls.

lowing the catastrophe of 1923. I recall, too, the Viscount's sympathetic commendation of the part my firm was able to play in this work of reconstruction through the great international loan made to the Japanese Government early in 1924.

That Viscount Shibusawa was truly a friend of America cannot better be illustrated than by the inspiration which prompted him to memorialize so beautifully half a century after the event, the visit to Japan in 1879 of our American President, Ulysses S. Grant.

Viscount Shibusawa died in 1931 on Armistice Day. And despite the doubts and perplexities which still beset our world civilization I cannot but believe that the date of November 11, 1918, will still be marked as the end not only of the World War, but of any general armed conflict throughout the world. I cherish the hope that America and Japan will be able to work together to preserve the peace of the Pacific basin and of the world itself. Abstinence from aggression, the maintenance of good will towards our neighbors, cooperation towards a more orderly and stable world—those are the ideals which Viscount Shibusawa worked for so faithfully, and which our countries must work to attain if we are to maintain civilization itself.

March 2, 1936   *Thomas W. Lamont*

SHAILER MATTHEWS

February 3, 1936

My dear Dr. Obata:

My acquaintance with Viscount Shibusawa began in 1915 when, as president of the Federal Council of the Churches of Christ in America, I visited Japan with Dr. Sidney L. Gulick to bring assurances of friendship and good will to the churches of Japan. Thanks to the cordial reception of this so-called Christian embassy, Dr. Gulick and I found our contacts were wider than had been expected. I have always believed that this was due in no small measure to the influence of Viscount Shibusawa whose devotion to the cause of international good will was everywhere recognized. He was not only the soul of courtesy but it was clear that his interest in the relations of Japan and the United States was that of a far-seeing statesman. Both in the meeting of Concordia, which he had founded, and in his repeated interviews he disclosed his profound interest in the establishment of mutual understanding and cooperation in the development of the new era upon which the world was entering.

In our various conferences he disclosed a concern for the ethical and spiritual elements of life which was very impressive. His nobility of mind was always apparent. His kindliness was so persistent and his loyalty to high ideals was so sincere that his opinions always had great weight with me. The same qualities gave him a very unique position in his visits to America. He was everywhere received with that respect which is given only to men of high purpose and sincerity. I shall always cherish the memories of this friendship and his devotion to that which is true and beautiful and good.

Very truly yours.

Shailer Mathews

JOHN R. MOTT

December 26, 1935

Dear Mr. Obata :

I have learned with the most lively satisfaction that you are preparing a biography of the eminent Japanese leader, Viscount E. Shibusawa. I can think of the story of no life in the Orient which will be awaited with keener interest, and perused with more pleasure by discerning people throughout the West, as well as the East, than the life of this man which so abounded in helpfulness to mankind. Among his many distinguished services I can think of none of greater timeliness and at the same time of more prophetic or far-reaching significance than what he accomplished to promote peace and good-will among the nations.

Viscount Shibusawa was an outstanding example of international-mindedness. His spacious mind took in not only his own great and expanding country but likewise the other nations of the world, both near and far. In my conversations with him I was always impressed by his intimate knowledge of the background of different nations, of their dominant characteristics, of their possibilities, and above all of their good traits. To my

mind he understood the nations of the West better than
the leaders of western countries as a rule understand
those of the Orient.

Viscount Shibusawa had not only an international
mind but, what I sometimes think is even more important, an international heart. He made the impression
upon me as actually sympathizing with the aspirations and
higher ambitions of different peoples. He was genuinely
sympathetic with reference to the burdens they were
bearing, and was ever responsive to the voice of human
need, no matter in what quarter of the world that need
was revealed. His generous cooperation with great unselfish projects was proverbial. Moreover, he made
foreigners feel truly at home in Japan. I shall ever
treasure in grateful memory my different visits to his
beautiful home and the great encouragement he gave
me in my various missions of service to the youth of
the world.

This great citizen of the world combined international action with his international feeling and international thinking. In other words, he had an international
will as well as an international mind and an international heart. He not only revealed intellectual comprehension of what is involved in promoting right international relations, and a heart large and sensitive
enough to feel for other peoples and to covet their
friendship, but also strength of purpose to bring about
right understanding and right feeling between the nations and races of mankind. He thus had the rare
quality of combining with the vision which commanded
him the steady action of the will. He did not shrink
from taking initiative and from assuming responsibility

for clearing up misunderstandings and ensuring practical and fruitful cooperation between the people of different nations.

It is a privilege indeed to pay this simple tribute to this noble character whose friendship I valued more deeply than I can express.

Very sincerely yours,

John R. Mott

D. B. SCHNEDER

Often when I pass the statue of the late Viscount Shibusawa opposite the Bank of Japan I take off my hat in respect for his memory.

My first meeting with Viscount Shibusawa was not long after his return from America and his meeting with John Wanamaker in Philadelphia. In the reception room of his business office he displayed the American flag and the Bible which Wanamaker presented to him. It was in evidence of his admiration for America and of America's humanest business magnate. My purpose in calling on him then was to solicit aid for my school, Tohoku Gakuin, in Sendai. I had an introduction to him from my predecessor in office. Very courteously but firmly he told me that he could not consider my request unless I had fuller recommendation—from the prefectural governor located in Sendai, or somebody of that standing.

That recommendation was secured, and then he responded, not only once, but later again and again, and he got other leading men of Tokyo to give. He became by far the greatest benefactor in Japan of the Christion school of which I was the head. Many thousands of *yen* were contributed by him and his business friends to meet dire needs.

I met him rather often after that first meeting. My wife sometimes went with me, and occasionally talked to him an imitation of the Sendai dialect, to his great amusement. Always just before going to America and soon after returning I would go to him. His desire for cordial relations between Japan and America was genuine and deep. Once my departure for America occurred soon after some anti-Japanese legislation had been passed. He was deeply disappointed and wounded. He said, "We must not be selfish; we must think of the interests of other nations as well as our own." It reminded me of the words of St. Paul: "Look not every man on his own things, but every man also on the things of others." But he believed that kind and fair treatment of Japan would redound to the welfare of America as well as Japan. The passage of the Japanese exclusion act was to him the severest blow. But he had the magnanimous confidence that America itself would eventually right that wrong. Thus far, unfortunately, his confidence has not yet been justified.

Viscount Shibusawa was a great man. Beyond his amazing business success he could see humanity itself, its needs and its aspirations, and he sympathized and helped to the utmost. He was one of the world's greatest philanthropists.

D. B. Schneder.

JULIAN STREET

January 4, 1936

Dear Mr. Obata:

I thank you most heartily for your invitation to contribute something to your forthcoming book, "An Interpretation of the Life of Viscount E. Shibusawa," and yet, when I face the problem of expressing something of the feelings that I had about the late Viscount, I find myself in difficulties. For to speak in praise of such a man seems an audacity.

It has been my privilege to meet many of the great men of the past thirty-five or forty years in my own and other countries, and this has perhaps engendered in me some understanding of the marks of greatness.

Of all the great men it has been my privilege to know the two who seem to me to have surpassed all others are Viscount E. Shibusawa and Theodore Roosevelt, former President of the United States. Dissimilar in many ways, these two nevertheless had certain qualities in common. Both were remarkable for their clearness of thought, their prevision, their realistic view of life and events, the simplicity and directness with which they met all problems, and their steadfastness of purpose.

To have experienced the same transitions that Viscount Shibusawa experienced, a man of the Occident must have lived five or six hundred years, for the Viscount's life encompassed everything from the feudal period of Japan to the modern period. Having seen so much, no wonder he was wise! The wonder is that any man—or nation—was able in a time so short to make so vast a readjustment.

In appearance Viscount Shibusawa suggested to me nothing so much as a Japanese portrait of the traditional figure of John Bull; and just as John Bull is supposed to represent the sterling qualities on which the British nation justly prides itself, so the figure of Viscount Shibusawa represented in my eyes the sterling qualities of the Japanese race at its best.

His charities, his generosities, were unnumbered. He was in the finest sense of the term a democratic gentleman. In the building up of modern Japan he played an important part, and his sense of world affairs was stupendous.

One of the great desires of his life was to improve relations between Japan and the United States. I have heard him tell how, as a youth, he saw Commodore Perry's ships anchored off the Japanese coast, and how he then flamed with hatred for the intruding foreigners. But later he came to believe that the breaking down of Japanese isolation was a good, or at least an inevitable thing, and no one saw more clearly than he the absolute necessity of friendly understanding between the two great nations facing the Pacific Ocean.

Born of a modest family he rose through his own ability to a position of greatness, and his greatness was of a kind that far transcends mere economic success, or titles of nobility. His greatness was of the spirit. He was the sort of nobleman who is a *noble man*—a sort

such as the Creator seldom makes. His greatness was
not restricted by a narrow nationalism, Japanese patriot
though he was. It was of benefit to the entire world,
and I am sure that countless others, from all parts of the
world, revere his memory as I do, and will continue to
revere it while they live.

Always sincerely yours,

Julian Street

HENRY W. TAFT

Dear Mr. Obata :

I received your letter of December 5th, and I very
gladly respond to your request that I make a brief
statement concerning Viscount E. Shibusawa.

I first met Viscount Shibusawa over fifteen years
ago, on the occasion of my visit to Japan as a member
of a party headed by Mr. Vanderlip. Our visit was at
the invitation of the Welcome Association, of which
Viscount Shibusawa was then the head. The Viscount's
chief interest then and during the remaining years of
his life, was to cultivate friendly relations between Japan
and the United States. He contributed much to achieve
that result, for he was so earnest and disinterested that
his influence was potent in both countries. At an
advanced age he several times visited the United States
and made many sincere friends in this country. I hope
that the effect of the Viscount's zealous efforts will

continue and that there may be in this country many who will cooperate with representative men of Japan in seeking to advance the cause of International friendship.

Very sincerely yours,

PAYSON J. TREAT

It is a privilege to be associated with the friends and admirers of the late Viscount Shibusawa in a tribute to his memory. The few occassions on which I had an opportunity to talk with him, on my several visits to Japan and during his last visit to my country, stand out clearly in my recollections. I treasure his influence among those which have been helpful in my own life. Of his services as an outstanding contributor to the achievements of the Meiji Era I need not speak. But two qualities of his mind and heart impressed me indelibly. I refer to his love of truth and to his firm belief that truth and justice will in due season prevail. As a student myself I was impressed by his active encouragement and support of historical scholarship in Japan. In this endeavor he was giving expression to a fine loyalty. But in a field which touched me more intimately he added courage and constructive leadership to his belief in truth. I refer to the improvement of relations between the Japanese and the American people. Like most thoughtful nationals of the two countries Viscount Shibusawa believed that the happiness of the people of the great Pacific nations depended upon good understanding and goodwill. He believed, I am sure, that each could contribute much to the benefit of the other, that there were no fundamental causes for harmful rivalry, and that the beneficent features of their relations far outweighed any harmful ones. But he realized how easy it was to create misunderstanding between peoples so different in culture and tradition and so recently brought into intimate contact. He did more than recognize these conditions, he did much to further good understanding and to inculcate good will. In this endeavor, which I believe was very close to his heart, he attached great importance to the search for truth. He believed that once the truth was discovered and made known it would triumph over the forces which sought to displace it. And no matter how discouraging the struggle he never lost heart. His fine courage should be an inspiration to every one who believes in international good will. I gladly testify to what it has meant to me. At this time when throughout the world the relations beteveen nations are more gloomy and threatening than at any time in recent years the world needs the inspiration and the example of the great and good Viscount Shibusawa.

Stanford University,
California
August 16, 1936

Payson J. Treat.

FRANK A. VANDERLIP

RECOLLECTIONS OF VISCOUNT SHIBUSAWA
FOR MR. OBATA

I think of Viscount Shibusawa as a typical good citizen, and in thinking that I do not regard him as peculiarly a good Japanese citizen, but rather an example of the type of citizenship which the whole world needs. Indeed, his breadth of comprehension, his sympathies and his desires for mutual understanding between alien peoples was such that he might well be described as a good citizen of the world.

I had the privilege of many conversations with him. There was the difficulty of being obliged to have these conversations carried on through an interpreter, but they were numerous enough for me to get, I felt, a pretty clear picture of his aspirations for better understanding between countries and their people. His views were never tinged by narrow nationalism, but had a breadth which always gave to me an added breadth of view. He had begun his travels early in life and kept them up almost to the end of his remarkable career.

His life covered almost the same range in world affairs. Japan has by no means been alone in coming to the realization that all the lives of all people are interwoven with the welfare of other people.

I think Viscount Shibusawa saw this truth vividly and that this insight led him away from a strictly nationalistic view and toward a view in which international fairness was predominant. I felt that he saw that immediate national well being should not alone be the aspiration even of an intense national patriot; that a reputation for all around fairness was as essential to a nation as to an individual; and indeed that the welfare of one's own country is related to the welfare of other countries.

Z. H. Vanderlip

GEORGE W. WICKERSHAM

My dear Mr. Obata:

I am glad to hear from your letter of the 5th instant that you are preparing a biography of Viscount Shibusawa in English. I wish I could contribute something which would be of value to you, but as a matter of fact, I never saw the Viscount but once, and that was at a formal dinner, where he was extremely gracious, but I had little opportunity for anything more than an exchange of formalities with him. Of course, I knew of his work in Japan, of his great devotion to the cause of international amity, especially friendship between Japan and the United States, and I always have looked up to him as an ideal type of man, who used his great position and his vast learning for the advancement of cordial relations between our two countries. I am looking forward with great interest to your book, and I only regret that I am unable to give you anything of value in the way of reminiscences to contribute to its make-up.

With sincere regards and compliments of the

Season, believe me to be,

Yours faithfully,

JOHN W. WOOD

Dear Dr. Obata:

In connection with a host of other friends, I shall always count it a great privilege that I knew Viscount Shibusawa. To know him was to have a deep respect and affection for him. I recall with gratitude his deep interest in, and the great help he gave to Dr. Teusler's plans for the building of St. Luke's Medical center in Tokyo. I am sure there must have been times when Dr. Teusler's stout heart would have despaired if it had not been for the friendship and the courage of the Viscount.

Of course, I did not know him as well as Dr. Teusler did, because, for one reason opportunity for fellowship with him was limited to my occasional visits to Japan and his even less frequent visits to the United States.

I think of the Viscount as a lover of beauty. I recall one visit to his home when with justifiable pride, he showed me his garden. That beautiful spot, marked him, I feel, as a lover of God's creation. I could not but feel that the beauty of nature drew him close to the heart of God, the Creator.

I know he was a lover of peace and of his fellow-men. Few men of any nation have done so much to further international fellowship and to produce the condition of heart and mind that makes armed strife between nations impossible.

I know he was a man who cherished with gratitude friendships of the past. I remember his telling me that as a boy, he knew Townsend Harris and counted him his friend. When the Viscount came to the United States about 1922 on a mission of international friendship, his first act upon reaching the city of New York, was to go to the cemetery where Townsend Harris had been buried many years before, and place a wreath upon his grave.

I know that Viscount was a lover of men, not merely in the mass, but as individuals. Among those to whom he showed this side of his noble character was our mutual friend, Dr. Rudolf B. Teusler. In March 1928, Dr. Teusler and I were planning to return to the United States to make a final effort to secure the funds necessary for the building of St. Luke's Medical Center. The evening before we started upon our voyage, Viscount Shibusawa made the long journey from his own home to Dr. Teusler's home in Tsukiji. He talked for a while of Dr. Teusler's hope of what St. Luke's might mean to the people of Japan. When he rose to leave, Viscount Shibusawa clasped Dr. Teusler's hand and said to him: "While you are away I shall be praying for the success of your mission." As they stood there, looking with respect and affection into each other's faces, there came back to my mind those lines of the English poet, Rudyard Kipling :

> " But there is neither East nor West
> Border or breed or birth,
> When two strong men stand face to face,
> Though they come from the ends of the earth."

With assurances of my best wishes for yourself and all that you are doing to preserve the memory of Viscount Shibusawa, I am,   Sincerely yours,

Tryon, North
Carolina
May 11, 1936   *John W. Wood*

The author is pretty sure that the reader will thank him for having introduced into this humble book a chapter symposium of these friends of the Viscount in the epistolary form. Indeed he takes pride in this chapter and in the Introduction, the two parts which he considers to be climax of the whole book.

CHAPTER XIV

BEIJU SHUKUGA KAI

(Celebration of the 88th Birthday)

FROM time immemorial, longevity has been regarded as one of the gifts heaven grants to virtuous men. With it happiness and good-luck are closely associated. This is our national belief, and the people observe in joy the return of their birthdays on the 60th, 70th, 77th, 80th, and 88th years. Public men are invariably feted by their clients who thus show their appreciation of the services for the promotion of their welfare.

Viscount Shibusawa was honored in an appropriate manner by his followers and admirers on these Epochal days in his career. The celebration of his 88th birth was the culmination of all the celebrations preceding.

Eighty-eight is quite a rare age for the average man to reach, and its rarity makes its observance or celebration an occasion of great importance in the personal history of the one felicitated. But there is another interesting reason for us Japanese in making much of the observance of the 88th birthday. We call the age of eighty-eight the " Bei-ju," " bei " meaning " rice " and " ju", " age", the two together meaning " the rice age." In Chinese character the word for rice is written as 米, which can be analysed into three parts, 八, 十, 八, signifying eight, ten, eight, respectively and together eighty-eight. Rice is our staple food, the most important product for the Japanese people. It is the symbol for fortune and vitality, and anything associated with it is certainly lucky.

Viscount Shibusawa reached his " Bei-Ju " (rice age) in 1928. His junior business men all over Japan had been anxious to find an opportune time for manifesting the highest possible appreciation of his long and useful life of service to the country and to the cause of industry. They felt that this was exactly the occasion on which they could carry out their cherished plan. So they appointed a committee to consider it and to prepare an appropriate program.

According to the program, the celebration was divided into three parts. The formal part of the celebration consisting of addresses; the banquet; and the entertainment. The date was fixed for October 1st, 1928, beginning at five o'clock p. m. The Imperial Theatre and Tokyo Kai Kan were engaged as the seats of the celebration.

The formal part was presided over by Baron K. Nakajima. At the banquet Ambassador Solf of Germany, the doyen of the diplomatic corps, together with nearly one thousand well-wishers felicitated the Viscount by drinking to his health. The entertainment consisted of plays performed by the foremost actors of Japan interspersed by a dance by a foreign troupe.

The reader will be astonished by going over the list of the names of the well-wishers who were present at the celebration. There were the Ambassadors, Ministers, and Charge d'Affaires of twenty-six nations; the Premier; thirteen Ministers of State; twenty-six members of the Privy Council, including the President and the vice-President; the Presidents of the House of Peers and of the

House of Representatives; the Chief Secretary of the
Cabinet; the Chief-Secretary of the Bureau of Legislation; the Superintendent-General of the Police; the
Governor of Tokyo Prefecture; the Mayor of the city
of Tokyo; Admiral Togo; seventeen retired Ministers
of State and Ambassadors; and twenty-two Presidents
of the leading newspaper firms of Tokyo, besides sixty-
five promoters (representative businessmen) and seven
hundred and forty-five supporters.   In addition the Viscount received nearly one hundred cablegrams of congratulation from friends and organizations in Hawaii and
the United States.   The words by Confucius most fit-
tingly summarize the life and character of the Viscount
now so highly extoled by this unique national and international gathering:

" Therefore having such great virtue, it could not but be that
he should attain the throne, that he should attain riches, that
he should attain fame, that he should attain long life."

We shall try to feel the atmosphere produced in the
celebration by reading the congratulatory addresses
delivered by Baron Dan, Premier Tanaka, Baron Goh,
and Ambassador Solf, and the Viscount's response.

Baron Dan representing the members of the celebration organization read the following congratulatory address:

" As Your Excellency Viscount Shibusawa reached the 88th
birthday last year, many of us, your admirers, intended to hold
a banquet for congratulation, but it so happened that we were
in the midst of the national mourning then.   This is the reason
why we postponed it till this year.   We have set this day to
carry out our cherished hope to commemorate your 88th birthday.

" We believe that your past life can be characterized with these words—self-sacrificing public service.   Looking back to the time of the Meiji Restoration, we notice that you discerned the signs of the time and caught a vision of the necessity of developing the nation's industry and elevating the position of businessmen.   From the day when you resigned the Government position, you have always devoted your time and energy to productive industry by creating financial organs on one hand and by organizing or assisting to organize cooperative institutions on the other.   You have championed the cause for the advancement of commerce and industry, and for the increase of the nation's wealth.   It is no exaggeration to say that the phenomenal advancement of the industry of new Japan extending through the three eras of Meiji, Taisho, and Showa is largely due to your management and guidance.   It is rather superfluous for us to touch on this point, because the public has a very decided opinion as to the great contribution you made to the nation.

" When Your Excelleney reached the age of 77 years, you saw it fit to retire from active life in the business world, and to pour your unabated energies into such public works as social, educational, and philanthropic, greatly contributing to the reconciliation of capital and labor and to the elevation and purification of the life of the general public.   There is hardly any public work which has not been either directly or indirectly assisted by you.   We are especially indebted to you for your international activity.   As the champion of peoples' diplomacy, you spared no pains to promote the peace of the world and the happiness of mankind.   Whenever a scholar, a statesman, or a businessman of repute came from a foreign country, you welcomed and entertained him, frankly exchanging ideas with the view of promoting better understanding.

" In spite of your advanced age, you made trips to America and visited many cities to establish closer relations between the peoples of our two countries.   You saw the imperative need of

a better understanding and closer relations. For this you organized a joint enterprise between the business leaders of both
countries, and you paid visits there. At times you have been
a Foreign Minister at large.

"For seventy long years, you have endeavored to promote the
nation's wealth and the people's happiness, foregoing personal
enjoyment and private comfort. Your robust health and vigorous mind may have had a great deal to do with your extraordinary activity, but such a steady and straightforward life could
not have been lived unless, you have had the innate nobility
which was trained and fostered by the application of the principles enunciated in the Confucian Analects.

"It was due to the effort of many strong men that the rapid
progress of Japan from the Meiji Restoratien has been achieved
until today she is ranked as one of the world's five great Powers. But you opened up a new field along the lines of industry
and economics, and developed social work according to the needs
of changing circumstances, thus contributing to the welfare of
the nation. In this regard you are peerless and the public gratefully concedes it. It is no wonder then that the reputation of
your meritorious deeds reached the Imperial Court, so that His
Imperial Majesty the Emperor was pleased to honor you by
elevating you to the peerage and bestowing on you a Decoration.
The older you get, the sounder your mental and physical condition grows. Your benign countenance and kindly words have
been a constant benediction to us. You have won fame as a
nestor in our business field and an authority in social work
throughout the three eras of Meiji, Taisho, and Showa. You
are indeed an outstanding figure in the brilliant reigns during
the periods just mentioned. You have now reached the enviable
age of 88 years, and we junior colleagues feel it a high privilege to felicitate you on this auspicious occasion. We most
earnestly desire that you may yet live long to serve the country you love, so that we may again be privileged to congratulate you at the age of 100 years."

Baron G. Tanaka, the Premier, representing the entire guests of the day, spoke thus:

" The summer clouds are now completely dispersed, and the fresh bracing autumn has come upon us. Just at this time we are invited to be guests to share the joy of this most auspicious occasion and to be filled with emotions that thrill us. When we pause to think of the courses through which the Viscount has reached this red letter day for him, we are reminded of his patriotic activities at the time of the Meiji Restoration which put an end to the Feudal system.

" He felt the political unrest, and planned to save the country from it by forming a band of his political sympathizers. He early saw that, in order to lay the firm foundation of the nation, it is important to cooperate with other nations. Therefore he visited Europe and came into contact with the Western civilization. He returned with certain ideas and plans. He was invited to serve the Meiji Government and assumed an important duty in the Department of Finance. This was the beginning of his public career—the career which made his life different from, and superior to, that of the average man. If we study the history of Japan's finance and economics we shall find that one half of it forms the biography of the Viscount. In the beginning of the Meiji Era the influence of the Feudal days was still persisting. The Viscount observed that the better class was still inclined to despise business and feel contempt for financial matters and that it was no easy matter to rouse the interest of the people in general industry. But he made it his mission to firmly establish the national finances and to promote the development of public and private economics. Hence as soon as he resigned his office in the Government, he published what may be called the general rules for the cooperative system, and stimulated the organization of trading companies. Also he endeavored to establish the First National Bank, (Dai Ichi Kokuritsu Ginko), which was the first bank ever established in Japan, and was made its super-president or General Superindent.

" Next, the Viscount assumed the responsibility of organizing the Tokyo Chamber of Commerce. He made an effort to open up the Tokyo Stock Exchange. He was elected the first chairman of the Bankers' Association. Then railway, steamship, spinning, paper manufacture, raw silk, coal mine, beer brewery, cattle breeding and many other industrial enterprises were started by his efforts.

" We cannot help looking upon the Viscount with profound admiration for his farsightedness, when we think that he laid a permanent plan for the country in founding a commercial school which became the forerunner of the present " Tokyo University of Commerce." He believed that the foundation of the perfection and unity of finance and economics rests upon commercial education. To conduct the life of industrialists with Lun Yu (Confucian Analects) and Soroban (calculating machine) was an innovation easy to understand, but hard to invent. When he saw that the industrial world had fairly been started, he turned his keen eyes to another direction—namely to the promotion of international relations.

" In order to accomplish this important task, he visited America, Europe, and China more than once. Especially he paid close attention to the promotion of a better understanding between Japan and America, and between Japan and China, as Japan maintains with these two countries close and important economic relations.

" His contributions to the Department of Foreign Affairs as an unordained diplomat, and to the extension of the national power, are recognized with gratitude at home and abroad. Just at present the Viscount is the president of the Japanese Association of the League of Nations, besides being connected with several other international institutions. Despite his old age the Viscount is giving his time and energy toward this international work. Moreover, the Viscount is paying attention to the elevation and maintenance of the dignity and culture of the city of Tokyo, which is the seat of the Imperial Palace. He has concentrated his best efforts in Tokyo. He directed his attention to the city government and rendered assistance to its improvement and progress. He has for a long time been looked upon by the citizens of Tokyo almost as their father. The Viscount's activity extends in every direction and permeates the whole city.

" As a champion of social work, he poured his energy into the work of philanthropy and the work of reconciliation between labour and capital, being deeply concerned about the relations of the two classes, which should be regulated as industry develops. He is the President of the Association of Central Social Work, the President of the Tokyo City Poor House, and the vice-President of the Reconciliation Society. He helped organize Hoko-kai (Gratitude Society), to look after and take care of the families of army men and the disabled soldiers, and served it as its president. There is no end to the enumeration of his contributions to the public welfare of the nation. His merit is broad as the sky, and deep as the ocean. It received the gracious recognition of His Imperial Majesty the Emperor who rewarded the Viscount with Decorations, elevation to the peerage and finally advancement to a Viscountcy. This last honor accorded the Viscount is an unprecedented recognition granted to a business man. He will soon reach the age of 90 years. He is enjoying his good name and genuine happiness. He and his kindred are indeed a center of envy. He is surrounded today by the hosts of his admirers in this auspicious gathering. We are greatly delighted to see him look so hail and hearty, with his radiant face like a ruby.

" We sincerely wish that the Viscount may live on to the age of 100 years, still to serve to promote national and international welfare, thus exemplifying the truth that a virtuous man lives long, and stimulating the future generation to take courage to emulate his life."

Then Baron S. Goh, representing the Promoters of the Congratulation Association, read the following resolution for the adoption of a plan for a congratulation-memorial :

" I have the great honor to announce in this auspicious gathering of leaders, consisting of officials and civilians, that there is a plan on foot to erect a bronze statue in honor of Viscount Shibusawa as a memorial work of this association, and to enlist your support.

" When some of us held a meeting to plan this gathering for felicitating the 88th birthday of the Viscount, we as promoters discussed how best we could express our appreciation to the Viscount for his contributions to the development of Japanese industry and economics, and to the promotion of public welfare work, thus letting the future generations long remember him. Various propositions were presented such, for instance, as the construction of a Shibusawa Memorial Hall, or the renovation of the Hall of Confucius, whom the Viscount highly admires. Views were exchanged about the future care of these projects in case either of them might be accomplished and possible difficulties were foreseen in their permanent preservation. After careful deliberation, it was tentatively agreed that the best way would be to erect a statue of the Viscount in a suitable place. Future generations may look upon his benign countenance, and thereby be influenced to love him and to wake up to follow in his steps.

" We first conferred with the Viscount about the project, but his modesty would not allow him to consent to it. He advanced more than once cogent argument for declining to accept the kind proposal. However, equally persistent was the attitude of the promoters.

" They argued that the Viscount is not only a benefactor in Japan's industry, but he is a great man of the world. His contributions to the public are incomparably great. There are great statesmen and renowned military men for whom statues are built. Compared with them there is something greater in the case of the Viscount for the reason that his merit has a national significance. Furthermore, there would surely rise a proposal in the future to erect a statue in his honor. If so, why should not the Viscount consent to have it built by those of us who have been in direct contact with him receiving his guidance. We almost coerced him in the matter to his great embarrassment and succeeded in obtaining his tacit consent.

"As to the design and other details decision will be reached after a suitable location is selected. At any rate it is our desire that we shall produce something compatible with modern art. Our idea of the location is that it should be a place which has a historic relation with the Viscount and which at the same time will be frequented by the people. The authorities of the city of Tokyo, with whom the Viscount has long held an official connection in promoting its social work, gladly consented to give us their best cooperation. We shall leave no stone unturned for bringing about the best possible result in selecting a location and in forming designs.

"This Congratulatory Society includes a large company of the industrial leaders throughout Japan who are closely acquainted with the Viscount. Therefore, we think it most appropriate for this Society to undertake to carry out the work of erecting the memorial statue of the Viscount as its accompanying enterprise. It is for this reason that I, on behalf of the promoters of the Congratulatory Society, announce the project. We earnestly request your hearty cooperation and enthusiastic support.

In the midst of deafening handclaps Viscount Shibusawa rose and responded :

"I am so overwhelmed by the honor you have conferred on me that I am at a loss to find adequate words to express my gratitude. Please accept my heart felt thanks. I have closely followed Dr. Dan's remarks made in the capacity of the representative of his colleagues. I feel that I don't deserve the high words he lavished upon me, and yet I shall accept them as a token of genuine expression of true friendship. Especially I take it a very high honor for me to receive such a cordial felicitation from His Excellency, the Premier, who minutely recounted my career in his written address. When I think of the great responsibility he shoulders and of the complicated problems he constantly has to deal with, his presence here on account of myself a humble citizen provokes within me a profound gratitude.

"There are many things I would like to tell you when I look back upon my past, but I am now so full of emotion that it disturbs my mental equilibrium to calmly arrange my thoughts in order. And yet the opportunity like this cannot be given me again. I shall, therefore, ask your indulgence for a while to hear me tell you briefly about my career.

"Most of you know who I am and what I am, so that I need not dwell npon the details of my life story. I was born in a conntry home as a son of a farmer. Up to the age of twenty-four I handled the plough to cultivate the soil. According to the custom then prevailing in the village, I had studied the Chinese classics under my father and relatives. I studied the Confucian Analects and other books, which stimulated me to take an interest in public affairs despite my position as a farmer. At the age of seventeen, an incident occurred which considerably stirred up my feelings and forced me to think of the harm the feudal system brings upon the country. The incident was this: I went to the official residence of the Governor and met the Deputy-Governor. I was ignominiously treated by him. This caused me to leave my home and almost made me desperate. The visit of Commodore Perry to Japan was made in 1853. I was fourteen years old then. The news of his visit did not disturb the average mind in rural regions, but men of education worried about the future development of this diplomacy. What might be termed the diplomacy of the day adopted by the Tokugawa regime was rather weak-kneed. Over it the strong men of the country were indignant. Men like myself, who deeply resented the attitude of government officials toward civilians, entertained animosity. Various incidents occurred in those days which whetted the spirit of revolt against the regime. The assassination at the Sakurada gate, and the attack of Sakashita, were conspicuous ones. At any rate violent deeds were quite prevalent among the so-called patriots. Some of us in our village were influenced by the atmosphere of the day and attempted to stage some radical movements on the ground that the country was in danger if it were left alone. Such an attempt was indeed absurd judged by the light we now have. It was nipped in the bud. The date of the plot was 1863 and I was twenty four years old then. There were about seventy of us. Today we hear much about socialistic movements. But in those days, the art of fencing was prevalent and those who were trained in the art were radically inclined. They aimed at the destruction of the existing regime.

"There existed a sharp rivalry in Kyoto between the Choshyu and the Satsuma clans, the former losing its power. Prince Sanjo and his colleagues were obliged to retreat to their own province. Satsuma, on the other hand, was propagating the idea of the union between the Imperial Court and the Tokugawa regime, Aizu endorsing the plan. The country people knew nothing of such an intricate movement then going on. Our naive notion was to hazard our lives at any cost. Just then my cousin, a senior member of our band Odaka by name, was in Kyoto to scrutinize the political situation there. We sent for him and he hurried back to us. I distinctly remember the date of his return. It was the 30th of October, 1863. As soon as we saw him, we proposed to him to join us in the plot. To our utter suprise he vigorously opposed it, saying that it should be given up as there was no hope for success in such an absurd attempt. We argued with him insisting that we could not give it up. Success or failure was not the question with us but that we were to sacrifice our lives for the sake of the country. Thus we furiously debated, but Odaka won the day and our plot was abandoned.

"Although our project suffered this abortive fate, yet the agitation was pretty well known. We had to dispose ourselves or we would be arrested. The situation obliged us, K. Shibusawa and myself, to betake ourselves to Kyoto. We left our village on the 12th of December of the same year. In Kyoto we paid our respects to one of the high officials of the Hitotsubashi family, whose name was Yenshiro Hiraoka. We did this because we had formed an acquaintance with him in early days. He was a well informed man about current topics concerning domestic as well as diplomatic affairs. In January of 1864 Mr. Odaka just referred to killed a man by some mistake aud was arrested. He was imprisoned. Among Mr. Odaka's personal effects was found a letter which I had written to him from Kyoto—a letter serious enough to involve us in arrest and imprisonment. Here it was Mr. Hiraoka who saved us in this critical hour and made us retainers to the Hitotsubashi. If his rescuing hand had not been stretched out to me at that time, I might have been imprisoned and died in the prison. A most unexpected thing happened in my case. One who had intended to destroy the Tokugawa regime and to drive out foreigners from the country completely turned round and became a ratainer to the Hitotsubashi. Prince Yoshinobu Tokugawa was the commander-in-chief of the Imperial Guards of Kyoto just at that time, and him was I to serve as a retainer. Two years afterward the Prince was inaugurated as Shogun and my status was changed from a mere retainer to that of a servant of the Shogunate. Not long after this, I was appointed to accompany Prince Mimbu, the younger brother of the Shogun, to France. The Prince was to represent Japan at the Exposition of Paris, and then to visit different countries in Europe. His ultimate object was to remain in France for study. This foreign trip of mine was made in 1867. About the time when I was appointed to accompany the Prince to France my ideas became much milder. I felt that I must follow the natural course of events, faithfully discharging my duty as a samurai of the Hitotsubashi clan.

"While staying in France we received the news that Prince Y. Tokugawa had surrendered his administrative power to the

Emperor and that the battles of Toba and Fushimi had taken place. Such political conditions at home made it necessary for the Prince to leave France, giving up the plan of remaining there for study. This was a deep regret to the Prince.

"During the Prince's stay in France and his trip to the five countries, England, Italy, Belgium, Holland, and Switzerland, I learned a most valuable lesson which impressed itself upon my heart. It was the way whereby officials and civilians mingled together—a way very different from what had been practiced in Japan. There were two Frenchmen who lived with the Prince. One was an army officer, Colonel Willette, whom Emperor Napoleon recommended to the Prince. The other was a banker, formerly a Consul-General, whom the Prince employed for the transaction of miscellaneous matters. His name was Flury-Herald. Their relations were admirably cordial and free. To me, who had drunk the bitter cup of contempt from that official years before and felt the distance between official and civilian to be unbridgeable, the social relations in France seen through these two men were a most impressive sight to my eyes. In the meantime the great restoration took place, and Prince Y. Tokugawa, receiving the foul name of traitor, was under the ban. We returned home just at that time.

"I told you a while ago, that though I was born in a farmer's family, yet I entertained an ambition to become a statesman. But that ambition became extinct leaving no trace behind. If anything was left in me, it was the impressions which I received during my journey in the foreign lands, especially the impression which enhanced my sentiment of deploring the attitude of aloofness between government officers and civilians. Out of these impressions an idea was born in me whispering that the country must increase real wealth and at the same time the discrimination between official and civilian must be done away. I might no longer be fitted to assume a political roll in the world but be able to contribute something along this line. Henceforth I must address myself to this cause. This desire dawned on me while I was in France and became more intense on my return.

Just about this time—namely in the winter of 1869, I was invited by the Government, especially by a strong appeal from Marquis Okuma, to enter into official life taking an office in the Finance Department. This start, however, was not my primary purpose. My sole purpose was fixed, as already stated, on industry. I wanted to improve and elevate the status of business men. I was convinced that unless business men can come to stand shoulder to shoulder with statesmen, scholars, and other public men, the true wealth and power of the county could not be realized. I worked under Marquis Inouye during the tenure of my office, and when he resigned his office, I followed him. This meant for me that I should be a banker.

" The Premier threw me a bouquet stating that I rendered a valuable service to the business world by publishing the regulations for business organization under the cooperative system. Really I felt the need of such regulations while I was travelling in foreign countries. Hence I gave my best effort to bring them out into a concrete form, but as I had no personal experience along these lines, I was shaky as to the outcome. My conviction on the question that the present condition existing between official and civilian must be improved was adamant, although it was somewhat vague in detail. I cannot claim any merit on my part as my ability was insufficient, but the trend of the time seemed to have coincided with my hopes. The result was the marvelous development of the business world during the last sixty years, far surpassing what I had imagined. I might say that the character of business men was improved rather than business itself. I am now an old man retired from business life long ago. And yet you are so generous as to invite me to this brilliant occasion celebrating my 88th birthday, honored by the presence of the Premier who gave a magnificent address. Would you charge me with impudence if I say that the Premier's participation in this function clearly demonstrates the close approach between official and civilian? (Applause). I believe that what I yearned for at the beginning of the Meiji Era, when I returned from France, was indeed vague. But looking back to it even now I can see that it was by no means a Utopia. There was truth in it, though the vision of it was not clear and distinct until today. But now in this very moment the vision is freed from any shadow of doubt and stands before me full-orbed. (Applause)

" When I look at this gathering from this angle, I must say that, by giving me this high honor, you have at the same time borne witness to the present state of our country.

" Perhaps I have bored you by my long story instead of expressing my thanks to you. But what a satisfaction to me as I am brought face to face to the fact that my vision of the dawn of the day when I could see the realization of human equality and the elevation of the business world was not an illusion I am almost intoxicated by genuine joy and gratitude. But in this moment of exuberance I must not forget that this congratulatory gathering is a demonstration which has a national significance and for which it should be felicitated.

" In the address, just made by Dr. Dan, he hinted that I should live yet longer, and he and his colleagues would again felicitate me. I shall be delighted to welcome such an opportunity, anticipating an occasion when I shall be able to tell you a still better story than I am telling you on my 88th birthday. It is my earnest desire to express the sense of my appreciation by continuing to do good. I fear that my response to your congratulations may not meet your approval. Be that as it may, I beg you to take it as my honest confession. Let me again thank you most heartily for this splendid function. (Applause) "

A brilliant banquet followed the afternoon celebrations. Dr. Willhelm Solf, the German Ambassador who was the doyen of the foreign diplomatic representatives, made a table speech in the evening, proposing a toast to Viscount Shibusawa.

The Ambassador thus spoke :

" Mr. Takuma Dan and Baron Goh in their speeches on the stage have dwelt on the eminent and distinguished services which our guest of honor has rendered to his country by building up in wise and conservative lines the financial and economic structure of Japan. The merits of Viscount Shibusawa not only lie in Japan itself, he has done great work also in furthering the relations of Japan with foreign countries. He represents in himself so to speak a ministry of the Interior and a ministry of Foreign Affairs. I consider it a great honor that the promoters of this august festivity have granted the privilege of proposing the toast of the day to a member of the foreign community and I am proud that I have been selected as speaker. Viscount Shibusawa has devoted his life rich in the experience of many decades to the task of making his country known throughout the world, and that in this he has succeeded brilliantly, we see in the position Japan has won in the whole world as a Power which plays a most important part in the concert of the nations. Although I am not authorized to speak in the name and on behalf of the Diplomatic Corps I am convinced that my colleagues, of whom I see many present here, gladly take part with me in celebrating our guest's 88th anniversary.

" Gentlemen, I call upon you to join with me in drinking to the health of Viscount Shibusawa."

Again receiving a thunderous ovation, the Viscount, the guest of honor rose and spoke :

" The high honor you have conferred upon me this evening in this brilliant banquet on the 88th anniversary of my birth is far beyond anything I deserve, and I am filled with such profound gratitude as I have hardly ever experienced throughout my entire life. Think of the present company. It includes not only the great leaders in the official and civilian circles at home but the Ambassadors and Ministers of the Powers of the West and the East. This is an international festivity, and to be favored with such a function is indeed the choicest honor of which one can justly be proud.

The words of Ambassador Solf so generously lavished upon me make me blush. I wish I were equal to them. However, I shall accept them as warning and encouragement to me for the future rather than the encomium on past achievement.

"As a token of my deep appreciation of this international gathering, I rise to the health of every gentleman present here this evening."

In concluding this chapter the author feels that further comment or remarks upon the theme under the review would spoil its value rather than increase it. Only he would challenge the future historian of Japan with this question: "Has any other single person in his life time built up such a huge structure of human culture in its broadest sense as Viscount Shibusawa has done?"

CHAPTER XV

ILLNESS, DEATH, AND FUNERAL

THERE is an old seventeen syllabled verse which
may be translated something like this:

> A raven perched on
> The dead limb of a tree
> At the dusk of autumn.

Can we imagine a darker and gloomier picture?
"Raven", "dead limb," "dusk," and "autumn" what
a quartet! Dante could not have heard a quartet
singing in Purgatory which would have sounded more
dreary than this one. And yet we are hearing this
sort of music in our daily life as a vital part of our
earthly existence. This time it is a trio instead of a
quartet—illness, death, and funeral!

From time immemorial mankind has been forced to
listen to this trio, but has never been reconciled to the
music. High and low; rich and poor; old and young;
men and women; clergy and laity; and even militarists
are requisitioned to attend the concert hall of this music,
free of charge. Many would gladly pay any amount
if by so doing, they could be excused from their attendance, but all in vain. Hence they reluctantly resign
themselves to the inevitability of this dreary music and
begin to prepare themselves against its poisonous effects
upon their minds and bodies. Hostipals, crematories, and
cemeteries have been prepared, and have become necessities just as much as clothing, food, and dwellings.

The living must surely die, and those who meet are bound to separate. So teaches Buddhism. Confucius airily explains away the problem of death by saying that as one knows so little about life how can he know anything about death.

Illness is a prologue to death, and the cemetery is its epilogue. An impenetrable mystery shrouds them all.

Viscount Shibusawa, a repository of sound common sense and practical wisdom, was well aware of the futility of delving into the mystery, and met it as such, when it stared him in the face. He knew that his family physician was the one to attend him when he was threatened by illness. When the illness was serious, and the doctor advised him to prepare for the inevitable hour, he calmly resigned himself to it, and gave instructions about his posthumous affairs.

He used to tell us in the evening of his life, that he had outlived the limit put on the average life, and was not inclined to ask for further longevity simply for its own sake. With every kind of comfort and pleasure at his command, and surrounded by a host of children, grandchildren and great-grandchildren, he was the happiest man on earth. The life in paradise could not be happier than what he was enjoying here below day after day. If possible, he would remain with them forever, and they would have him with them always. But Death, the tyrant of tyrants, proclaims the unalterable decree that there is no permanent existence for mankind on earth. He speaks to emperors, kings, generals, admirals, statesmen, philosophers, bankers, and millionaires, saying:

" As he came forth from his mother's womb, naked shall he

return to go as he came, and shall take nothing of his labour."

Confucius says :

" The wise are free from perplexities; the virtuous from anxiety; and the brave from fear."

Viscount Shibusawa in the latter days of his life was indeed an incarnation of the truth expressed by the Chinese sage. He was perfectly free from perplexities, anxiety, and fear, because he was wise, virtuous, and brave. There was that serenity, solidity, and dignity about him, which can be felt by one gazing at Mount Fuji late in the fall, when the air is clear and limpid. Nothing in this world ruffled him. He transcended the threat of death in that he took it as one of the many mysteries fastened to the life of men. So was he prepared to respond to the last roll call, ready to give up all his fame, power, prestige, wealth, and even his family ties.

Several months preceding the end of his earthly pilgrimage, he had been somewhat ill, but showing no particular sympton.

Mr. Shiraishi gives the following description of the Viscount's movements :

" We would inquire into the activities of the Viscount in the year 1931 (the year he passed away). On the New Year morn, he received callers in his Ai-i Sonsô, but as he had contracted a cold toward the close of the year, he did not attend his time honored gathering of Dai Ichi Ginko for the New Year felicitation. He quietly spent the New Year days in recuperation. On the 26th of January, he, though not quite himself, attended the ordinary General Meeting of Dai Ichi Ginko, as President Sasaki (the Viscount's right hand man for many decades in the bank, and his immediate successor as its president) was to resign the office. He spent the whole month of February at home for rest; on March 1st, he held in Ai-i Sonsô a gathering in honor of the outgoing and incoming Presidents of Dai Ichi Ginko; on the 3rd, he attended the councillors' meeting of Chu-Nichi Jitsu-gyo Kaisha (China-Japan Industry Company); the next day, the 4th he attended the anniversary luncheon of the opening of the Imperial Theatre. Then another recuperation period; on the 8th of April, he held an extraordinary meeting of the Board of Trustees of Nihon Joshi Dai Gakko at Ai-i Sonsô; on the 13th he attended the wedding reception of Mr. Nobuo Shibusawa (one of his grandsons); and on the 30th he called on Prince Tokugawa at the Peers' Club.

" In May, the Viscount showed improvement in his health; visited the Art Gallery known as the Shunyô Kai where Mr. Hideo (the last and favorite son of the Viscount) won the competitive award to hang his painting on the walls. On the 5th, he attended the trustee meeting for the Prevention of Leprosy.

" On the 12th, he was received in audience by Her Imperial Majesty, the Empress Dowager, at the palace of Her Majesty.

" On the 19th, he presided over the Japanese American Relations Committee; on the 26th, he attended the meetings of the Board of Directors for the Prevention of Leprosy, and the Board of Directors of the Reconciliation Society; on the 30th, he attended the trustee meeting of Japan's Association of the League of Nations. On the 10th of June, he paid his respects to Prince Tokugawa (the descendant of Prince Yoshinobu Tokugawa, the last Shogun of the Tokugawa Regime, whom the Viscount had served as retainer); on the 13th, he visited the Tokyo City Poor House (the regular monthly day on which the Viscount, except in time of illness, made his visits during more than sixty years); on the 18th, he attended the directors' meeting of the Hôkô Kai, and the trustee meeting of the same (the Hôkô Kai is the Society organized to look after needy families of veterans), and also the tea party of the Jo Sui Kai (the Alumni Association of the Tokyo University of Commerce); on the 19th, he held a luncheon party at Ai-i Sonsô, in honor of Dr. Herbert S. Houston who with Mrs. Houston was visiting Tokyo as the guests of the Japanese American Relations Committee; on the 22nd, he attended the welcome and farewell meeting of the Nihon Joshi Dai Gakko for the incoming and outgoing Presidents.

"During July, on the 4th, he invited the Directors of the Ishikawa Jima Ship Building Company to Ai-i Sonsô; and on the 27th, he attended the ordinary General Meeting of Dai Ichi Ginko, for the explicit purpose of doing honor to Mr. K. Ishii at his debut as the new President.

"In August on the 5th, he held a farewell tea party in honor of Dr. and Mrs. Houston at Ai-i Sonsô.

"In September he made a radio address from Ai-i Sonsô as the President of the Sympathizers' Society for the Flood Disaster in China, on the evening of the sixth.

"Thus recounting his late activities, we are painfully surprised at the paucity of his daily program."

Mr. Hideo Shibusawa describes his father in those days:

"Father used to sit comfortably on the rattan armchair, often resting his feet on a rather thickly made cushioned stool. When the weather was inclement and too cool, the lower part of his body was wrapped in a black blanket. The darkly varnished and coarsely made rattan arm-chair was placed almost against the wall of the north side of the room, over-shadowed by the mantle piece on the left side. As he leaned back in the chair, his head almost touched the wall. The relaxed wrists peeped out of the sleeves of his plain Japanese clothing, and the five fingers of each hand assumed a most natural position placed on the arms of the chair as though they were slightly grasping the arms. His large head of fine profile; the wide nose; the lustrous skin somewhat like that of a European; and the stomach like that of the painted Hotei (a deity of good luck)—all manifested a perfect contentment. Truly his posture gave forth an atmosphere of profound peace and unassailable solidity. When I read a book to him, sometimes he innocently smiled and at other times asked questions. At still other times, he would pause for a few minutes to drink deep the meaning of a sentence or two just read. His alertness and tireless endurance could not make us believe that he was an old man of ninety two years. While I was thus reading a book to him, I was reminded of the words found in the closing of the Kuei Chu Lai (歸去來) of Tao Yuan Ming (陶淵明) which father was specially fond of reading in his declining years. They read : ' I am resigned to fate through change, taking delight in the Ordeal of Heaven and doubting nothing.' Not infrequently was I clearly convinced that father had definitely reached both in mind and body the state of life here described."

This delicate picture painted by Mr. Hideo Shibusawa revives the memory of the frequent experiences the author encountered during the three months visit to America as interpreter and English secretary of the Viscount at the time of the Washington Conference for disarmament. The Viscount wore neither moustache nor beard. He kept his face cleanly shaved. This meant his frequent visits to barber shops. His interpreter always accompanied the Viscount like his shadow. After the shaving, or the hair cut, the Viscount was always taken to the manicurist, invariably a young woman, who was as a rule agreeable and sociable almost to the point of coquettishness.

She would say to him : ' What a beautiful hand !' This attracted the author's attention to the finger nails of the Viscount. In them he found the strength and beauty which characterized the entire physical constitution of the Viscount. The strength consisted of his well proportioned large finger-nails of smooth, thick and concave shape, and the beauty of their pink colour and rich new moons which we Japanese call kai-zume (shell nail). While we are on this point, it would be interesting for the reader to listen to a quaint story told by the Viscount about himself in his younger days and also to the testimony of the family physician about the health condition of the Viscount when beyond ninety.

The Viscount says:

"The height of my body was just about the same as now. Though small in stature, yet I was quite stout and had much strength. What I am telling you is an old story. It was at the time when I was studying Gekken (fencing), under the tutorship of Heibei Okawa. Once he and I lived as travelling fencers (a travelling fencer in those days journeyed from place to place to challenge fights with the leaders of that art in the training institutions). I had a hard time travelling more than twenty miles on foot carrying on my shoulders the fencing instruments—both his and mine.

"Teacher Okawa was tall and imposing. I was fat and small. It was quite a task to keep pace with him. And he was empty handed while I had to carry a heavy load. It was no joke for me. However I succeeded in keeping step with him because I had the strength in me."

Dr. Hayashi, the family physician, tells:

"The Viscount possessed a fine physique. His nutrition was perfect. The skin of his body was white, elastic, and beautiful, rarely seen among Orientals. The flesh of the body together with the lustrous complexion reminded one of the constitution of a young woman of typical health, so much so that we could find no sign of decline in his health in any part of his body."

Mr. Shiraishi continues to describe the Viscount's movements and says:

" The Viscount was greatly narrowed in the scope of his activities by the charge of his physician to stay much of the time at home. He had a chronic trouble of asthma, which compelled him to sit in the rattan chair, instead of lying on the bed. This habit had to be increasingly resorted to from August to September. In October his daily program became more and more lonely. At the beginning of the month the discomfort in his bowels took a bad turn and produced even pain. Finally it was aggravated into an intestinal obstruction which could not be left unattended to. The best medical authorities Japan could afford were summoned, and they together with the family and close relatives of the Viscount held a conference regarding the treatment of the patient. They reached the conclusion that he should undergo an operation. It was conveyed to the Viscount who acquiesced in the decision, and the date of the operation was set for the 14th of October. But two days before the date fixed—that is on the 12th, the Viscount expressed the desire to give up the operation for the reason expressed in the following words: ' I am an old man of ninety two years of age, who should already have been dead from the average standard of life. I have lived long enough not to covet further pilgrimage. Of course, there remains for me plenty to do, and I do not wish deliberately to shorten the natural course. What I desire is to avoid any artificial method to prolong my life. I know nothing about the kind of trouble in my intestines, but I do not wish to seem to have such a passion for life as to prolong it even through an operation. I am prepared to go, and if possible would prefer to pass on in the condition just as I am. Although I yielded to the kind counsel of you all, yet I would forego the operation, because I cannot free myself from the notion that I am undergoing it from a lingering attachment to the earthly life.'

" The thought expressed here by the Viscount was characteristic and worthy of him. But his plea could not be honored with ready acceptance for the obvious reason that he would suffer intolerable pain if not operated upon. So another conference was held and Mr. T. Shibusawa, the eldest son, was asked to convey to his father what was decided in the conference. It was briefly this; that it was perfectly understandable that he would forego the operation if the motive for it were as he construed it; but it was necessary for the speedy relief from the awful pain surely to come upon him. The operation is of no special type. It is a well known method to be applied to the case like that of the Viscount. In order to avoid publicity, it could be performed at home.

" In this the Viscount acquiesced and the operation was to take place on the 14th of October. Dr. Shioda the best surgeon in all Japan took charge of it."

It was said that Dr. Shioda showed a grave concern over the operation. So much so that he almost hesitated to apply his surgical knife to the Viscount, not because he was afraid of the physical constitution, the vitality, and the soundness of the internal organs of the patient, but because of his unprecedented experience of operating on a patient over ninety years of age. Therefore Dr. Shioda warned the attending physicians and nurses to give the most careful and best possible attention to the condition of the patient. The operation was satisfactorily performed, and the recovery favorable, although a slight rise of fever was observed. But the deepest concern was the lack of appetite on the part of the patient. No effort to restore it was spared, but all in vain. The weakening of the patient was daily increasing.

The kinsfolks and the physician in charge agreed that the public should be informed of the condition of the Viscount, as the public through newspapers had begun to show restlessness, no less than those who were near to the patient. So on the 31st of October, eighteen days after the performance of the operation, the following statement of his condition was published in all the papers of the city :

"Since the spring of this year the patient has been suffering from an obstinate constipation hard to cure. As a pertuberance was observable on the left side of the bowels, the Roentgen ray examination was made at the beginning of August, which clearly showed that there existed a stricture in the colon. In the early part of October he felt pain in the bowels which had swollen. For a while the symptoms looked like a stoppage of the passage of the intestines, giving him an intolerable pain. Hence as a final resort Dr. Shioda was requested to conduct the operation of forming an artificial rectum at the home of the patient on the 14th of October. The result was satisfactory, but later on a light fever rose. The appetite became dull which deprived the patient of nourishment. Failing symptoms began to manifest themselves."

The publication of the news soon brought streams of anxious visitors to the Ai-i Sonso. The newspaper correspondents spent days and nights to send out to their papers the bulletins given out by the physician in charge every few hours.

The official bulletin issued on the evening of the last day of October at eight o'clock stated ;

"At half past one o'clock, a chill siezed the patient, lasting nearly one hour. At three o'clook it changed into a high fever, which did not go down even toward sunset.

"Temperature	Pulse	Respiration
39	112	36

The bulletin of the morning of the first day of November at 10 o'clock gives the following account :

"Though the temperature fell symptoms of bronchopneumonia appeared. Poor appetite continues."

On this day, Her Majesty the Empress was exceedingly gracious to bestow upon the Viscount a gift of fresh vegetables through her imperial messenger. Soup was prepared from them and given to him which he took with profound gratitude.

On the next day, the 2nd, the Viscount was favored with gifts of chrysanthemums, quails' eggs, and milk from Her Majesty, the Empress Dowager, through her imperial messenger. He most reverently received them.

No improvement was noticeable. The poor appetite continued. In the spacious sick room no outsiders save the close relatives, the attending physicians, and nurses were admitted. But there was one exceptional case and that was the visit of Mr. Y. Sasaki, ex-President of Dai Ichi Ginko. About this incident Mr. Keizo Shibusawa, grandson and heir of the Viscount, gives the following account :

" I believe it was either on the third or fourth of November that I requested Mr. Sasaki to step into the room by the permission of the physician in charge. In the room there were present the physicians, Mr. Hayashi and Mr. Sakurazawa, besides Dr. Irisawa. Grandfather at that time was lying on the bed with the head slightly raised and lying on his right side. He was not sleeping, but closing his eyes lightly. No sign of discomfort was shown. In order to look at the face of grandfather one had to go around to the back of the bed. Mr. Sasaki assuming a tender attitude as if he dreaded to squarely look into the face of bed-ridden grandfather, quietly approached him, bowed to him to pay final respect, and seemed quickly to leave the room. I told grandfather : ' Mr. Sasaki is here to inquire after your health.' Grandfather lightly opened his eyes, and gazed at Mr. Sasaki for a while. He stretched out his right hand. Mr. Sasaki with a certain hesitancy grasped the hand of grandfather with his right hand and then with his left warmly enfolded the patient's hand. Mr. Sasaki saying ' Doka o daiji ni' (Please take great care) withdrew his hands. Deep silence, and the time seemed quite long.

" There were no tears in the eyes of the two men. The utterance of only a word or two, and the rest dead silence, calm and serene. As the interview between the two men who had weathered the storms of life for a common cause in profound mutual trust during the last sixty years and who were now fully conscious of the fact that this was the last moment to see each other, it looked to me first rather cold and sadly dry, but No. The atmosphere in the room was permeated with a great solemnity, so that even the faint rustle of handkerchiefs was audible. I turned back and found that all the doctors were struggling hard to repress the flowing tears."

Thus hour by hour the condition of the Viscount was growing worse until the crisis of his earthly career became a question of time. This boding news reached the Imperial Household. His Imperial Majesty the Emperor graciously granted to the patient a gift of wine, and inquired after his condition by dispatching Mr. Murayama, the court physician at fifteen minutes past twelve o'clock midnight. On the next morning, the 10th, at 11 o'clock Baron Hozumi, a grandson of the Viscount paid a visit to the Imperial Household to express on behalf of the Viscount the gratitude for the visit of the court physician. On this day beginning atbout 7 o'clock in the morning the change for the worst became visible, and those who had kept vigil day and night began to quietly walk into the sick room to bid the patient final farewell.

Meanwhile the Viscount was without much pain, but breathing uneasily though assisted by the application of a lung-motor. At a little after eleven o'clock, an Imperial message was solemnly read by Mr. Keizo:

"Viscount Eiichi Shibusawa: The First Class Order of Merit, Second Court Rank, Junior Grade, is by special grace promoted to the Second Court Rank, Senior Grade."

The temperature was gradually rising from forty degrees to a little over forty-three; the respiration was getting difficult; and the atmosphere in the room unbearably heavy, when a clock on the mantle piece struck twelve.

The 11th of November—the Armistice Day of the Great World War was soon to dawn.

At fifty minutes after one o'clock of this memorable day, the stout heart which had steadily beaten for nearly ninety-two long years suddenly stopped its work, and the end came....

A mighty soul took its flight, leaving behind its earthly tabernacle, through which it had achieved incomparable good in promoting a healthy civilization, based on and controlled by the principle of the harmony of economics and morality. The entire nation from the highest to the lowest were in mourning over the departure of Viscount Shibusawa. As soon as the sad news was flashed over the country through radio announcement and the newspapers, streams of mourners began to surge into Ai-i Sonso.

As it is customary in case of the death of a public man, the formal announcement of the death of the Viscount was made public through the leading papers of Tokyo, signed by Keizo Shibusawa, the heir, the Shibusawa Household, and Mr. Yunosuke Sasaki.

The announcemnt read :

" We respectfully announce in place of personal notice that Viscount Eiichi Shibusawa, First Class Order of Merit, Second Court Rank, Senior Grade, who has been ill died today at fifty minutes after 1 o'clock a. m. The farewell rites will be conducted at the Aoyama Funeral Hall according to the Buddhist form on the 15th from one to three o'clock p. m. In conformity to the Will, friends are requested to withhold from making any gift of flowers and other offerings."

It was through careful consideration that the Funeral Committee finally decided to have the services conducted at the Aoyama Funeral Hall. Ai-i Sonso was first considered, but it was not sufficiently spacious to accommodate automobiles and the host of visitors. The family temple, near which the interment was to take place, was mentioned, but the lack of transportation facilities, especially if it might rain, was a strong objection against the choice. The temporary arrangement at Hibiya Park was suggested.

It was ruled out, as such an elaborate plan might not befit the will of the departed. The bereaved members all agreed to this. Thus final choice fell on the Aoyama Funeral Hall, although much anxiety was felt as to its adequacy to hold the funeral services of so great a man of national fame.

But the police and municipal authorities in one accord offered their best possible assistance to make the funeral procession orderly and dignified. The chairman of the Funeral Committee, vice-chairman, two executive secretaries, forty advisors, and six hundred committee men were severally assigned to such duties as reception for foreigners, ceremony, intermediary, ushers, gifts, finance,

Four Generations of the Shibusawa Family.

The Late Viscount.   Viscount K. Shibusawa.
Late Mr. T. Shibusawa
Master, M. Shibusawa

Aii Sonso (Asukayama home) consisting of:

Gate

Houses in the Japanese and Foreign Styles,
Sei-en Bunko (library),
Bankoro (hall for tea party),
Airendo (memorial hall brought from Korea)

Mushin An (cottage for tea ceremony).
View of Garden.

meals, recording, correspondence, transportation, and headquarters. Each group of the Committee held conferences and the full range of discussions resulted in faultless preparations.

The group meetings were held frequently until the very morning when the funeral procession was started.

The committee on gifts had a most difficult task to discharge in the enforcement of the non-acceptance decision of gifts of flowers, wreaths, and other offerings. As soon as the sad news was known by the public, some big families vied with each other in expressing their condolences accompanied by offerings.

Although the Headquarters allowed no time to be lost in making this non-acceptance announcement, yet it took some hours to make it fully known to the public. Placards of non-acceptance were erected in places where various gifts were to be brought in. Some of the gift-bearers would not listen to the courteous refusal of the usher, and the Chairman or vice-Chairman had to come out to solve the question.

Even after the public announcement was made through the city papers distinctly stating the non-acceptance of any gift, a host of mourners presented their condolence offerings all of which were firmly but most courteously declined.

There was excuse for disregarding the non-acceptance announcement on the part of the mourning public, because in many cases the announcement becomes a dead letter, or a mere formality, and offerings are accepted in spite of the public declaration.

The funeral committee in this case really meant what it publicly stated and was determined to enforce it how-

ever embarassing a situation the act might create. The
reason for it was plain and simple, and at the same
time was a cogent one. It was the wish and will of
the Viscount that in death as well as in life he should
in no wise cast even the least burden upon the shoulders of others.

But there was an exception as there is always an
exception to rules.

With Japanese citizens an invitation or a gift from
the Imperial Household amounts to an absolute command
to be accepted with profound gratitude. In case of an
invitation no other excuse is permissible but illness,
mourning, and absence from the country. The Committee on the funeral therefore most gratefully accepted
the condolence gifts from the Imperial Household. This
attitude was also assumed towards the gifts from the
Princes of the blood. The condolence gifts from the two
Tokugawa families of Tokyo, and the Tokugawa family
of Mito, were treated with special regard, because the
Viscount was a retainer of Prince Yoshinobu Tokugawa, the last Shogun of the Tokugawa regime. Then
floral and other offerings from Ambassadors and Ministers of foreign countries, and from the chief mourner, the
other members of the bereaved family and close relatives,
were placed in the category of "exceptions".

It would seem somewhat out of place to make any
comment on the events which transpired during those
days of mourning and deep sorrow. Yet that firm
consistence on the part of the funeral committee, especially on the part of the Chairman and vice-Chairman,
to the public announcement of the non-acceptance of
gifts and offerings from general mourners, fully anti-

cipating confusion, difficulty, and even hurt feelings, should highly be commended. On the one hand it was a deed worthy of the followers of one whose supreme concern in life was the persistent maintenance of moral integrity, and on the other it was a valuable lesson incidentally thrown before the public, intimating that people should be careful not to drift into the moral laxity which has frequently been tolerated as a matter of course in funeral events among the well-to-do classes. This business-like, nay moral-like, reform which seemed on the surface so eccentric and bold, was achieved by the committee and admired by thoughtful men, only because of the spirit of the central figure who " being dead, yet speaketh." Only because of the thorough understanding of that spirit by the committee, especially by its Chairman and vice-Chairman, were they able to carry out the determination at any cost. Who were the Chairman and vice-Chairman? They were the surviving lieutenants of the Viscount in Dai Ichi Ginko—ex-President Sasaki and President Ishii respectively.

On the morning of the 11th, Mr. Keizo Shibusawa, the heir and chief mourner, received the following letter from Baron Ikki, the Minister of the Imperial Household :

" Being informed of the death of Viscount Eiichi Shibusawa, First Class Order of Merit, Senior Grade of the Second Court Rank, I have the honor of communicating to you that, by special grace,

His Majesty the Emperor's messenger at thirty minutes after 2 o'clock in the after-noon

Her Majesty the Empress' messenger at forty minutes after 2 o'clock and

Her Majesty the Empress Dowager's messenger at fifty minutes after 2 o'clock
will be dispatched to his residence today for condolence.

The appointed hour came and the kinsfolks stood on both sides of the hallway to receive the Imperial messengers. Mr. K. Shibusawa attended the special visitors.

At 10 o'clock, a. m. Her Majesty the Empress Dowager granted offerings through the Imperial messenger. Their Majesties the Emperor and Empress granted a culinary gift for one hundred persons. Princess Takeda, Prince Fushimi, and Prince Kuni in their capacities as President of Tokyo Jikei Kai (The Tokyo Charity Society), President of Shibun Kai oyobi Tokyo Ri-Ka Gaku Kenkyu Jo, (The Chinese Culture Society and the Tokyo Research Institute of Physics and Chemistry), and President of Shōtoku Taishi Hosan Kai (The Patrons' Society of the Prince Shōtoku) granted offerings through the messengers of their Highnesses.

The day swiftly wore on as the committees on the funeral preparations and reception were kept busy. Eight o'clock p. m. was fixed for the ceremony of placing the body in the coffin. Preceding this ceremony, the bereaved members gathered together to bid the final farewell. The rites were conducted by the Chief Priest Otaki, and incense was burned by the mourners present.

After the rites of utmost tenderness were finished, the coffin which consisted of double caskets—inner and outer—was taken into the main hall. It was covered with snow-white silk cloth and placed on the supports. On the coffin a large framed photograph was placed, literally buried by gifts and flowers granted from the

Imperial Household, the Princes of the Blood, and the Tokugawa families. The following decorations were arranged in order : the Grand Cordon of the Rising Sun with the Paulownia Flower ; the First Order of Merit ; the Order of the Sacred Treasure ; the Legion d'honneur of France ; and the First Royal Crown of Belgium.

At nine o'clock the messenger of Prince Takamatsu paid his visit and burned incense. After the chanting of the Buddhistic prayer, the incense burning ceremony took place. A wake was held by many friends of the Viscount besides those whose names were specially mentioned for the purpose. The night of the 13th was spent in attendance on the remains by the friends whose names were specified and also by volunteers. On this day Her Majesty the Empress Dowager granted a culinary gift, and Prince Kan-in as President of Onshi Zaidan Saisei Kai (the Philanthropic Institute of the Imperial Donation, Inc.) also granted offerings.

The 14th—the day before the funeral came, and the committees of funeral arrangements held several conferences to make thorough preparation for the occasion. Every detail was discussed. On the other hand the reception committee and ushers were kept busy confronted now and then with the question of non-acceptance of gifts.

It was previously heralded through the Imperial Household that the Imperial messengers for condolence were to be dispatched to the Shibusawa residence on the morning of this day and the preparation for their reception was made.

As was arranged, at ten o'clock the messenger of His

Majesty the Emperor arrived. Mr. Keizo led the messenger into the parlor. After a little while Mr. Keizo most reverently received the following gifts from the hand of the messenger:

A Scroll of Imperial Message.
One Enclosure of a grant for Religious Service, from
    Their Majesties the Emperor and Empress.
Five Rolls of White Silk.
Eight Trays of Cake-offerings.
A Pair of Floral offerings.

The scroll was borne by Mr. Keizo and the other gifts were carried by Baron Morimura, Baron Furukawa, and Mr. S. Asano. Mr. E. Tanaka prepared an incense-burner and at the signal given by Mr. T. Hara all the mourners present stood up. The Imperial messenger led by Count S. Hashimoto walked into the room. The entire scene was stillness itself. Every member of the Shibusawa family and the others present on the occasion were profoundly impressed by the high honor bestowed upon the Viscount. Again ushering the messenger into a reception room Mr. Keizo expressed to him sincere gratitude.

At 10:20 a. m. the messenger of Her Majesty the Empress appeared. Her Majesty granted the gift of a pair of floral offerings through the messenger who also burned incense.

At 10:30 a. m. the messenger of Her Majesty the Empress Dowager made his appearance, through whom Her Majesty granted the gifts of one enclosure of a grant for religious service and a pair of floral offerings. He burned incense and retired.

Then Mr. Keizo most reverently unrolled the scroll of the Imperial Message and read:

" *With lofty purpose he accepted a high office in the Government. With rare foresight he entered into the business world. Many were his creative activities in that sphere. His social work was full of various enterprises. Rich were his contributions to the advancement of culture. He strove to promote international friendship. He devoted his entire life to the improvement of public welfare. His career was permeated with truthfulness. He was indeed a peerless authority in the field of economics, commanding confidence of all classes. He was a model of citizenry, worthy of admiration of men at home and abroad. His death is sincerely deplored. Let these articles be a token of condolence.*"

It is needless to say that it was a most impressive moment causing many to sob.

The day passed quickly and night came on. This being the very last night for the mortal part of a great soul to linger, a larger number of mourners kept the vigil.

At last the day for the funeral came. The farewell rites were performed at 7 o'clock in the morning by the bereaved members of the family, the close relatives, and other mourners in the midst of the chant of Buddhist scriptures led by the Chief Priest Otaki. The coffin was transferred to the hearse. The automobiles for the use of the procession were numbered. At 8:40, the preparation for the procession towards the Funeral Hall was completed, and at 9 o'clock the signal of trumpet for the start was given. All along the route through which the procession passed the entire traffic was stopped. Every house had flags at half mast and both sides of the road in the Takinogawa ward were lined with an immense number of citizens and the stu-

dents of schools with which the Viscount was vitally
related. The cortege arrived at the Hall on time and
the preparation for the last public rites was completed
at 9 : 55 o'clock.

At the further side of the platform of the Hall,
the palanquin was placed, and on its front a large
picture of the Viscount in a frame was set up. Then
various offerings were arranged. In front of these a
stand was placed and on it three incense burners
were laid. In the middle, the burner for the use
of the Emperor's messenger, on the right, one for the
use of the Empress' messenger, and on the left another
for the use of the Empress Dowager's messenger were
arranged.

On the right and left, close to the stand, the offerings of the close relatives were arranged. In front
of them, the floral offerings of the three Majesties, the
Emperor, the Empress, and the Empress Dawager were
arranged on both sides. Behind them and on both
sides fifteen pairs of sakaki (sacred trees), the offerings
from the households of all the Imperial Princes, were
arranged. Facing the seats where the bereaved members
and the relatives sat, the floral offerings from the French
Ambassador, a wreath from the American Ambassador,
and the floral offerings of Prince Iyesato Tokugawa,
Prince Yoshimitsu Tokugawa, and of Prince Kuniyuki
Tokugawa were arranged in a row. At the front of
the seats on the left a wreath from the Minister of the
Republic of China, and the floral offerings of the three
Tokuwaga families stood in line.

At the front of the seats of the members of the
bereaved family, Prince and Princess Iyesato Tokugawa,

Prince Yoshimitsu Tokugawa and his mother, and Prince and Princess Kuniyuki Tokugawa took their seats. Behind them, the bereaved family and relatives were seated. On the opposite side, Mr. Yunosuke Sasaki, Mr. Kengo Ishii, Mayor Nagata, Baron Seinosuke Goh, Baron Takuma Dan, Baron Toranosuke Furukawa, Baron Kishichiro Okura, and other advisors were seated.

Now the preparation of the Hall for receiving the Imperial messengers was completed. The prearranged hour 10 o'clock came, and the Emperor's messenger, Chamberlain Honda, arrived. Led by Count Hashimoto, the messenger walked into the Hall as all present stood and approached the incense burner and performed the rites. At 10:05 o'clock, the messenger of the Empress, Mr. Noguchi led by Mr. Takemaro Kaneko, and at 10:10 o'clock, the messenger of the Empress Dowager, Mr. Nishimura led by Baron Okura, performed the rites. As soon as the Imperial messengers finished their solemn duties, the Chief Priest Otaki and his attendants began to perform the ceremony. In the meanwhile, condolences were brought in and laid on the altar. There was a large number of them. At the end of the chant, Mayor Nagata proceeded to the altar and read his condolence. Baron Goh, representing the Japan Chamber of Commerce and Industry, did the same.

Thus the entire ceremony for the funeral services was concluded at 11 : 30 as was planned. What remained were the rites of farewell by the public mourners. Two hours for the performance of these rites were allowed.

At noon they had begun to pour in and wait for the door to open. From the street to the Hall, along the left side of the passage as they walked in, the reception committee sat behind tables covered with white cloth. On the tables were trays to receive the cards of mourners.

At one o'clock, the door of the Hall was thrown wide open and the mourners two in a row at first, then three, and finally four walked in. They walked up to the front of the altar and bowed before the palanquin.

It is customary that each mourner should burn incense on the table, but in order that the services should be hastened that part was omitted by the visitors, a priest constantly burning incense for them. It was estimated that 40,000 mourners paid their last honor to the Viscount within the two hours. Thus the ceremony in the Hall was concluded. The next rites to be performed were the interment rites at the grave.

It was after sunset when the cortege reached the cemetery, where everything was in the perfect order to conduct the burial rites.

Another rite of the chant of the Buddhist Scriptures was performed by the Chief Priest Otaki. The ceremony of the incense burning by the family, the relatives, and other mourners was repeated before the casket was lowered into the grave.

The time was the evening of November 15th, late in autumn. A cold wind was blowing and the leaves of trees around were falling, reminding one of the peculiar custom of self-immolation practiced in ancient days by the courtiers at the burial of their sovereign.

CHAPTER XVI

THE MEMORIAL STATUE

IF Viscount Shibusawa could have had his own choice, he would not have had any memorial statue erected for him. He persistently maintained this attitude. Perhaps his child-like simplicity and sense of modesty made him feel that he did not deserve such high honor, for he was almost too extremely plain in his habits.

During his tour in America in the winter of 1921–22, his toilet paraphernalia consisted only of a tooth-brush and an old fashioned Japanese comb carried in a folded black paper called *tato*.

In midsummer days, he used to carry a *tenugui* instead of a regular handkerchief. There is nothing wrong for a gentleman wearing a frock coat to use *tenugui* to mop his brow. It is only an innovation. The Viscount undoubtedly preferred *tenugui* to a handkerchief, because the former is softer and more absorbing than the latter. There is another illustration which demonstrates his taste for plain living. It was his long accustomed usage to carry all letters and documents in *shingen-bukuro* or in *furoshiki*. They were put together in a good order, but it had not infrequently happened that important letters or documents were either mislaid or mixed up with other papers, so that considerable delay in finding the missing ones was incurred.

Mr. K. Shibusawa, who made it his pleasant duty to watch over every movement of his grandfather and make his life easy, comfortable, and satisfactory, had seen more than once such confusion and disturbance in this use of a *furoshiki*. So he conceived the idea that if a good size valise with several partitions were bought for the use of his grandfather, it might save him from the troubles above mentioned, as the documents could be classified in the pockets of the Valise. The Viscount, always appreciative of any courtesy shown him, was very grateful to his grandson for this new and improved substitute, and made a good use of it for some time, but again reverted to the use of a *furoshiki* in such a way that even his close attendants hardly knew when the change took place. The Viscount was also known as a man without a summer or winter villa. Mr. Shiraishi comments that the Viscount did not care for a villa because he was so healthy and active that he preferred to be in constant touch with the busy world. The author gives full credit to the soundness of the observation of Mr. Shiraishi, believing at the same time that this trait of simplicity and modesty of the Viscount had much to do in denying him the common pleasure and recreation men of his class enjoy.

Then the question arises why was such an elaborate and grand statue erected for him? Was the Viscount compelled to bow to some irresistible power to change his mind? As no independent or self-respecting person allows himself to yield to coercion or oppression, the Viscount never accepted for himself or imposed upon others anything that savoured of impertinence or coercion.

Was the Viscount persuaded by his friends to acquiesce in the proposal of having a memorial statue erected in his honor even though he could not welcome

it with enthusiasm? This is a different proposition and
it is rightly conceivable that a man like the Viscount
possessing rare common sense and sound judgment might
have well afforded to yield to a strong appeal of his
friends, who though they fully understood and appreciated the moral embarrassment on his part in this
matter, yet felt that they could find no better and more
adequate way than to erect a memorial statue to express
their profound recognition of the great deeds of national
significance achieved by him and also to perpetuate the
memory of the man and his deeds for the good of
future generations.

This was exactly the situation which arose at the time
of the celebration of the 88th birthday of the Viscount,
sponsored by the leading business men of all Japan,
on the first day of October, 1928. As set forth in the
earlier chapter under the subject " Celebration of the
88th Birthday of Viscount Shibusawa, one of the most
important and significant events of the day was the
unanimous adoption of the resolution to erect a bronze
statue in honor of the Viscount.

Pursuant to this resolution, the promoters held a
conference at the Japan Industry Club on the same
day the celebration was held. The conference appointed
a committee of seven with full power to act. The late
J. Inouye was made the chairman of the committee,
although Baron Goh succeeded to the chairmanship when
Mr. Inouye became a cabinet member as Minister of Finance. While the committee was steadily working toward
the goal the Viscount died on the eleventh of November,
1931. Not long after his death nearly one hundred
business men, including most of the promoters of the

celebration of the 88th birthday of the Viscount, organized " Zaidan Hōjin Shibusawa Sei-en Ō Kinen Kai " (The Viscount Shibusawa Memorial Foundation, Inc.) The application to the Government for the organization was made by Baron Goh, representing the organizers on the 20th of December 1932 and the recognition was granted on the 12th of January 1933. Thus the organization was achieved and the work of erecting a memorial statue for the Viscount was transferred to the Foundation, which agreed to promote several other enterprises in addition to this one. The following is the translation of the prospectus of the Foundation :

" Early in November of the year 1931, when it dawned upon the mind of Viscount E. Shibusawa that his illness might prove fatal, he with his wonted graciousness asked his close attendant to transmit to junior friends of the business world the following words :

" ' I am now seriously ill, and deeply regret that I cannot live on to the age of one hundred years, so as to further serve my country in her progress. The country is now being confronted with many vexing problems, and is calling for your loyal support. Although I may soon be removed from this world into the Great Beyond, yet I shall abide with you in spirit to guard your health and the prosperity of the business world.'

" On the 26th of June of the same year, the Viscount prepared a will in which he charged his family that the buildings and compound of Ai-i Sonsô (Asukayama home) where he had lived more than thirty years should be donated to Ryumon-sha, the organization whose membership is composed of his admirers. A part of the Testament reads as follows :

" ' From the very time when I left my native place in my twenties, I have always kept in mind the sense of obligation to the State and Society. I have earnestly striven for the improvement of moral and social life ; the development of economy and industry ; the progress of business education as well as of women's education ; the advancement of social work ; the reconciliation between Labour and Capital ; and for the promotion of international friendship and world peace. I am now painfuly conscious of the fact that what I have accomplished falls far short of my eager expectations, and yet I can comfort myself in the thought that I poured my soul into whatever work I undertook to do with such determination as to let nothing but death halt my activities. Hence it will give me unspeakable joy if my heart's desire will be perpetuated even after my departure. The Asukayama villa, with its buildings, and gardens, has been my abode for the latter half of my life, but it was not built to satisfy my personal pleasure. I rather intended to use it for the purpose of carrying on the work above mentioned. For this reason I sincerely wish that the buildings and gardens should be similarly utilized in the future as in the past, making it a center where my deep concern for the State and Society may permanently be fostered.'

" The distinguished services and magnificent accomlishments of the late Viscount Shibusawa along the lines of industry and culture through the greater part of his long life of ninety two years are, without controversy, an object of emulation for us all. But great as are his numerous achievements, yet greater by far is his lofty patriotism—patriotism with which he stirs our emotions and which was already demonstrated in the remarks he made, even while he was hovering between life and death, utterly forgetting himself and his own interests. Can any one who reads these remarks of the Viscount remain unmoved by his transparent sincerity and not try to renew a stronger desire to serve his country better ? Is it any wonder then that the Viscount was, at his death, honored by His Imperial Majesty the Emperor with a gracious message of condolence.

" ' With lofty purpose he accepted a high office in the Government. With rare foresight he entered into the business world. Many were his creative activities in that sphere. His social work was full of various enterprises. Rich were his contributions to the advancement of culture. He strove to promote international friendship. He devoted his entire life to the improvement of public welfare. His career was permeated with truthfulness. He was indeed a peerless authority in the field of economics, commanding the confidence of all classes. He was a model of citizenship, worthy of the admiration of men at home and abroad.'

"The age in which we are now living is full of unrest both at home and abroad. At home many troubles beset us. Extreme and radical thoughts fill the air. Moral quality of fidelity and devotion is waning to a fearful degree. In such a time as this, we firmly believe that it is of an imperative necessity to lift up high before the eyes of the drifting world a great life like that of the late Viscount Shibusawa, which is characterized with unimpeachable honesty and genuine tenderness, thus stimulating moral and business life. Therefore, we who are of the same mind concurred to organize the Viscount Shibusawa Memorial Foundation, Inc., by appealing to friends in different parts of the country for subscriptions, and intend on the one hand to help build, through this institution, a bronze statue of the Viscount, to publish his biography, to permanently maintain Ai-i Sonso, and to astablish on the other hand works after the pattern he left behind, which will keep alive his influence for a long time. In this manner, we shall be able to remind the coming generations of a great man who will inspire them to a higher life and a nobler work.

"We anxiously await your enthusiastic and generous support in this cause."

Then the appeal for subscriptions was made signed by the constituents of the Foundation. The statement of the appeal reads as follows:

"Dear Sirs:

"We, the undersigned, agreed upon a plan to organize the

Tomb.

Zaidan Hojin Shibusawa Sei-en Ô Kinen Kai (The Viscount Shibusawa Memorial Foundation, Inc.) for the purpose of cherishing and fostering the memory of the noble life and towering achievements of the late Viscount E. Shibusawa. We are herein enclosing the prospectus and the outline of the accounts for the subscription and the enterprise, soliciting your kind consideration for and generous support of this project.

"Nothing would please us more highly than to receive your enthusiastic response in the matter."

On the other hand the preparations for the erection of the memorial statue were progressing. By the consent of the city of Tokyo, the site for the statue was fixed on a lot owned by the city near by the old Tokiwa Bridge, Marunouchi, Kojimachiku, Tokyo. The lot covers an area of 999 *tsubo,* one tsubo being six feet square, and 270 *tsubo* of its southeastern part was given to the statue and to accessories. The statue itself is 12 feet high, measuring 29 feet from the ground up. The front of the floor of the statue extends 122 feet along the bank revetment of the outer moat, with a width of 9 feet and height of 2 feet. In a space of 62 feet along the outer moat a wisteria-trellis and a bench were built. The floor of the statue is 35 feet square with the height of 4 feet. It is surrounded on the back and two sides with a stone wall 3 feet one inch high above the floor. The pedestals consist of two strata. The base pedestal is 14 feet square and the pedestal proper is 5 feet square the total height of the pedestal being 13 feet from the floor. On the front of the pedestal proper "Sei-en Shibusawa Eiichi" was carved, the characters being Chosen from among his hand writing and arranged in order. On the back of the pedestal "The Viscount

Shibusawa Memorial Foundation, Inc. built this on the 11th of November, 1933" was carved. At the front of the Square, a round fountain with the diameter of 22 feet was constructed, having in its center a water-spout with the height of 7 feet. In the compound trees of various kinds were planted and electric lamps illumine it at night. Special stones were used for the construction of the floor pedestals and the steps. The maker of the statue was F. Asakura, Professor in Tokyo Academy of Fine Arts; the superintendent of the plan, G. Tamura, Doctor of Forestry; and the builders, the Shimidzu Gumi Co. The work was commenced on May 10th, 1932 and completed on the 9th of November 1933.

The bronze statue is in a standing posture with the Viscount supporting his right hand on a cane and looking down upon the city as though he were anxiously watching what is going on.

The Square is called Tokiwa Bashi Kōen, (the Tokiwa Bridge Park), because it is located near the old Tokiwa Bridge. Across the moat stands the building of the Bank of Japan, the very heart of Japan's financial system.

The ceremony of the unveiling of the memorial statue took place on the 11th of November, 1933, the second anniversary of the death of Viscount Shibusawa, but the third anniversary according to the Japanese usage.

The chronicler of the scene at the unveiling ceremony summarizes what transpired on that day in the following words:

"The unveiling ceremony of the statue of Viscount Shibusawa took place at the Tokiwa Bashi Park on the third anniversary, the 11th of November 1933. It was a rainy day. Those who were present on the occasion numbered more than seven hundred, consisting of the members of the Shibusawa family, relatives, and notables both official and non-official. The ceremony began with the opening address of Mr. S. Ohashi, the chairman of the day, at 2.30 p. m. Then followed the address of Baron Goh, the President of the Viscount Shibusawa Memorial Foundation, Inc. Mr. K. Nishino, representing the Committee for the erection of the memorial statue, made a report concerning the business side of the construction work. After that Master Masahide Shibusawa, a great grandson of the Viscount, unveiled the statue amidst great applause. The benign countenance of the Viscount appeared in the mid air. After the congratulatory address by the representative of the guests of the day ; the response by the representative of the Shibusawa family ; the presentation of a list of gifts consisting of the statue and its accessories to the city of Tokyo ; and remarks by the Mayor of Tokyo ; the ceremony was concluded at 4 o'clock with closing remarks by the Chairman.

Mr. Ohashi, the Chairman made an opening address as follows :

Excellencies, Ladies and Genthemen :

" I have now the honor of opening the unveiling ceremony of the memorial statue. What the Viscount Shibusawa Memorial Foundation, Inc. was trying to bring about as its work— namely the construction of the memorial statue of the late Viscount—has been completed under your enthusiastic support. We have decided to perform this ceremony on the third anniversary of his death.

" As you are well aware this is the anniversary of the Armistice Day of the great World War, and it is most significant to have the unveiling ceremony performed on this day knowing as we do how deeply interested the Viscount was in the promotion of international good will. We are sincerely grateful to the members of the Shibusawa family and the host of distinguished friends both official and civilian for your presence here today.

"The statue and its accessories will be donated to the city of Tokyo to become a park belonging to the citizens under the supervision of the city authorities. The formal presentation will be made following the unveiling ceremony.

"In conclusion I wish to remind ourselves of the words spoken to us junior business men by the Viscount when he realized that the inevitable hour was approaching him : 'I am now seriously ill, and deeply regret that I cannot live on to the age of one hundred years, so as to further serve my country in her progress. The country is now being confronted with many vexing problems, and is calling for your loyal support. Although I may soon be removed from this world into the Great Beyond, yet I shall abide with you in spirit to guard your health and the prosperity of the business world."

Baron Goh, President of the Viscount Shibusawa Memorial Foundation delivered a ceremonial address :

"As the bronze statue of the late Viscount has been completed, we are now to observe its unveiling ceremony on this day of the third anniversary of his death.

"Five years ago, we younger friends of the Viscount celebrated his 88th birthday, and passed a unanimous resolution to erect in his honor a statue for the purpose of immortalizing his various achievements, such as industrial, financial, social, educational, and cultural. The resolution was strongly supported by leaders, official and non-official, and native and foreign. Since then the work for its construction was smoothly progressing when the Viscount passed away before its completion. It was an irreparable regret for us that we could not finish it while he was alive. However, for us now to be able to see the statue, produced by the famous artist and erected in the heart of our great city, is the next best whereby we can comfort ourselves under the circumstances.

"Of the meritorious deeds the Viscount accomplished during his life time of 92 long years, the public is well aware. It is also true that his sincere and magnanimous character is widely appreciated as a model for business men. The world in which we are now living is full of confusion and perplexities; and it calls for the presence of such a prophetic genius as the Viscount, who wisely counselled us and in whom we placed our boundless confidence. Hence it is no mere accident that at such a time as this our admiration and love for him are crystalized into this statue, which is going to be presented to the citizens of Tokyo, with whom the Viscount held close relations. We hope that there will be many who, looking upon the benign countenance of the Viscount reproduced by the statue, will be reminded of his wonderful achievements and may be stirred to rise to do something for their country.

Then Mr. K. Nishino, representing the committee on the erection of the statue, made the following report of the work :

" May I make a report on the work of the erection of the statue? The plan of erecting a statue in honor of the Viscount began with the resolution adopted on the occasion when the celebration of his 88th birthday was observed three years ago. While the investigation for the selection of a site was being made, unfortunately the Viscount passed away. Later Zaidan Hojin Shibusawa Sei-en Ô Kinen Kai (The Viscount Shibusawa Memorial Foundation, Inc.) was formed and it undertook as a part of its work to erect the memorial statue of the Viscount. By a special favor of the city of Tokyo, the permission to use for the site of the statue the old Tokiwa Bashi Ko-en in the center of the city was given. Hence the work was started two years ago with the appropriation of one hundred thousand yen (¥100,000.). Mr. Masaki, formerly the president of the Tokyo Academy of Fine Arts, consented to act as an adviser; the production of the statue was entrusted to Professor Asakura of the Tokyo Academy of Fine Arts; the design of the work to Mr. Tamura, Doctor of Forestry and Mr. Inoshita, Director of the Park Department of the city of Tokyo; the actual work of construction to the Shimidzu Gumi Co. The work of the bank revetment and the lay out of the park were carried on by the city authorities. Through the cooperation of the agencies above mentioned we have realized our object. Further details are described in the reports distributed.

"In conclusion I take this opportunity to express our deep gratitude to the self-sacrificing services rendered by Messrs. Masaki, Asakura, Tamura, Inoshita, Shimidzu Gumi and the members of its out-door staff. Special thanks are due to the office of Tokyo City and to the departments of park and rivers of the City office.

Baron T. Yamamoto, the Minister of Home Affairs then made a congratulatory address:

"Two years have passed since a great genius, Viscount Shibusawa, passed on. Just now we are confronted with perplexing problems rarely seen in the history of our country, and it is a time for us to make a desperate effort in order to conquer all these difficulties. At such a time as this, our thoughts go back to him, whose presence is greatly desired. Early in the Meiji Era the Viscount entered into public life, devoting himself to the promotion of the welfare of the State and Society. He labored hard for the improvement of social justice; the development of economics and industry; the advancement of education and culture; the promotion of social work; the harmony of Labor and Capital; international goodwill; and for world peace. His long life of 92 years was wholly given to services for his country and the general public. Even after his departure, he wanted to continue his unselfish devotion to public weal by bequeathing all his estate to that purpose.

"It was perfectly natural for him to command confidence from official and non-official circles while alive, and to be highly respected by the coming generations after death. At his death he received gracious condolence from His Imperial Majesty the

Emperor—a great and immortal honor.

"The erection of this bronze statue by the host of his business friends is indeed a genuine demonstration of their appreciation of his useful career. The Viscount and I were good friends for many years which fact renews in me at this particular occasion an irrespressible emotion of bereavement.

Next Viscount K. Shibusawa rose and responded:

"In behalf of the members of the bereaved family, I desire to speak a few words at this time. We do appreciate most deeply that the Foundation made it possible to celebrate the unveiling ceremony of the bronze statue, erected by it as a part of its work, on this occasion of the third anniversary of my grandfather's death.

"As was expressed by the President of the Foundation a while ago, its officers have given their best thought and hardest efforts for the construction of the statue. The result is what we see now with admiration. We cannot be too grateful for this. We feel it utterly impossible to find adequate words to express our gratitude to Mr. Asakura for his choice work; to Mr. Tamura, Mr. Inoshita and many other participants in this work and its accessories as the statue and its setting are so plainly and dignifiedly constructed as can rarely be seen elsewhere. When we look upon the statue, as the members of the bereaved family, we cannot help but feel that grandfather is still alive. We have resolved that it is our sacred duty to walk as grandfather did, and this resolution will be increasingly strengthened by seeing the statue. The best response and gratitude we can offer to our kind friends will be to do our utmost for the promotion of the welfare of the State and Society. Whenever we pass by this place and glance at the statue, we shall receive stimulus to live worthily and act nobly. In this connection I am reminded of Mr. Makoshi who would surely have rejoiced to witness this scene.

"We express our hearty thanks to the parties who have shown

such deep interest in this enterprise and made it a grand success. Especially we are grateful to His Excellency Minister Yamamoto who delivered an address full of tenderness and appreciation.

Mayor Ushizuka concluded the ceremony with the following remarks :

" I am deeply moved by looking at the statue of the late Viscount Shibusawa, which makes us feel as though we are standing in his living presence. It is superfluous for me to say that the Viscount was a citizen of the world, but there is a peculiar relation between him and myself, which helps me to understand him as a great citizen of Tokyo better than any one else. You know that the autonomy and enterprises of Tokyo had been conducted under the designation of Tokyo Prefecture, until the change of administration as Tokyo City called for the turning over of all the work of Tokyo Prefecture to Tokyo City. Every important work which was started during the period of Tokyo Prefecture and which was later transferred to Tokyo City, was planned and directed by the Viscount. The present structure of Tokyo Prefecture and the Tokyo Gas Company are monuments to his untiring effort. Besides these, there are many more such enterprises.

" As I served first as Governor of Tokyo Prefecture and am now serving as Mayor of Tokyo City, I know well what I am talking about. The Viscount made invaluable contributions to the prosperity of Tokyo City, beginning with the accomplishment of its perfect autonomy and promoting the city administration. I stand here this afternoon filled with profound respect for this great citizen. I understand that the statue was erected by the joint effort of business men who hold the Viscount in admiration. It is now presented to the city. I accept the gift. I shall cause it to be maintained, supervised, and preserved, so as to meet the conditions under which it was presented. I shall let it stand before the eyes of 5,000,000 people of

Memorial Statue.

Viscount Keizo Shibusawa.

the city as a model of citizenship and a representative of an outstanding citizen to inspire them with the strong sense of autonomy and cooperation.

The address of Mayor Ushizuka concluded the ceremony for the day. Every guest was presented with the souvenir of a large photograph of the statue. Refreshments were served before the audience scattered.

There are several statues in the different parts of the city of Tokyo, honoring modern and ancient heroes and commemorating their great deeds, but there is no statue thus far erected in the city which can be compared with the statue dedicated to the memory of Viscount Shibusawa so far as the superiority of the latter's location, setting, and surroundings are concerned.

A similar project of erecting a memorial statue in honor of the Viscount was launched in Korea under the leadership of Baron Inyo Ri. It was erected in the park called " Kei-Jo Fu Sho Dai Chyu Dan Koen " and the ceremony for unveiling took place on the 11th of December 1933. Baron Ri made the ceremonial address. The following is an excerpt from it :

" .... As early as 1878, the late Viscount Shibusawa established a branch office of Dai Ichi Ginko in the peninsula, thus contributing to the stabilization of currency and the development of banking here.

" Another vital contribution of the Viscount to the peninsula was the construction of the railway trunk line which is called the Kei-Fu railway. He encountered and overcame numerous obstacles and difficulties in pushing this enterprise, but counselling with leading officials and civilians, he finally succeeded in it.

" The Viscount always kept in his mind the development of Korea. He showed his deep sympathy and gave his careful guidance to it. It is the gift of the Viscount to the peninsula that Korea is so prosperously faring today in its economic life. Truely he was a great benefactor of Korea. Two years have elapsed since he passed away. We find ourselves in the midst of unrest and turmoil. There was no time in the past as now when we need a leader like the Viscount who had character and ability. But he is gone, which fact makes us feel drawn to him, hoping against hope for his presence. What we should do now is to perpetuate his great name by erecting a monument with the inscription of his great deeds, as a token of our deep indebtedness to him."

In concluding this chapter, special reference should be made to Zaidan Hojin Shibusawa Sei-en O Kinen Kai (The Viscount Shibusawa Memorial Foundation, Inc.)—the monument of all the monuments so far raised in honor of the Viscount, and one which we believe highly acceptable to the spirit of the Viscount. It will grow in its efficacy as the years roll on, and numerous public works, in which the Viscount was interested will be perpetually carried on.

The Foundation will be a resuscitation of the late Viscount in the form of a legal person, not as a mere memory of him, but as an active, creative, and initiative leader in the ever expanding fields of public activities.

Baron Goh, the President of the Foundation, and its Directors and Councillors will have a tremendous responsibility to increase the endowment in order that the Foundation may amply meet the demands and appeals pouring in from various kinds of organizations and parties, covering educational, social, and international work.

May the Foundation fulfill its misson, worthy of one whose memory it aims to keep forever alive!

EPILOGUE

Epilogue is a relative term finding its complement in the term prologue or foreword. A thing or an event has its beginning and its ending. In the case of this book the prologue is written by Baron Goh, the President of Zaidan Hojin Shibusawa Sei-en O Kinen Kai (the Viscount Shibusawa Memorial Foundation, Inc.), and by Dr. Obata, the author, both of whom are so eminently fit for the purpose that one can hardly find their equals.

Imagine that I am one of the spectators in a cinematic show illustrating the life and work of my grandfather. There can be no one more interested in viewing the gradual unfolding of the picture than I. But the deeper and keener interest will be roused in me when I come to the scene of his activity within ten years before and after his eightieth birthday. There is a threefold reason for this: In the first place there was a great difference between his age and mine. He was fifty six years old when I was born. Of course a mere difference of age should not necessarily separate a younger person from an older in congeniality and companionship. There are many grandfathers and grandmothers who are fond of their grandchildren, and whose companionship is constantly sought by the little ones.

My grandfather was the kind of a man who was

never dull nor a scarecrow to us little tots. Instead he was the best of friends to us grandchildren. He had a capacity to welcome us and make us feel perfectly at home with him.

But children are children the same everywhere. They have a limited capacity to appreciate the love or caresses of their older companions. The capacity is superficial and makes it difficult for them to catch and appropriate the influence shed upon them by the matured ones. Such was the case between my grandfather and myself. In the second place, my days were fully occupied in completing my school education, while my grandfather was a very busy man. He returned home late at night and went out early in the morning. Days and weeks would pass by without seeing him. Hardly a chance even to get a glimpse of him! So near yet so far was he to me. Thirdly, I finally reached a stage where I could be near him more frequently than before, and this was during the period above referred to.

Then there was a habit which entitles me to write an epilogue about my grandfather. I invariably used to walk behind him whenever I accompanied him, looking at him from behind.

Grandfather had soft bushy gray hair quite unusual for a man of his advanced age of ninety years. The back of his head was like that of child lovely and attractive. He kept his body straight like a trained athlete. As he walked he slightly turned his head toward the left, and for a reason unexplainable he gave a more forcible step to one foot than to the other. In his healthy and robust frame viewed from behind, I could see a wonderful repository of the comprehensive and complex experiences he underwent during those eventful periods covering nearly seventy long years. His advancing figure symbolized to my mind his matured life full of strength and beauty.

Friends of my grandfather have been extravagant in pouring on him their eulogies and their appreciation of what he achieved for the country and the business world of Japan and we as his kinsfolks are deeply grateful to them. We feel utterly helpless to adequately express our profound gratitude. But frankly speaking I feel that what was accomplished by him must have fallen far short of what he intended to achieve. He always aimed more at the quality of an enterprise than at the quantity. His business attitude was to pay attention to the nature of an enterprise and to the personality of the man involved. In this as in other cases we can see his insistence on the moral side rather than on the material. Therefore, he must have been not only scrupulous in selecting the work and the worker, but also must have given up any enterprise at any time when anything hypocritical and unfair in it was found out. This is a reason why I suspect that there must have been many enterprises which suffered premature death. He was energetic and tireless. His brain was full of plans and projects. It truly might be said of him that comparatively speaking he planned much and realized little.

Any future biographer of my grandfather would do well to dwell quite at length on the facts in his life which would explain why and where he failed, because that kind of treatment would not only reveal hitherto undiscovered fields of his activity, but also point out to the future generations the shoals whereby some ship of enterprise was wrecked, thereby giving a warning to them to avoid what is wrong.

I saw a marked change in the life of my grandfather after his eightieth year. Up to that time he was more materialistically minded. He ate sumptuously. He worked hard. He was explosive and almost intolerant in dealing with sluggish ones. But later his life was greatly purified from any tinge of worldliness. His character became transparent and gradually mellowed. He scattered around him the air of heavenliness. His life long precepts, Chyu Jo (忠恕), completely took possession of him. He was sternly true to himself and was kind to others.

He utterly forgot himself in helping others. He was never satisfied until he had poured out and exhausted his ideas and suggestions to the visitor who sought his counsel. We, who were anxious about his health in his latter days, were often placed in embarrassing positions in asking him to abstain from comparatively less important interviews. A writer once wrote this sentence " Love relentlessly plunders." But in the case of my grandfather " Love ungrudgingly gives " was true.

This brings me to mention some of the experiences I passed through while attending on my grandfather during the illness, to which he finally succumbed on the Armistice day of the great World War. He suffered from it nearly a month, and the time was full of boding. But there was a positive relief from that heavy and suffocating atmosphere, which is generally characteristic of a room filled with the smell of medicine and occupied by physicians and nurses. There was brightness and optimism in the room. Sorrow did not enter into my heart even when the inevitable hour came to him. It was so natural for me to see him go. It seemed to me that I desired for him to choose no other way than what he was subjected to. It never occurred to me to commit his soul to some supernatural being or to pray for his future. I was so completely taken by the naturalness of the scene that I was entirely indifferent to the subsequent loneliness to be felt from the realization of the fact " he is no more."

This extraordinary equanimity or sense of victory over death must have been created by the strength of personality of the patient. He transcended death. In his life time he faced death several times and tested its strength. I must have been captivated by his strength.

He was humorous and remained so till his death. He was attended by several nurses. One day when he was somewhat relieved from complaint, he said to one of the nurses: " I am sorry to trouble you so much. I thank you for the care you are giving me. But I am not the one to be blamed for troubling you. The blame must rest on Disease." All the nurses were unanimous in the verdict that my grandfather was the most complacent patient they had ever nursed.

Another matter which surprised the nurses as well as the physician in charge was the fastidious cleanliness of the patient. He not only was suffering for a month, but he had a high fever lasting three days in the last part of the month before he breathed his last, and yet his body was immaculate. When I was thinking of this, there came to me a sentence from a Buddhist scripture :

"Less virtuous a man is,
       filthier   still   is   he."

To me his passing was like the setting of the sun,
which leaving behind a trail of beautiful after-glow,
returned to the home prepared by Nature. It was a
solemn and beautiful scene which will never fade away
from my life.

For a few months following the funeral rites of my
grandfather, memorial services were held by various
organizations at different places. We the members of
Shibusawa family were invited to be present at them.
Words of sympathy and appreciation were spoken by
the sponsors of the meetings. I, being heir of my
grandfather, had to represent the rest of the family in
thanking the speakers. Thus I was always the last
speaker in the programme—a true epiloguist.

Here again I am invited to write an epilogue for the
book to be made public on the seventh anniversary of
the death of my grandfather, whose meaningful "back
view" is once more vividly revived in my memory.

In closing I would like to say a few words about
the relationship between Dr. Obata and my grandfather.
Dr. Obata was in close contact with my grandfather
during more than a decade as interpreter and English
secretary—an interpreter of grandfather through pen
and tongue. As such Dr. Obata could take not only
the "front view" and "back view" of my grandfather,
but also the "inner view" of him, thus becoming an
interpreter of the soul of my grandfather. In other
words, Dr. Obata came to know him as few men did.
It is for this reason that I am highly pleased to see the
book written by him. I owe him a great debt of

gratitude for this fine work, and take this opportunity to express to him my hearty thanks.

Viscount K. Shibusawa

INDEX

INDEX

Imperial Guard, Commander-in-Chief of, 28, 33
Imperial Edict, 73.
Imperial Hotel, 216
Imperial Theatre, 221, 322, 342
Industrial Bank of Japan, 212
Indemion, 49
Ino, T., 68
Inokashira School, 147
Inoshita, Sei, 373, 374, 375
Inouye, Marquis Kaoru, 71–79, 81, 87, 88, 89, 108, 130, 160
Inouye, Junnosuke, 209, 214, 228, 297, 365
Inouye, Tetsujiro, 297
Institute of Pacific Relations, 291
International Exposition of Paris, 189
Irisawa, Tatsukichi, 349
Isaka, S., 53, 55
Isaka, Takashi, 211
Ishii, Kengo, 355, 361
Ishii, Viscount Kikujiro; Introduction, vi; 211, 212, 228, 343
Ishikawa Jima Zosen Jo (Ishikawa Jima Ship Building Company), 275, 343
Itabashi, 142
Itagaki, Count Taisuke, 121
Italy, 4, 5, 48, 173, 217, 262, 334
Ito, Prince Hirobumi, 68, 69, 38, 97, 160
Iwakura Mission, the, 78, 79
Iwakura, Prince Tomomi, 88
Iwasaki, the, 162
Iwasaki, Yanosuke, 123
Iwasaki, Yataro, 113, 114, 115, 117, 118
Izu, 41, 229

Japan; Introduction, iii, vii, viii, xii–xv; 2–4, 8–10, 15, 21, 26, 32, 41, 51, 53, 85, 86, 97, 103, 107, 114, 117, 124, 125, 130, 132–134, 136, 138, 141, 143, 146, 151, 153, 160. 161, 169, 171, 173–175, 178, 179, 182, 184, 187, 188, 191, 195, 198, 200, 203, 204, 206, 208, 212, 215, 219, 226, 228, 231, 234, 270, 272, 273, 279, 290, 291, 293, 299, 300, 306, 308, 310, 312–314, 316–319, 322, 324, 327, 330, 331, 337, 338, 365; Epilogue, 380
Japan-India Society, 226
Japan International Children's Society 229, 234
Japan Mail Steamship Company, 113–116
Japan Society of New York, 300
Japanese Advisory Council of St. Luke's International Medical Center, 207
Japanese American Joint High Commission; Introduction, xiii
Japanese American Relations Committee; Introduction, v, vii, xiii, xiv; 180, 186, 206, 207, 210, 213, 217, 342, 343
Japanese American Ship-Steel Exchange Arbitrator, 228
Japanese American Treaty of 1851, 189
Japanese American Unofficial Conference, 214, 216
Japanese English Dictionary, 226
Japanese International Association, 185
Japanese Radio Company, 182
Japanese Relations Committee; Introduction, vii; 213, 223, 224
Japanese Roumanian Commercial Relations Committee, 226
Jessup, Morris K., 196
Jiyu To, the, (Liberal party), 121, 122
John Bull, 311
Jo-I, 10
Jordan, David Staar, 109, 110, 271
Joshi Kyoiku Shorei Kai (Society of Girls' Education), 160, 161
Josui Kai, 342
Jyudo, 15, 236

Kagami, Kenkichi, 127, 211
Kaishin To, the, (Reform Party), 120
Kakisaki, 229
Kamiya, Tadao, 205
Kanagawa, 42
Kaneko, Count Kentaro; Introduction, xv; 79, 209, 211, 212, 214, 272

昭和拾貳年拾壹月 五 日印刷
昭和拾貳年拾壹月拾壹日發行

定價金參圓五拾錢

著作兼
發行者　小畑久五郎
　東京市澁谷區緑岡町二二

發行所　財團法人 澁澤靑淵翁記念會
　東京市瀧野川區西ヶ原町一〇三六

印刷者　木下　憲
　東京市豐島區高田南町一ノ一九五

印刷所　美術印刷所
　ダイヤモンド事業株式會社
　東京市豐島區高田南町一ノ一九五

賣捌所　丸善株式會社
　東京市日本橋區通二ノ六

支店出張所
【東京(神田・三田・早稻田・丸ビル)仙臺・大阪
神戶・京都・名古屋・橫濱・福岡・札幌・京城】